[PRAISE FOR]

party of one:
the loners' manifesto

"A witty essay about things best done on your own. . . . A founding manifesto for an organization of self-contained people. . . . A clever and spirited defense."
—*Kirkus Reviews*

"This brilliant book, filled with wonderful asides and insights, has convinced me that there is something terribly wrong with calling a loner a deviant. Terrific, learned, and ferocious, *Party of One* brings all kinds of wonderful ideas to mind, so don't be put off if you happen not to be a loner. I am not, and I learned an enormous amount."
—JEFFREY MOUSSAIEFF MASSON,
author of *The Nine Emotional Lives of Cats*

"Anneli Rufus is a stylist of the first order, a lyrical and evocative writer with a big heart and keen intellect who turns to gold any topic she touches. And now with her latest book, *Party of One*, Rufus has hit upon the perfect subject to match her considerable talents. The result is an original, provocative, and passionately written plea on behalf of all those who want to be left alone. *Party of One* is muckraking of a different kind, exposing the tyranny of the mob while delving deep into the human psyche."
—GARY RIVLIN, author of *The Plot to Get Bill Gates*

party of one

party of one

THE LONERS' MANIFESTO

[anneli rufus]

marlowe & company
new york

PARTY OF ONE: *The Loners' Manifesto*
Copyright © 2003 by Anneli Rufus

Published by
Marlowe & Company
An Imprint of Avalon Publishing Group Incorporated
161 William Street, 16th Floor
New York, NY 10038

Library of Congress Cataloging-in-Publication Data
is available.

ISBN 1-56924-513-4

9   8   7   6   5   4   3   2

Designed by Pauline Neuwirth, Neuwirth & Associates

Printed in the United States of America
Distributed by Publishers Group West

To Fuzzy, for being,

To Matthew, for believing,

To DM, a friend
from 1965 and beyond

&

To EK, a friend
from 1982 and beyond

contents

[CONTENTS]

[CONTENTS]

introduction

I WENT TO FISHERMAN'S Wharf to watch daredevil navy pilots do stunts over San Francisco Bay. The six sleek planes dove and spiraled and sped off wing-to-wing, trailing curlicues of white smoke like whipped cream from aerosol cans. The roar of their engines drew call-and-response roars from the crowd below.

It *was* a crowd. Spanning two miles of waterfront on the last sunny Saturday of the year, a sea of spectators lined the railings along docks and piers, jamming walkways and lawns and traffic islands and restaurant roofs. Clots of people in colorful T-shirts waved at the sky from hotel balconies, streamed off tour buses and streetcars. Stuck in traffic, drivers and passengers craned their necks as seagulls swooped and snatched at fallen onion rings as if mocking the planes.

I thought, What am I doing here? As a rule, I avoid crowds. I am not an agoraphobe, but dislike crowds on principle. The inevitable if unwitting poke of strange elbows into breast and back. The potentiality—and it has been realized—of someone throwing up onto my shoes. The premise, the presumption implicit in any crowd, from concert hall to kaffee klatsch to office party, that shared experiences are the only ones that count. The only experiences toward which everyone aspires.

The only *real* ones. I never liked the circus as a child, and the audience was as much the cause as the clowns. But I was in the neighborhood the day the planes came. So I said *What the hell.*

The spectators rippled and swirled, particolored, like clouds of confetti. Flesh to flesh. A happy crowd, as crowds go. And like all crowds, it drew from its hugeness a shared frisson. A sense of collective self. A jubilation in assembly, in the very fact of its existence. Jubilation in the fact that all those persons were in one place at one time, as if their numbers, their consensus on a sunny Saturday under a sky crisscrossed with jet streams, the air redolent of fish, proved—what? That anything worth doing is not done alone.

I found a spot between a car and a family from India. I stood watching the planes, together with the crowd and yet apart.

APART.

Such a simple concept. So concrete. So easy to represent on charts or diagrams with dots and pushpins either in or out. Yet real life is not dots. Some of us *appear* to be in, but we are out. And that is where we want to be. Not just want but need, the way tuna need the sea.

Simple: an orientation, not just a choice. A fact. To paraphrase that Boston song, *more than a feeling.* We are loners. Which means we are at our best, as Orsino says in *Twelfth Night,* when least in company.

We do not require company. The opposite: in varying degrees, it bores us, drains us, makes our eyes glaze over.

Overcomes us like a steamroller. Of course, the rest of the world doesn't understand.

Someone says to you, "Let's have lunch." You clench. Your sinews leap within you, angling for escape. What others thrive on, what they take for granted, the contact and confraternity and sharing that gives them strength leaves us empty. After what others would call a fun day out together, we feel as if we have been at the Red Cross, donating blood.

This is not about hate. I did not hate the individuals in the crowd at the air show. Not the man leaning over the rail, a tattoo on his back of a baby-faced devil above the words Born Horny. I don't hate my relatives or those whose names fill my address book. But I do not want to have lunch with any of them. It is not personal. I am not angry. Nor is this about being afraid. I am not shy. I do not have terrible manners.

Do birds hate lips? Do Fijians detest snowplows? Being a loner is not about hate, but need: We need what others dread. We dread what others need.

HOW MUCH BETTER if I had known from the start, if someone had said, *This is what is different about you.* It would have been so simple, would have explained anything. But no one ever said. That is the point. We will not—cannot—hail each other on the street and ask, *Are you this way?* We will not take each other into confidence on line at Safeway.

Being as we are is just a way to be, like being good at sports or being born in Greenland. If only it were not dorky to quote

Robert Frost, if he were Sufi or had died young in the Spanish Civil War, then we could seize as our motto the final three lines of "The Road Not Taken":

> Two roads diverged in a wood, and I—
> I took the one less traveled by,
> And that has made all the difference.

This way to be, this way we are, gets us into trouble. We are a minority, the community that is an anticommunity. The culture that will not on principle join hands. Remote on principle from one another—this is in our charter and we would not have it any other way—each of us swims alone through a sea of social types. Talkers. Lunchers. Touchers.

Nonloners. The world at large. The mob.

The mob thinks we are maladjusted. Of course we are adjusted just fine, not to their frequency. They take it personally.

They take offense. Feel hurt. Get angry. They do not blame owls for coming out at night, yet they blame us for being as we are. Because it involves them, or at least they believe it does, they assemble the troops and call us names.

Crazy. Cold. Stuck-up. Standoffish. Aloof. Afraid. Lacking in social skills. Bizarre. Unable to connect. Incapable of love. Freaks. Geeks. Sad. Lonely. Selfish. Secretive. Ungrateful. Unfriendly. Serial killers.

THEY BRIDLE WHEN we turn down invitations. They know we are making up excuses, but they can't handle the truth.

They cannot fathom loners any more than birds can fathom lips. The mob makes definitions and assigns identities based on the sorts of clues loners do not provide. We are elusive, not given to dressing and behaving such that we would be in stadiums raising giant foam-rubber hands proclaiming anything. We frustrate our observers, try their patience, make ourselves amorphous. Make ourselves either unintentionally scary or invisible. With the blithe assurance of a majority, the mob nods knowingly when Justin stays home alone on Christmas Day. He is depressed, they say, or else he has something to hide. The clerk who goes home after work to have a bubble bath instead of joining the gang at the bar is declared undeserving of a raise, afraid of men, afraid of women, too smart, too stupid, scary, a pervert.

The mob posts jokes on the Net—for instance, a page called "The Loner's Home Companion," which begins: "Ever had lots of spare time, a .357 Magnum burning a hole in your pocket, and an unhealthy obsession with Heather Locklear. . . ?" And like the mock interview with "a loner" who muses: "I spend most of my free time by myself. I steer clear of crowds and social functions . . . I'm just a normal, average guy who will go to great lengths to avoid unnecessary human contact. Is that so wrong? No, it's not. Human beings are nasty, disgusting, germ-infested vermin."

The l-word, as we hear it most often today, sounds nasty. It is the sound of a nervous music, a whine of mistrust, the hiss of fear, the dull growl of incomprehension. Animals make that sound when foreign species invade their dens, or when they find a rogue within the herd. Loners live among the mob, so the mob mistakes us for its own, presuming and assuming. When the mob gets too close, the truth is revealed. Running or walking away, chased or free, any which way, we tell the mob in effect *I don't need you.*

Hell hath no fury like a majority scorned.

YET HERE WE are, *not* sad, not lonely, having the time of our lives amid their smear campaign.

We are the ones who know how to entertain ourselves. How to learn without taking a class. How to contemplate and how to create. Loners, by virtue of being loners, in celebrating the state of standing alone, have an innate advantage when it comes to being brave—like pioneers, like mountain men, iconoclasts, rebels, and sole survivors. Loners have an advantage when faced with the unknown, the never-done-before, and the unprecedented. An advantage when it comes to being mindful like the Buddhists, spontaneous like the Taoists, crucibles of concentrated prayer like the desert saints, esoteric like the cabalists. Loners, by virtue of being loners, have at their fingertips the undiscovered, the unique, the rarefied. Innate advantages when it comes to imagination, concentration, inner discipline. A knack for invention, originality, for finding resources in what others would call vacuums. A knack for visions.

A talent for seldom being bored. Desert islands are fine, but not required.

We are the ones who would rather see films than talk about them. Would rather write plays than act in them. Rather walk

Angkor Wat and Portobello Road alone. Rather run cross-country than in a relay race, rather surf than play volleyball. Rather cruise museums alone than with someone who lingers over early bronzes and tells us why we should adore Frida Kahlo.

Alone, we are alive.

Alone does not necessarily mean *in solitude*: we are not just the lone figure on the far shore. This is a populous world, and we are most often alone in a crowd. It is a state less of body than mind. The word *alone* should not, for us, ring cold and hollow, but hot. Pulsing with potentiality. Alone as in distinct. Alone as in, Alone in his field. As in, Stand alone. As in, like it or not, Leave me alone. This word wants rescuing, this word wants pride. This word wants to be washed and shined.

There *are* books, out there, about solitude. They give instructions on being alone. These books talk of "stealing away," of "retreats" and of "seeking sanctuary." They pose solitude as novelty and a desperate act: the work of thieves and refugees. But for loners, the idea of solitude is not some stark departure from our normal state. *We* do not need writers to tell us how lovely apartness is, how sacred it was to the sages, what it did for Thoreau, that we must demand it. Those books are not for loners, not really. This is not one of those books.

By the way, I am sane. People whose job it is to know these things have told me so.

WE LONERS DO not know each other by sight. Every day we pass our brethren in the street unwitting. Sure, you might notice the solitary figure on the subway car and think, *Aha*. But we do not exchange glances or high-fives or have our own slang or symbols. What would those be, anyway? The tarot's Hermit card? A stick figure wearing a party hat? A tiny, tightly rolled scroll in a silver capsule like Jewish mezuzahs, inscribed with the names of famous loners? Henry David Thoreau, Emily Dickinson, Alec Guinness, Erik Satie, Sir Anthony Hopkins, Stanley Kubrick, James Michener, Greta Garbo, John Lennon, Piet Mondrian, Franz Kafka, Hermann Hesse, Janet Reno, St. Anthony, Batman. Even that would be reductive. Would leave out so much.

Because it is all too easy to generalize. About them. About us. If this is a manifesto, it speaks for all of those—and we know who we are—for whom no one has yet spoken and who, by nature, do not seek to call attention to themselves. As a journalist, I have covered hundreds of subjects, reported on thousands of people, ways of life, cultures, subcultures, cults, habits, hobbies, ripples, rites, beginnings, ends. Towns where on certain days every year, snakes deluge the streets, then slither off at dusk. Towns whose most famous incidents are massacres. Towns whose churches are built under the surface of the earth, whose hotels are carved out of ice, whose residents are waiting for spacecraft to land. Towns burned to the ground and towns drowned. And yet, in all this, never did I hear the voices or see phalanxes of what is as surely my own kind as rock 'n' roll fans or Jews or people from Los Angeles. No one had linked us, threaded us like beads on one strand. Someone should. Because we have a point. We form a chorus, but the oddest chorus in the world, a willful antichorus. In saying entirely different things, usually not saying them aloud to anyone at all, we are saying a lot.

Which is why a manifesto for loners cannot pretend to speak for every last loner, word for word. Generalization is impossible. It is an insult. Instead, what you will find here—the fact, opinion, research, interview, reportage, analysis, and observation— is a periscope. *This is the world from here.* Held up to every loner's eye, the view will be the same, but different.

THE MOB IS not as actively hostile as it is intolerant. Even this accusation would surprise the mob. It prides itself on having evolved beyond prejudice. It parades proof of its enlightenment: its multicultural government cabinets, legal rights for same-sex partners, wheelchair access, plus-size models. Those are surely prideworthy. But no one wants to own up to the bias that thrives in full flush as the others go down in flames. This bias does not show itself in laws against us, antiloner legislation, unless you count tax breaks for married couples with kids and higher taxes for the self-employed. It mostly shows itself— surprise, surprise!—in attitude.

Such as the fact that anything done alone is discredited, demeaned, devalued, or at best, simply undiscussed. People talk about other people, and of things they do with other people. What is done alone is presumed dull or embarrassing. Or abstruse, like quantum physics. A gauzy veil hides what is done alone: its warp is shame, its woof incomprehension. When nearly all you do is done alone, it makes the effort that is conversation that much harder, and all the more fruitless.

And consider all those phone calls at all hours from relatives and others who presume that because we are home alone we are always available, up for a chat. Being home alone, they presume, could not possibly also mean being busy. Or contented exactly as you are. Unwilling to be interrupted. Different standards apply to the nonloner at a desk in an office tower. No one questions that *she* is really employed.

At 10 A.M. and 8 P.M., loners' voice-mail recorders collect evidence. *I know you're there. Pick up the phone.*

The bias shows itself in nosy questions. *What are you doing in there?* Hurt feelings. *Why are you avoiding me?* Catcalls. *You're weird.*

Say what they will, do what they will, we still know where the party is. A terribly small party, *they* would say.

We are part of the human race. We need our space. Get used to it.

THE MOB WANTS friends along when doing errands, working out at the gym, seeing a movie. The mob depends on advice. Eating alone in decent restaurants horrifies the mob, saddens the mob, embarrasses the mob. The mob wants friends.

The mob needs to be loved.

It lives to be loved.

Or hated, with that conjoined fervor with which mobs face their enemies. Both love and hate are all about engagement. About being linked with humanity generally, as a policy. Loners have nothing against love, but are more careful about it. Sometimes just one fantastic someone is enough. As a minority, we puzzle over nonloners, their strange values. Why do they require constant affirmation, validation, company, support? Are they babies, or what? What bothers them about being alone? What are they so afraid of? Why can't they be more like us?

Well, they cannot, nor can we be like them. Behavioral geneticists claim that human temperaments and talents—skills, preferences, modes—are inborn, like eye color. This science is comforting insofar as it frees our parents from feeling that having loners as children is their "fault," that they "did something" to "cause" this.

Was I born this way? Or am I a loner because I am an only child? My friend Elaine is one of seven children, and she is the most lonerish loner I have ever met. Stephen Zanichkowsky is a loner. His memoir, *Fourteen*, is about growing up with thirteen siblings.

Does it matter how I got this way? Not if I am happy. I am. Loners need no more to be cured, nor *can* be cured—the word is gross in this usage—than gays and lesbians. Or people who love golf.

AT EIGHT YEARS old I was appalled at Bluebirds meetings where the girls were idiots who did not know that France was next to Germany or how to spell *Thanksgiving* on the cards we made from paper bags.

Halfway through every Bluebirds meeting, I longed to go home. It was not my house I missed so much, not the orange sofa with its squeaky plastic cover or the thick pong from my grandfather's cigars. Rather, I wanted distance from the jabber and the dullness, the blue-skirted girls arguing over whose mother was the prettiest. They ganged up, they loved games, they were easily bored. They yawned when we went to the tide pools. They shouted that the sea anemones looked like barf. I would rather be anywhere than with them, I thought, anywhere, even in prison or a hardware store.

I knew, even then, that I could not get away. My mother murmured with the troop leader. They had their heads together. *Troubled . . . antisocial . . . hopeless at games, does not seem to want to win.* My mother, in a sort of panic, paid my dues a whole year in advance. I could not quit. The message was, I must learn to like Bluebirds, before it was too late.

How could I know, then, when nobody told me, that I had a heritage? Beyond race or religion: another kind of sameness that bonded me with all those who had gone before, and bonded them with one another. A sameness of personality that set us apart from the majority as cleanly and as surely as the stroke of a Damascus sword. In emotion, in interest, in achievement—not that anyone would tell me, not that anyone would dignify it with a name or call it a line of succession. Its rich legacy lay everywhere, and nonloners lapped at that legacy though its true flavor, its core and meaning, were meant just for me. And for my kind, not that I knew I had a kind.

The legacy shimmered in art museums, galleries, libraries, concert halls. In every home with electricity, with a TV. In algebra classes and cinemas. Since the beginning, loners had been out there, on their own, making and doing things. They had kept to themselves, liked their own company, thrived on their days alone. They had produced the *Mona Lisa, Jungle Book,*

Taoism, *Walden*. How could I have known? In that nonloner world of teams and troops and congregations, who would have said, *Psst, hey, loner. Here is a grand roll call of your forebears. Protoloners.*

Down the years, around the world, they form a shining line—in single file, of course. Da Vinci. Michelangelo. Isaac Newton, who as a boy would rather have tinkered and solved math problems than play. René Descartes, the pioneering mathematician and philosopher who did his best work alone in his bed and said, "I think, therefore I am." Kipling. Thoreau. Beatrix Potter. Dickinson, who stayed home for sixteen years and wrote two thousand poems of startling passion. Lawrence of Arabia.

Crazy Horse, whom his own Sioux tribe called "the Strange Man" but loved him for his laconic air of mystery. Austrian-born philosopher Ludwig Wittgenstein, who lived as a hermit. Philo T. Farnsworth, who invented TV single-handedly. *Silent Spring* author Rachel Carson. Brian Epstein. James Michener. Alec Guinness. Albert Einstein, who wrote in 1932: "Although I am a typical loner in daily life, my consciousness of belonging to the invisible community of those who strive for truth, beauty, and justice keeps me from feeling isolated." The same Einstein who observed wryly, "To punish me for my contempt for authority, fate made me an authority myself."

All those for whom two was a crowd. Who braved the ridicule, rising time and again to the clear view through their own eyes, the wonder and horror they found and explored in themselves. Of course I would not meet them. We are not the type who meet. We do not wish to, in the flesh. We do not need to.

. . .

NONLONERS BORROW A term from Jung and call us introverts. They think it makes them sound intelligent to say so. At
the dawn of the twentieth century, Jung devised it along with
"extravert." (He spelled it with an a.) Humankind, Jung asserted, is divided into these two types, extraverts comprising three-
fourths of the total. The difference between the two, he said,
lies in the way they perceive and interpret information.

Extraverts concern themselves with facts, with the objective,
Jung said. By contrast, the introvert concerns himself with the
subjective. Confronted with an identical scenario, the extravert
will deduce its meaning based on what can be seen and what is
recognized as true. The introvert, meanwhile, conjures a complex meaning based on individual and largely immaterial details.
Impressions and opinions. He feels his own deduction to be correct, Jung wrote in 1921, yet the introvert "is not in the least clear
where and how they link up with the world of reality."

Acknowledging "the normal bias of the extraverted attitude
against the nature of the introvert," Jung added that, for the
latter, "work goes slowly and with difficulty. Either he is taci-
turn or he falls among people who cannot understand him;
whereupon he proceeds to gather further proof of the unfath-
omable stupidity of man. If he should ever chance to be understood, he is credulously liable to overestimate. Ambitious
women have only to understand how advantage may be taken
of his uncritical attitude towards the object to make an easy
prey of him; or he may develop into a misanthropic bachelor
with a childlike heart. Then, too, his outward appearance is

often gauche . . . or he may show a remarkable unconcern, an almost childlike naiveté."

Yet introverts and loners are not one and the same thing. Surely some who gain information from within and not without still enjoy company. And what of all those countless scientific loners? All those loner hackers, loner programmers, loner inventors? Surely they rely on facts. My father was an engineer without a subjective bone in his body. Yet he was a loner all his life. He taped handmade signs on the door to his den, a door he always kept shut. *Abandon Hope, All Ye Who Enter Without Knocking. Confucius Say: Get the @#! Out of Here.*

LONERS ARE ALL types, subjective and objective thinkers, religious and atheist, soldiers and screenwriters and supermodels. We are the group that is never a group, that sneers at groups. In number theory, we might be described as "the set of units that are not associated with any other unit." We are the confraternity whose members would rather chew Brillo pads than gather in some rathskeller to plan a strategy. We will never stage a protest march, a rally at which loners chorus, *Do not call us on the phone! Leave, leave, leave us alone!* We cannot lend each other our support. It goes against our nature—in body, at least, if not in mind.

America trembles in fear of loners, yet Charles Manson is a social butterfly.

The mob needs loners. It might never know how much. For its own sake, for entertainment and advancement, it needs what we have. What we do and make in our worlds hidden within the world.

• • •

WHEN PARENTS ON TV shows punished their kids by ordering them to go to their rooms, I was confused. I loved my room. Being there behind a locked door was a treat. To me a punishment was being ordered to play Yahtzee with my cousin Louis. I puzzled over why solitary confinement was considered the worst punishment in jails.

School startled me. Crowds made it hard to think, and teachers rebuked me for not liking to share. The oddest thing was that my classmates never minded how boring they were, nor minded each other's incessant attention. They sat whispering wetly into one another's ears, eagerly awaiting recess when they could ram each other or throw balls to one another, sharing their dullness like a secret handshake. There was one wild boy whom the teacher exiled to a remote desk in the corner. He sat, writhing, desperate to return. I wished that desk was mine.

My father was a loner, disdaining everyone but Jacques Cousteau and the men on *Wild Kingdom*. My mother was not a loner by nature but had come to act like one, having been fat as a girl and having faced cruel taunts in an era when fat kids were fair game. She had learned to keep away from what might hurt. Imagining that I was taking after them, my parents pictured me grown up, mad in a garret, hair a mess, listening to Radio Free Europe on a fold-up chair.

This is why Mom enrolled me in Bluebirds. Two or three of the other girls combined, as I saw it, barely amounted to a complete person. They *needed* each other because they were not whole. This is how I learned to feel superior.

The creed we chanted at each meeting called us "sisters," to whom each of us was pledged to "cleave while faggots are brought from the forest." Not that I cared all that much whether they liked me. But the *reasons* they chose for disliking me: such as the way I worked at projects, gluing every last sugar cube and pebble into place when making dioramas of castles and the bottom of the sea, whittling Popsicle sticks into dragonfly wings, mixing red and white into hot pink long after everyone else had quit and left the paints uncapped.

Not that I was incapable of friendship. *Don't be shy*, the teachers coaxed. I was not shy, only extremely choosy. And Denise shone like a diamond. If you had asked me to define paradise, I would have said a desert island which Denise could visit, on a boat.

But when she did the other thing, the social thing, throwing her head back in a crowd and laughing, she looked like a stranger to me. Afterwards all she could talk about was people. *Jeff said Patti had a hickey when they went to Tim's with Julie.* It was jealousy, but more, a suspicion that she was right and I was wrong, that she was well and I was sick, a premonition that the world would not dole out its rewards equally to both of us.

In high school I wanted to be a foreign-exchange student. After several interviews and essays, the judges declared me an ideal candidate. Clever but curious, polite, brave in strange places. Then they turned me down. I was not social enough, they said. So they chose a girl who belonged to seven clubs and tutored small children after school.

This is how I learned to feel inferior.

For years and years.

Because being a loner does not, in this so-populous world, guarantee confidence. Maturity. High self-esteem. To this day, I make no claim on maturity. Ours is a path marked with wonders of our own making, but also with barriers, baffles, and border guards, and even land mines. Being one's own friend—sometimes one's only friend—is not always easy. Drawing validation and fun from within is all well and good, but hard when we see nonloners scooping up all the prizes. My father used to say *It's not what you know, it's who you know,* and I did not want to believe him. He said it ironically, wistfully, loner that he was. Networkers get promotions, commendations, raises, he said. *Ass-kissers,* he said. Not smart guys like himself, he meant. *The schmoozers always win.* In his career and mine and most, of course it's true. The whole world is a personality cult.

WHICH IS WHY loners must remember how it felt to glue those sugar cubes. Each of us loners is a point on a vast continuum. At one end is the hermit in the hut or cave, subsisting on wild herbs and water, and speaking to no one for years at a stretch. At the other end is the urbanite juggling job and family, and hoarding moments alone like pearls.

At one end are misanthropes. At the other are do-gooders: doctors, for example, and philanthropists. In the middle are all the rest: a throng as diverse as the glass bits in kaleidoscopes. Happy, sad. Shy, laughing at danger. Sprinting, languid. Contemplative, reckless. Cool, uncool.

But here. There. Having millions of tiny parties everywhere.

party of one

I.

village people

[COMMUNITY]

Groupthink was a survival tactic when sieges and plagues
threatened the futures of clans and cultures. Now it's an
evolutionary remnant that we are free to discard.

IMAGINE YOU'RE A loner whose ideal home would be a cottage on the beach, miles from the nearest neighbor. And your ideal day would be one in which you slept from noon to dinnertime, worked half the night, then split the rest between raising pigeons and walking—alone, of course—on the beach.

In some places and eras, you could get away with it. Not most. In most you would be loathed, surveilled, suspected of perversion, called a witch, hauled out, spat at, set afire—or something like that. With luck you might only be laughed at, mercilessly, all your life.

Time, place, and culture have crushed countless loners. Fancy having been born in an Anasazi cliff dwelling, cheek by jowl with kin and neighbors in a small confined space cut off from solitude by a long sheer drop. Or as a woman in a wealthy

Ming Dynasty household, consigned to see only relatives for years on end, and only in the house and courtyard. Villages with thin-walled huts side by side, face to face, surrounded by wildernesses too fearsome to assail alone. Tenements. Communes. Call it anthropology or sociology but, for most loners, call it hell.

It makes sense that when a group is struggling to survive, a loner is a liability. We are the acid that dissolves the glue that bonds communities. We are the loose thread in the weave, for all intents and purposes the poison in the pot. From the dawn of civilization onward, *inter*dependence has been the best weapon. Concordance fuels work, faith, folkways, and the future—and, as countless loners have been chagrined to realize, identity. Cooperation, by the old rules, guards against starvation—*you* chop trees with which *I* build a boat in which *he* catches fish which *she* hawks and *they* buy. Loners who step out of the loop exempt themselves from mercy. It is the cooperative ant that survives famines, not the selfish loner grasshopper. *Whoever isn't with us is against us* is the old shout. That puts loners right down there with pillagers and rapists. When extinction looms, loners who shun the family way might as well be murderers, too. Each time, place, and culture makes its own rules for how to be a model citizen. Being a loner usually means smashing all those rules, simply by breathing.

But just as Homo sapiens no longer need prehensile toes, we no longer all need to be social animals in order to survive as a species. Mandatory social interaction is an evolutionary remnant which those who wish to may discard. The world has changed since barns needed raising. Our military forces are already so populous that you do not *have* to join the army in order to keep your hometown safe. Unless you want to. There are systems in place to take care of criminals and children and the ill. There are so many people out there, doing so many things, that your being a loner, or my being one, or that guy over there's, will not hold back the human race.

THE VERY NOTION of the self as a separate entity, unique from others, is a luxury and a fairly newfangled one at that. The psychologist Anthony Storr posits that the notion of the self emerges only when populations begin to feel solidly secure about their future as a whole. As individuals acquire more free time, they are allowed more choice about how to spend that time and with whom, if anyone, to spend it. These exponentially expanding options make for a loosening of traditional relationships. Less is demanded of the traditional bonds between kinfolk, between neighbors, between the flock and its clergy and its deities. It is exactly this—the dissolution of old-style communality, and the rise of what Margaret Mead called "the fragmented life of the city"—that social critics blame for soaring rates of crime, suicide, depression, and divorce.

In his exhaustive study of villages around the world, journalist Richard Critchfield—employing the observer-participant method adopted by many anthropologists—voiced a yearning to "recapture" the dynamic of "mutual help that so typifies village life" but which, in the late twentieth century, seemed obsolete. Wistfully, Critchfield conceded that to do so "would demand an unacceptable return to subsistence agriculture."

But to applaud that lost era of barn raisings and harvest homes, to insist that *it takes a village,* is to disparage loners. The tight weave of traditions that makes a comfortable hammock for some just as surely makes a noose that strangles others. Loosening the stranglehold and throwing away the noose is, for loners, the beginning of culture rather than the end of it. If the notion of the self is a product of human confidence and security, of free time and free choice, then it is nothing less than a product of civilization. Individualism is a reward, like the printed word and manicures, for millennia well-spent. By this logic, those who draw their sense of identity from within—from the self, as loners do—rather than from a group and its folkways, are basking in the glory of advanced civilization. By this logic, loners are also carrying that momentum forward. And by this logic, group behavior is a bit retrograde, a bit primitive.

NOTHING CAN STOP loners from being born, wherever and whenever. But living happily as a loner, fulfilling one's destiny as a loner, is another story. Working in Africa for more than thirty years, Polish journalist Ryszard Kapuściński recognized that its geography renders close communities a virtual necessity: "The problem of Africa is the dissonance between the environment and the human being, [and] the immensity of African space," he writes.

A Ghanaian colleague explained to Kapuściński how, among his own tribe, the Ashanti, "time spent communally is highly valued. . . . It is important to live together, or near one another: there are many tasks which can be accomplished only collectively—otherwise, there is no chance of surviving." The traditional Ashanti manner of greeting friends and strangers alike, Kapuściński observes, is a complex ritual that celebrates interdependence. "It is essential to exhibit from the very beginning," he writes, "from the very first second, enormous, primal joy and geniality." Hands are extended with "a large, vigorous gesture" so that "these extremities, bursting with tremendous energy, now meet halfway . . . with a terrifying impact of collision." All the while, the owners of the hands "share a prolonged cascade of loud laughter. It is meant to signify that each is happy to be meeting and warmly disposed to the other." This segues into a series of sincere how-are-yous. On a visit to Uganda, Kapuściński observed night falling so rapidly and so unrelievedly that in the space of "one instant . . . you can see nothing, as if somebody has pulled a sack over your head" and, he notes, "darkness separates people, and thereby intensifies all the more their desire to be together, in a group, in a community. . . . Being alone? That's misfortune, perdition!" He received that message wherever he traveled on the continent. In Nigeria, for instance, "let's say that you have found a small room somewhere, and you want to shut the door to work. Shut the door? This is unthinkable. We all live together in a family, in a group—children, adults, old people; we are never apart. . . . Shut yourself alone in a room, in such a way that no one can enter? Ha! Ha! Ha! This is impossible!"

My friend Eve, who studied music in Ghana as a Fulbright scholar, is a loner.

"It's considered a sickness," she says. "I found it excruciating to be me in West Africa.

"One of the hardest parts about being a loner in a foreign culture is vulnerability. This is worse in Africa, where as a white person I couldn't possibly hide because of my color. I felt traumatized just walking out the front door and down to the corner market, bracing myself against all the gawking and laughter and shouts of 'white person' and people asking for money. Part of being a loner is not wanting to stand out, right?

"And what makes it even worse," Eve reflects, is that Ghana lacked any "infrastructure to maintain your anonymity. You have to interact socially in order to get anything done at all, because there are no impersonal systems and institutions to handle things—there are only people."

Since she was there to film traditional musicians, "much of the high drama came from finding myself way out in some middle-of-nowhere village with a gang of complete strangers in some attempt at ethnographic field recording, with an expensive video camera and suddenly losing my nerve. I pissed a lot of people off because I'd start off all gung-ho, and then realize I was way out of my league and defenseless, in the event they decided to jump me and steal everything I had. So it would be wonderful for a while, on a new adventure to some remote place, but then my courage would start to fail. Then I'd grab the next taxi back down the road in the opposite direction, followed by a horde of very angry Ghanaians whose plans I'd just ruined."

She hoped to find a bit of comfort among the fellow Fulbrighters with whom she shared an apartment compound, "but as usual I just couldn't make any of those relationships 'stick,' either. Most of them traveled as couples or even families, and the ones who didn't quickly found a safety net of Ghanaian connections. One by one they all left the compound. I can still hear the sound of that heavy, rusty, iron gate creaking in the middle of the night. At that point, I would even have welcomed the company of the angry African-American roommate who despised me for being there in the first place and moved out soon after he arrived.

"The Ghanaians seem to regard it as a form of perversion if a person has no friends, lives alone, and goes around by themselves. It was like you were a *bad* person, an outcast—possessed. There was no such thing as an individual in our Western sense, a person who existed outside of any social group—i.e., a loner—except maybe shamans, the sick, and the insane."

She discontinued her scholarship, gave up on a dream, and flew home early.

IN OTHER CULTURES she would have suffered less. Her loner nature would not have become an issue. Prague-based travel writer Tim Nollen explains that in the Czech Republic, "interaction with strangers—in shops, on the metro—are generally kept to impersonal comments and curt replies, if anything at all." Czechs "don't put too much effort into getting to know one another," he observes. Compared even to most other Europeans, they "have a strong sense of privacy," he declares, and "tend to stay home."

By at least partial way of explanation, Nollen cites those long Cold War decades during which Czechs "lived in dull fear of being observed or judged." For several generations, societal monitoring was a, ubiquitous feature of Czech life. After that period was over, the nation's president, Vaclav Havel, recalled it bitterly, decrying a Communist leadership "that finds it convenient when people keep an eye on each other, watch each other, are afraid of each other . . . that sees society as an obedient herd." As a result, Nollen warns, "Don't expect, upon moving into your new home, to be welcomed by your neighbors, or even to be greeted in a friendly way the first few times they see you. In fact, don't expect to get to know your neighbors at all." Nothing personal, he points out; "it's just how it is." Calling Czechs "reserved" and noting that they present a detached air as they "focus on what they are doing with their own lives," Nollen urges the visitor who wants to fit in to "keep a low profile." As the cold war ebbs ever farther into the past, some of this might change. But the notion of a loner culture, of automatically fitting in by virtue of *not* having to do what is expected of one elsewhere—smile, say hello, gush to strangers about how much you adore their country—is compelling.

Most urbanized cultures, in Europe as anywhere, are for loners a mixture of heaven and hell. Finding one or the other is a matter of knowing where and how to look. The rugged shores and misty hills of Ireland have long enchanted hermits, even transplanted ones such as Wittgenstein, who for a while adopted the seclusion of a seaside hut near Galway. Writers and monks tend to be reclusive. Ireland prides itself on spawning writers and monks. Do the math.

At the same time, "[t]he ability to talk easily to strangers is very noticeable in Ireland," observes Patricia Levy, a longtime resident of West Cork. "Unlike many cultures which go to great lengths to not have to recognize the existence of another person, the Irish consider their day a success if they have chatted to a foreigner or someone from another part of Ireland." The result is "interminable conversations" in the pub, at the bus stop, in the shops, in which each conversant is "politely but ruthlessly questioned," less out of suspicion than out of endless curiosity. This constant round of talk, Levy believes, "is part of the Irish myth-building process, part of the sense of an essential history." Any stranger "seems incomplete until some of their story is known and they have become a part of the oral tradition which helps form the historical identity of a region."

Ireland, then, is shining proof of what loners know is true: We exist in every culture, every country. We are here. And there. And everywhere. And every culture, every country has a place for us. Whether this is a comfortable place or not, or a visible place, a place free of meanness or shame—well, that depends. Ireland makes no attempt to discredit its bards and seers, mystics and beachcombers. With pride and gratitude and simple tolerance, it knows enough to know how anemic its heritage would be without them.

OTHER CULTURES DISAVOW their loners, just as they also disavow their gays, their disabled. Keep them under wraps. Pretend they aren't there. *What? Loners? Here?* Or, presented with evidence: *Okay, that guy's a loner but it's only him. And he's a freak.*

The Japanese word *kata* means "form." American journalist Boye DeMente, a commentator on Japanese culture for over forty years, notes that from earliest childhood onward, "every situation is expected to have its own known *kata*"—a precedent, a way in which it is known to be done. Being out of *kata*, DeMente warns, amounts to "a sin against society." He goes on to add that "groupism . . . prevails in every profession" and "there is relentless pressure for [the Japanese] to join groups and stay in them."

To outside observers, Japan seems an almost impossible place in which to be a loner. Signs of Japan's famous conformity are everywhere—from its phalanxes of uniformed schoolchildren and identically suited salarymen on trains to its fashion-conscious teens all emulating the same idol-singers, to its *kata*-ized systems for eating, bowing, shopping, and even handing a colleague your business card. (Use both hands.) Japan is "a conformist society where a clear line is drawn between inside and outside, strange and normal," declares *Time* magazine, joining the international media chorus. Foreign loners might be able to swing it, if only because the Japanese tend to view foreigners as such aliens that normal behavior is not generally expected of them. But within the herd, formalities so thoroughly govern speech, gesture, and intent that human interaction—anticipating it, participating in it—plays a crucial and constant role in nearly every aspect of Japanese daily life. It matters very much which gift to give and which not to give, which colors to wear in which season. To slip up is to run the unconscionable risk of offending others.

What in Japan constitutes stepping *outside*, acting *strange*, would, in many cases, in many other countries, go entirely unnoticed. Yet in Japan the punishment is dire. The national press abounds in stories of *ijime*, or bullying—in which a child is singled out for mistreatment by his or her classmates. Any sort of "differentness" can spark *ijime*: severe acne, an unemployed father, the wrong color hair—one fourteen-year-old in Kanagawa killed himself in 1994 after his classmates relentlessly called him ugly. Loners beware.

YET THE OTHER side of this coin is that in Japan many loners have thrived, most notably in the arts. One of Japan's best-loved contemporary novelists, Haruki Murakami, is both elusive and reclusive, yet the reading public adores him no less.

"Japan has a long tradition of treating loners with respect or at least tolerating them," *Japan Times* columnist Hiroaki Sato tells me, "even though as in any society there has also been a strong pull toward keeping members of a community in line." Bristling at Western journalists who wax "gleeful" about "the dichotomy between Japanese conformism and American rugged individualism," Sato contends that the solitary figure bent over a writing tablet in a seaside shack or mountain hut is just as Japanese as any salaryman on the bullet train. "Buddhism," he reminds me, "at least as it was transmitted to Japan, insisted that enlightenment required solitude."

The pull of solitude directly contravenes the crowd mentality that is Japan's most visible feature. It almost seems as if no middle ground is allowed. And a growing shift among ordinary citizens—not Buddhist monks, but kids and workers—toward solitude has the country's social critics worried. "More of us are spending more time alone," frets the writer of an editorial in *Mainichi Shimbun*. "People do not socialize in public spaces as much and seem to show less interest in their fellow human beings. The more people feel that they are bystanders with no connections to other human beings, the less capable they will be of applying limits to their interactions with others."

THIS IMPLIES, OF course, that loners are wild beasts, out-of-control maniacs who flick the hats off strangers' heads and rant incessantly about the best way to peel beets or lance boils. Loners, the columnist implies, have no limits. The idea, in Japan, that being a loner makes you sick is most strikingly illustrated by the increasing concern over a social phenomenon that first seized the attention of the local press in the mid-1990s, then gathered momentum and became a hot topic in newspapers worldwide.

Hikikomori, meaning "social withdrawal," refers both to the individual and the syndrome now said to affect as many as a million young Japanese. *Hikikomori* barricade themselves in their bedrooms, refusing, often for years at a time, to come out. Typically it begins when a student quits school abruptly, then holes up with TV, computer, and Gameboy behind a locked bedroom door, emerging to raid the fridge only when the rest of the family is asleep. Calling this "a national mental health problem," *Asahi Shimbun* gave as one example a twenty-nine-year-old man "whose only communication [with the outside world] over the previous five years had been in the form of written notes left on the kitchen table with instructions such as: 'Get me a video game magazine.'" *Asahi* has also reported on parents who move out of their homes, leaving the recluses alone there for fear that, if they stay, their *hikikomori* children will murder them. Commentators on the phenomenon say *hikikomori* simply would not have been possible in an earlier, less affluent era. A generation ago, kids' bedrooms were not outfitted with arrays of electronic toys and equipment—and parents and teachers wielded more control.

The foreign press shines its curious klieg lights on what it sees as more proof of Japan's bizarreness. "Missing: the hermit closeted behind the bedroom door," is the headline of an article on *hikikomori* in an Australian daily. Dubbing it "Japan's lost generation" and "one of the most perplexing mysteries in Japan today," *Time* quotes the director of a Tokyo-area *hikikomori* outreach center who offers this explanation: "It's Japan. Here, you have to be like other people, and if you aren't, you have a sense of loss, of shame. So you withdraw." The editor of a magazine for and about *hikikomori* speculates that a childhood spent trying desperately to please others leads some to profound alienation and social burnout. By her account and others, theirs is a far-from-idyllic seclusion. It is merely, apparently, by the *hikikomori*'s own logic, a manner of coping, a last resort. Arguably, their extreme response would not be necessary if Japanese culture was more tolerant of loners in general, less eager to pounce on those who—from the mainstream point of view—drop the ball. It is as if, from behind their bedroom doors, the *hikikomori* are taunting their tormentors: *You want to pretend we don't exist? Okay. We'll hide so well that the whole world will hear about it, to your shame.*

IF THE WORLD at large tolerates lonerism barely, if at all, throughout the rest of the year, it is relentless at holiday time. Holidays vary from culture to culture, and many an American loner traveling or living abroad has spent a serene, guilt-free Thanksgiving or July 4 at work or at the beach or preparing a favorite dinner far from home in a country to which those days do not matter. Far from home, the loner is far from that social pressure which even nonloners detest about holidays. There is this presumption that on holidays we need to be somewhere. Need to be with people in general and in particular with relatives who have a way of bringing out the worst in us and in each other. *Need* in whose opinion? Theirs. The faceless they. Of all the conventions agreed upon by the majority and thus taken for granted as the will of some even greater authority, assumed to be right and true, the idea that holidays must never be celebrated alone is ironclad. Holidays mark milestones whose importance entire nations and religions recognize. So who could say such days, infused with spiritual and political meaning, are *too* profound to share? That sharing dilutes sensation, thought, meaning? That holidays are thus best savored in a concentrated form: alone? Who could say so? Loners. Blasphemers.

Criticism comes to those who beg off family holiday gatherings. *How could you do this to us? Aunt Doreen wants to see you before chemotherapy makes her lose all her hair. You used to love Easter. I want the whole family together for once—you haven't seen your brothers and sisters all year. Why do you hate us? This is going to kill your father.* And criticism comes to those without families and who beg off celebrating with friends or coworkers who imagine themselves kind to ask us. "No One Should Have to Spend Holiday Alone," declares a headline in *The Compass,* a Catholic newspaper. "Alone for Christmas?" asks another, in a Mennonite paper. "If you are part of a wonderful family, and have good friends near, then this will be a Christmas to look forward to. . . . If you're facing the prospect of a Christmas alone . . . take comfort in Christ, our Saviour, who knows your anguish."

Granted, for nonloners the prospect of holidays alone is truly horrifying. The media feeds into this horror by reporting, as Christmas approaches, that the national suicide rate always soars at this time of year. That the claim proves untrue and is more urban legend than fact only makes clearer the nonloner bias, the contagion of nonloner belief. A team of researchers at the Annenberg School for Communication collected sixty-seven newspaper articles with a holiday theme that appeared between November 1999 and January 2000. While two-thirds of the stories created the perception that this is a deadly season, only eight of the stories cited any research attempting to back the claim. The researchers found that in 1996, the most recent year for which statistics were available, December actually saw fewer suicides than any other month.

Holidays serve a sociological and anthropological function. In that sense, they exist purely to unite people—compatriots, members of any given faith—who by sharing celebrations cement their shared values and customs. In that sense, too, holidays are an effective means of showing and teaching tradition. All of this goes out the window if holidays are observed by an individual, alone. *Then* what function do holidays serve, if not a purely communal one?

A ritual one. And rituals are too often snatched out of the hands of the individual, where they would mean more, and could be tailored to fit. And what of those days that are, for whatever reason, red-letter days for the loner alone? The anniversary of the first time he won a marathon? Of the first day she saw the Eiffel Tower? Who has the right to decide what everyone should celebrate? Maybe what matters most is the day you survived a car crash. That is your holiday, yours alone.

AND IF THE world levels a basilisk's eye at holidays spent alone, neither does it give any quarter to undergoing, alone, those minuscule celebrations observed every day: meals. The act of eating, it is generally understood, is another of those endeavors that bespeak human fulfillment when shared, but when performed alone are evidence of failure, an Eleanor Rigby-ish last resort, shameful and even sinister: It cannot possibly be fun. The chef Alice Waters once told me she believes Americans "just aren't happy," and that both a reason for and a symptom of our national sorrow is the fact that "we aren't sitting down at the table anymore." The implication was: sitting down with others. She cited a recent study that determined that 88 percent of American children no longer share even a single daily meal with their families. Whether or not this is making America fat and sad, as Waters suggested, the comment reveals how deeply set, even at the very vanguard of culinary culture, is the notion that meals eaten apart and alone are somehow inferior.

Granted, wolfing a bag of Funyuns while watching *Porky's 2* on video in an otherwise deserted apartment is one thing, and relishing a mesclun salad at a candlelit table in the same apartment so alertly as to pulp every leaf ever so gently between the teeth is another. But loners, no matter our taste, eat many meals, if not most, alone. At home, this affords the essence of choice and spontaneity, thus the essence of loner experience: the true meaning of "having it your way." Jell-O eaten from a toy pail with a toy spade while taking a bath? A beef-tongue omelet? Why the hell not?

It is when loners go out that the going gets tough. Dining alone in restaurants invites stares: furtive, curious, pitying. *That poor man! Did his date stand him up? Did the wife who used to cook his meals die?* My friend Nicholas dines out alone all the time. He has found that sitting at a restaurant's bar, ordering and eating there, is easier and provokes less unwanted attention than asking for a table all to himself.

"It's fine to sit at a bar and not talk to anybody," Nicholas says. Conversation and eye contact are not expected there, as they would be at, say, the long refectory-style tables featured in some upscale new restaurants. Nicholas first adopted his strategy years ago at Jeremiah Tower's Stars Café in San Francisco, where he discovered that, sitting at the bar, he could order off the same menu as did diners at tables. And rather than facing those tables, seated at the bar he had a direct view of bartenders and dishwashers and the restaurant's hustle and bustle.

"It was like a show. So I was fine sitting there just being with myself."

Dining alone elsewhere, he says, "I've been eyed a little warily. And as experienced as I am, it still summons an act of bravery from me, and I like that. I like the idea of setting an example—proving that it is acceptable to be alone in a public place where everyone else is in groups, and to just be sitting there eating, not having to be engrossed in anything else."

On a visit to Las Vegas, I once ate breakfast alone at the Circus Circus buffet. I just wanted to see if it was possible, how it might be done. After waiting on line for my first serving of eggs, waffles, cantaloupe, hash browns, and coffee, I made my way to a booth that had been designed to seat at least four. There weren't any smaller ones, and the sea of tables crammed into the huge ring the booths made were too close together to bear. Jingly ambient music mingled with the clatter of dishes, the thud of ketchup bottles and mugs and the shrieking of children who have eaten too much syrup. Nibbling the waffles, I took out a book and began reading. Coffee. Eggs. Turned the page. It was hard to sit still. Something in the experience, in the very fact of sitting alone at a booth made for many, in a vast restaurant built to seat hundreds in a format that encourages eating fast, had an almost physical effect, a propulsion, as if the pink vinyl seat would eject me. Very deliberately I finished what was on my plate, left my book open, facedown, and went back on line for seconds. Slowly. Meaningfully. As if it was the most normal thing in the world.

But it was not. And I could feel that with every bite: that I was bucking a tide, that it took great will to stay. That I was dining on borrowed time.

And this is why loners love takeout.

CIVILIZATION WILL GO on whether you attend the block party or not. It will, whether you say hello and talk to anyone today or not. Whether you get married today, or ever, or have kids or not. Its momentum is strong. It will go on.

And on and on and on until it sucks up the last resources of the planet that birthed it, according to ecophilosopher Pentti Linkola, a loner who believes Earth is doomed because there are too many people on it. Linkola, whose writings have sparked fierce controversy in his native Finland and around the world, compares the planet to a ship that is filled beyond its capacity with passengers and is capsizing. There is only one lifeboat, and only a fraction of the passengers can fit into it. The best thing to do, he insists, the only reasonable thing, is to hoist a few worthy survivors into the lifeboat, then grab an ax and resolutely whack off the hands of any others who try to climb on board. In Linkola's ideal vision of the world, its population would be reduced to about five million—roughly one-tenth of one percent of the current figure. This should be achieved, he insists, by the issuing of parenting licenses only to those select adults who prove themselves qualified. In Linkola's future, mandatory schooling would last only four years, advertisements would cease to exist, handtools would replace electric ones, forests would replace parking lots, hunting would replace other forms of food acquisition, bicycles and rowboats would replace cars. Linkola practices what he preaches. He lives alone near an isolated lake in which he fishes for his meals. Not surprisingly, he has a lot of critics.

WHILE THE PRIMARY foes of Linkola's radical vision are consumerism and industry, he is also saying that society in its current state—greedy and growing larger—is a form of planetary suicide. Civilization's old habits, learned in bygone times when survival depended on our all sticking together, have in fact become liabilities.

At the very least, whether or not those habits bring about the death of the planet as Linkola fears, they are clearly no longer required.

Your participation is now optional.

2.

listen to us

If it's popular, then what in the world has it got to do with us?
Well, that's a secret.

GROWING UP HALF an hour from Disneyland meant being taken there at least once a year, some years many more. Under a bubblegum-blue sky I glided through its gates, slipping under the silvery belt of the monorail, then into the crush, a solid sunburned mass capped with felt pirate tricornes and Goofy hats, trailing two-eared balloons all the way to the slate turrets of Sleeping Beauty Castle.

Queuing up to ride the Matterhorn, its fiberglass snow twinkling in the Orange County sunshine I would fall into a stupor. Like a hophead, I stared blankly as tinny yodels pumped from the speakers, submarines plied the sparkling bay across Tomorrowland, and all around me visitors cried, "Look! There goes Daisy Duck!"

The jungle boats were bliss. The Inuit automatons singing *it's a small world* made my blood surge. Not that I knew it then, but mine was a different euphoria than others felt. For them it was just fun, all rocket ships and tape-recorded xylophones. For me it was a trance, a transmission: the heady buzz of mysteries vouchsafed. I was the channeler. The chosen. Not that I, whirling almost nauseous in a giant teacup, realized this.

Messages for me breathed from every cable, from the very asphalt. The secret, though it took years to translate, was: *This is what imagination can do. Minds made this pirate ship. Minds made those flying elephants.*

Not just plain minds but special minds, the minds that can.
Yours.

Wink. It was an invitation. A challenge. Seduction. Obligation. Troth. The invisible partnership whose secret sign you always wear.

Not that I knew this then. Not that I realized, then, that there were those who were creative and those who were not. That the creative made what the others consumed. That the creative were few and answered to summonses that no one else could hear. That this meant many—if not most—of the creative must be loners. That there was such a thing as loners at all.

Or that the minds behind Disneyland were in large part the minds of loners. How was I to know about the loner Ub Iwerks, Walt Disney's early partner and master animator, who created Mickey Mouse and whose innovative animation techniques set Disney productions light-years ahead of anything the entertainment world had ever seen? Or Walt himself, a self-promoter whose success depended on shepherding the workers he called his "Imagineers"? Like me, he needed few friends and, like me, he got a reputation as aloof.

SUPERMAN IS A loner. Tarzan is a loner. Batman, Spider-Man, Davy Crockett, and Xena are loners. Elvis Presley tried to pass himself off as one. The Lone Ranger, Tonto not withstanding, was a loner.

In the playground and the classroom and the office, we are mocked and feared. The loner who goes home to feed his iguana when the rest of the Crate & Barrel staff goes out after work for beer is despised, not idolized. Yet on the screen, stage, and page, it is a different story. Here we see heroic loners. Self-reliant, sexy loners. Rebels. Sages. Mages. Stars. The mob worships imaginary loners. Pays to watch them. Wears T-shirts depicting them, adopts loners' catchwords, dresses as them for Halloween. Frat boys love Spider-Man, and so do Girl Scouts.

It is make-believe, but in that land of make-believe, we rule. We fucking *rule*.

Now why is that?

In each nonloner lurks a tiny loner struggling to get out. Just as many if not most loners possess, within them, an uncanny knack for entertaining others, many nonloners possess, deep down in *them,* a secret touch of lonerism. An impulse, a yearning—it lies dormant nearly all the time, knowing that the outside world would hardly make it feel welcome. It knows, this loner within, that it is safer hidden. Yet now and then it is confronted with a rare welcome in the form of some song or comic book, and it springs out: clumsily, a bit insecurely, but hungrily.

There is another reason. Made-up loners capture mobs' hearts because, being made-up, these rebels and righteous punks and rocketmen are made to please. They are not heroic by accident but because they were created that way. Created, often enough, by loners.

If loners are a minority in the world at large, we swell the ranks in the creative world. The creative process lends itself to loners and vice versa. And there is the key. This is why so much of what winds up in art museums, movie houses, music venues, bookshops, theme parks and on TV has a loner slant. Unlike fine art, popular culture targets the broadest possible audience. But what no one wants to admit is how much of "popular" culture has always been the work of a tiny, maligned subset of the population. The subset that will not join hands. That does not know itself by name. Wink. Nudge. It is not, perhaps, really the Jews who run Hollywood.

A loner who fashions a fictional character who is a loner will not make that character a sleazy, ugly, hateful, unredeemed killer. A loner given the chance to fashion a loner for the public eye will make that loner hot. Smart. Strong. It stands to reason. And given our disproportionate presence among those whose dreams and visions end up onscreen, on the billboards along Sunset Strip, it stands to reason that so much of what has turned into American popular culture over the last two hundred years has been loner propaganda. We dish it up.

And nonloners devour it like it was pie.

Loner values once played a much larger role in American culture than they do now. A nation founded by iconoclasts, a revolution won by outnumbered outsiders. A wild land settled by rugged individualists: the cowboy and the pioneer against the unknown, the uncharted, the frightening creatures whose home it was. A protagonist on his own, brave and resourceful, making claims and righting wrongs, misunderstood, a stranger in a strange land, pure at heart. Loner values.

But the rugged-individualist-as-American-hero has been more or less eclipsed in the culture, in general. A settled land functions on teamwork. A slow but sure antiloner sentiment has crept into every chamber of the American honeycomb. Loners, as portrayed in the media, have turned from saviors to terrorists. Loner heroes are less obvious onscreen and on the stage today than fifty or even thirty years ago. They no longer enjoy uncontested pride of place. But frat boys still love Spider-Man.

It is easy to resent them for this. Eyeing the nonloner humming loner anthems by Nirvana or wearing a Batman T-shirt, we think *What the hell do YOU know?* Nonloners can just fleetingly grasp the meaning of those anthems and those heroes. Sing though they might, wear what they might, nonloners are ultimately left behind. They serve a purpose, though. They pay the bills.

NOT ALL LONERS are creators. Many of us are consumers, and as such we are devoted fans, after a fashion. Each of us in our own tiny way has loved some next-big-thing. But loners as fans do not serve the purpose that the entertainment industry wants fans to serve. We do not feed the industry because, by nature, we do not proselytize, do not actively convert new fans, do not create new markets. Early adopters, as trendsetters are called in the industry, declare their love for something or other and become vortices, passing the flame from friend to friend and follower to follower. Loners stand apart from this relay race.

For most fans, it makes all the difference in the world that there are other fans. Part of the thrill of those arena concerts is the fellowship, the frisson in the *fact* of it, just as it is in war and church. The more fans share a love for anything, the more valid that love looks. This is classic nonlonerthink. This is one of those things bred in nonloner bones which loners fail to understand. Nonloner fans compete over which of them can show their love the most, in other words which of them can buy the most branded merchandise, attend the most shows, tell the most friends.

Unmoved by the mass hysteria, immune to the contagion by which nonloners spend fortunes just proving they like a certain song or style, we do not give the entertainment industry what it seeks. We do not do as it would wish. Neither spending the money nor sporting the outward signs of what we love, we slip under the corporate radar, slip outside its gunsight. We are invisible fans, the purpose of our fandom having just to do with us and the objects of our affection, not with fellow fans.

We tend to react to these things we love in our own ways, which tend to have more to do with feeling and imagining than with buying. This harks back to the way I felt at Disneyland:

that it was not simply a pleasure dome, but an implicit challenge. Not an end in itself, but an inspiration. *Now that you have learned about imagination, go and use your own. Do not waste your time in the gift shop loading up on souvenirs. They will not bring you what you need.* Nonloners take being entertained for granted. For the mob, entertainment is a finished product, not a starting point.

LONERS NEED POPULAR culture and need it badly. You might say that is a contradiction in terms. You might say that what is popular by definition is not meant for you. Yet even in these tricked-up versions of reality lies information. TV gives no more an authentic reading of the real world than a zoo gives an authentic view of animals. But we need clues. We scry mass entertainments not as members of the mass, but in the interest of acquiring snatches of its language.

And loners need information. Nonloners learn from flesh-and-blood role models. They find these everywhere, hitching their wagons to teachers and friends and mentors with an ease that shocks us. And we might mock nonloners for this, for being role-model sluts. But lacking that easy way out, loners are forced to learn a lot from non-flesh-and-blood sources. Sure, we burn with questions. What does a monsoon feel like, we wonder, but will never bring ourselves to ask Mr. Singh down the block. What would it be like to live through civil war, in a harem, on a submarine, as a doctor, raising a family, being knighted, going over Victoria Falls in a barrel, falling in love with a blind man, breeding baboons in the jungle, burning down a house, battling pirates, plundering Egyptian pyramids?

We cannot find out firsthand, at least not yet. So we soak it up secondhand. We trust what comes across to us on the screen, on the page because it comes to us pure. It asks nothing of us. Interaction is work, is not our natural mode. Why should the getting of wisdom involve an extra barrier, be an ordeal? Why put it behind murky glass, as it is when it requires interaction, and attach a ball and chain?

AT THE DAWN of the twentieth century, political economist Thorstein Veblen wrote about the rise of a new American leisure class to whom seeing and being seen meant everything. It was Veblen who coined the phrase "conspicuous consumption." A wealthy man's "own unaided effort will not avail to sufficiently put his opulence in evidence," thus only by the showy expenditure of money will others be sure to see and understand. "The aid of friends and competitors is therefore brought in," Veblen explained, "by resorting to the giving of valuable presents and expensive feasts and entertainments." Such displays, such sharings of wealth, were nothing new. Native American tribes of the Pacific Northwest had long since been engaging in potlatch rituals based on the same principle. But high visibility gave the new leisure class an unprecedented power, setting in motion what has by now become a knee-jerk reaction and a main mechanism of the style-making machinery: the masses imitating the privileged, either with merchandise or manners or activities.

In Veblen's day, "privileged" meant rich. Today it means cool and good-looking—and sometimes rich. By the mid-twentieth century, "keeping up with the Joneses" had already become a vicious cycle.

With the emergence of urban life, Veblen wrote, "the means of communication and the mobility of the population now expose the individual to the observation of many persons who have no other means of judging his reputability than the display of goods (and perhaps of breeding) which he is able to make while he is under their direct observation." It is now customary, and instantaneous, to identify strangers by their style, their choice of mass-produced popular culture. Thus loners who eschew fads and movements are elusive, offering few dead-giveaway clues. By Veblen's reckoning, we give no evidence. Our observers "have no other means of judging" us. They do not know what to make of us. Fancy their frustration.

In 1939, when Bill Finger and Bob Kane created their superhero, Batman, they decided that the black-clad crime-fighter would be nearly a hermit. In the earliest episodes he broods alone in his cave, laying plans for punishing the bad guys of Gotham City. Only later did Batman get a sidekick, young Robin, for whom the loner was a mentor. As a representative of the "normal" world, Robin makes Batman appear all the more marvelous.

Steve Ditko, the artist who cocreated Spider-Man with Stan Lee in 1962, deliberately made teenage Peter Parker a loner: a nerdy, intelligent, reclusive, orphaned teen who was not popular at school. His arachnoid alterego was daring and courageous, though in his dark windowless room after a dramatic adventure,

Parker sometimes mused wistfully about his own obscurity. The world could never understood him and didn't want to.

Something in the nature of comics—perhaps the sheer low-tech physicality of drawing or the way words and pictures feed each other—makes them a startlingly intimate mirror for an artist's soul. For his comic *Ghost World,* Daniel Clowes created a loner heroine in the alienated teen Enid Coleslaw, whose view of the world is that only two people in it—herself and her best friend, Becky—are at all worthwhile. Enid's name is an anagram of the artist's. When the screenplay of the film version of *Ghost World,* which Clowes coauthored with director Terry Zwigoff, was nominated for an Academy Award in 2002, the cartoonist told me he couldn't wait for the celebrity luncheons, publicity events, and even the ceremony to be over so that he could go back to drawing in the quiet seclusion of his California home.

"Everything was going great until this happened," he told me, not entirely joking, a few days before Oscar night. "The minute this thing's over, everything will be back to normal. I can't think of anything more torturous than having to give a speech in front of a billion people." Laughing drily, he mused that a book about loners could easily be all about cartoonists. Clowes had been profiled shortly before in the *New Yorker,* and he still felt the sting of having had a stranger in his house watching him work and asking probing questions. "There's a reason that we aren't actors," Clowes says of cartoonists.

· · ·

NO POPULAR-CULTURE medium is aimed at a larger audience with a lower common denominator than television. Worldwide, a billion viewers really *do* watch the Academy Awards. This reality, the astoundingly massive group consciousness that is entered at the flick of a TV's "on" switch, has been reflected in countless ensemble shows—from soap operas to police dramas—whose crux is the relationships between their multiple characters. Yet even from the living-room screen, a few important loners have emerged.

Riding the shirttails of cinematic Westerns, which we will investigate elsewhere in this book, no less than two dozen TV Westerns were airing during prime time every week by the end of the 1950s. Apropos of the Western genre, many of these series spotlighted singular heroes in a time and place whose openness and lawlessness made individualism iconic and made self-reliance romantic. Launched in 1958, *The Rifleman* was the tale of a single-dad loner perpetually setting things straight with an innovative rapid-cocking rifle. *Have Gun Will Travel* is the story of another loner in the form of a highly ethical hired killer. The tellingly titled series *The Loner*—created by *The Twilight Zone*'s Rod Serling—featured an ex-Union soldier on a solitary sojourn in search of personal meaning.

In these programs, guns flash. Stunning Western scenery sweeps past. But what matters most is the man. We watch his eyes. We wonder what we would do in his shoes. Historians such as Frederick Jackson Turner have said that the American West is the key to our national identity, that from its man-against-the-wilderness dynamic sprang our pluck, our independence, our inventiveness. As we have seen, the paradigm of the Wild West is a loner paradigm: the outsider, the self-reliant carver of his own future, the screw-you individualist. Nonloner viewers feel that inner cowboy stirring deep inside, and in him they feel a wistful anguish at what has been lost. Actual loners see Wild West adventures as transparencies to be fitted over our own lives. Lariats aside, is navigating a tricky stretch of Jackson Hole alone on horseback all that different from plotting a course through a day at the office when time clocks, bosses, and coworkers are the rattlesnakes, the rapids, the Sioux on the warpath?

LAUNCHED IN 1972, the TV series *Kung Fu* introduced Caine, a half-Chinese, half-American martial artist. Solitary and con-summately circumspect, Caine kicked and spun his way through dangerous encounters on the frontier, forever guided by Buddhist wisdom learned in boyhood at the feet of his old master in China. True-life martial-arts star Bruce Lee had inspired the TV series, whose dreamy but lethal-footed fictional loner soared to prominence as an unlikely role model for adolescent boys.

Adolescent boys, loners or not, tend to like to kick things. That they would, en masse, filter their kicking fervor through a quiet, gunless character such as Caine gives pause for thought. Because he must fight unarmed, Caine is more independent than other Wild West heroes and, in effect, more potent. With only his limbs as weapons and with ancient philosophy elevating his fighting above mere brutish ferocity, Caine exemplifies heroism refined to its essence. By this logic, the ultimate hero is the ultimate loner. So by virtue of being loners, we, too, are all heroes. Like Caine, we are strangers in a strange land, outnumbered, out-armed. Like Caine, we look defenseless, but our secret, like his, is that we are not.

BULLHORN THAT IT is for rebel voices, rock music has from its outset attracted loners. Like comics, rock at its roots is primal, minimal, a body and, maybe, an instrument. Nostalgic critics lament that rock was co-opted after Woodstock, when greed and cynicism poisoned its rebel ideals. True enough, later rock has a less and less lonerish sound. At the turn of the millennium, hip-hop was the world's top-selling musical genre, and almost universally its lyrics laud togetherness. We be clubbin'. Gangbangin'. Gangsta love. Rock the party. A Snoop Dogg hit in the autumn of 2002 features the singer urging a woman to share her sexual favors with his friends: "It ain't no fun," goes the refrain, "if the homies can't have none." A far cry from the tattered outsider pleading, *Oh Lord, please don't let me be misunderstood.*

Ever media-savvy, Elvis crafted his public image carefully and consciously, vaunting himself as a loner—more of a loner than he actually was, some insiders say. But he knew the new genre he was spawning was all about alienation. About being misjudged. He worked it.

His fans seized onto this ethos as well. Posing as outrageous fringe-dwellers, early rock stars launched one of the most powerful pop phenomena the world has ever known: youth culture. And while it is a mass movement, conformist nearly to the point of fascism, its core message—rock's creation myth—is that of the loner. Of Bob Dylan turning his back on society with a sardonic croak: *Don't think twice, it's all right.* Rock lyrics lend themselves to lonerism: disenfranchised, individual, poetic, emotional, personal. Youth culture, thus pop-music culture, is a very strange animal because it is a collective loner culture. How much of its lonerism is a put-on, is artifice, depends on the performer. The star is spotlighted and amplified. The star is set apart, untouchable, glorious, gifted, driven.

DESPITE THE CAMARADERIE in the Beatles' early public image, from the outset John Lennon was assessed by insiders as aloof and—a typical charge thrown at loners—standoffish. Lennon kept to himself. "The smart Beatle," as he was known, wore a distant smile that suggested he inhabited a rich but private inner world of which his songs and stage persona offered only fleeting, tempting glimpses. The photographer Jürgen Vollmer, who worked with the group in its early Hamburg days, recalls Lennon as a "mystery behind sunglasses." By contrast, outgoing Paul McCartney was "a very nice, warmhearted man. Always smiling. . . . But that wasn't the case with John. He was much more complex and I didn't feel completely comfortable with him . . . he was never that accessible as a person. He was very guarded." Onstage, Vollmer reflects, Lennon forced himself to seem at least a bit more social "in order to play to his audience."

The concert stage is at once the world's most private and most public place. It is a bridge: On one side lies the dreamy, solitary netherworld where art is born. On the other lies the fleshy crush of fans, the press, the public image. For loners whose success depends on navigating that span, disaster always lurks. Tales are told of legendary rockers who, at crucial points in their careers, slipped out of sight, sometimes out of life.

After founding Pink Floyd in 1964, singer-songwriter Syd Barrett was one of Britain's most promising young voices. A former art-school student, Barrett reacted badly to touring and the social pressure it entailed. He started ingesting drugs, one cohort later recalled, "by the shovelful." Throughout one concert, Barrett remained absolutely motionless onstage, like a mannequin. Shortly afterward, in 1968, he quit the band. During his last-ever interview, in 1971, Barrett told a reporter, "I'm disappearing. I'm full of dust and guitars." He promptly went into permanent seclusion, though fans worldwide remained fixated on Barrett's short but blindingly bright trajectory. In 1988, his brother-in-law Paul Breen was interviewed on British radio. "Contrary to public opinion," he declared, Syd—who had gone back to using his birth name, Roger—was "not living in a field in a barrel somewhere. He is living in a semi-detached house in a suburb of Cambridge . . . I think the word 'recluse' is probably emotive. It would probably be truer to say that he enjoys his own company now rather than that of others." Barrett had stopped playing music, but had once again taken up painting, his old love. As the years wore on, backpackers periodically camped outside his home, but he pointedly ignored them.

Releasing a solo record in 2002 after years spent in seclusion at his Minneapolis home, the Replacements' Paul Westerberg told the *San Francisco Examiner* that he had written his new songs "to entertain myself. After four years holed up in my house, I didn't want to watch TV anymore and I was sick of reading books. So I just sat down at home and began playing." To the reporter, who called him "an avowed recluse," the influential songwriter explained his own loner philosophy: "Nobody thinks so, but I actually do love the people who care about me, and if I'm in a room with them I feel very protective. If it's a room full of chowderheads, though," Westerberg said, he will simply "walk out."

Guns N' Roses became the biggest-selling band of the late '80s before its aggressive vocalist and cofounder Axl Rose left the public eye and went into seclusion. In 1999, MTV reported that Rose had turned from "the rock world's most notorious star to its most puzzling recluse," noting that "sightings of Rose have been virtually nonexistent" since the band's last tour eight years before. In 2000, *Rolling Stone* dubbed Rose "rock's most famous recluse" and ran a probing interview in which the "recluse locked away mysteriously at his Malibu estate" told the reporter: "I don't find it's in my best interest to be out there. I am building something slowly, and it doesn't seem to be so much out there as in here, in the studio and in my home." He was to reappear two years later at the Grammy Awards ceremony.

Others have not survived the crossing. Folk-rocker Nick Drake became a posthumous sensation after a 2000 Volkswagen Cabrio commercial featured his moody song "Pink Moon" as its background music. Ironically, the commercial showed a carful of attractive young friends enjoying a moonlit drive—Drake himself was a notorious loner. Little appreciated during his lifetime, he died at twenty-six of an overdose that may or may not have been deliberate.

Nirvana's Kurt Cobain sang wrenchingly of a loner's angst in songs like "About a Girl," whose shouted refrain is: "But I can't see you every night—free!" Here, the singer acknowledges his attachment to the lover in question, yet repeatedly declares his need for private time and space. Never, he warns, must she expect more of him than he is willing or able to give. His tone is not sneering, not taunting, just desperate, as if he has exhausted himself striving to establish boundaries which others refuse to respect. A song on the band's *Nevermind* album is titled, tellingly, "Stay Away." The more numerous and adoring Cobain's fans grew, the more alienated he felt from them. He killed himself at twenty-seven in 1994.

ROCK STARS ARE *expected* to be tortured loners. Alienation and separation go with the territory. This, too, is a nonloner fantasy: for fleeting moments, playing air guitar, nonloners visualize themselves onstage, holding the hordes in thrall, making them scream, cream, sweat. Just as they do when watching *Batman*, they picture themselves getting a loner's glory but, because they cannot comprehend it, not his pain.

For famous ballplayers, the virtual opposite applies. Nobody wants *them* to be loners. Their every move watched by millions, these are team players in the most literal sense. Professional team players are paid handsomely for acting like anything *but* loners. They must cooperate, follow instructions, and anticipate the thoughts and actions of others. Basketball, football, and soccer would be entirely different games, albeit more interesting ones, if every player made up his own rules.

So when an occasional exception to the rule makes the big leagues and plays like a dream but remains an unrepentant loner, neither fans nor the press are very willing to forgive. Joe DiMaggio led the New York Yankees to ten American League pennants and nine World Series championships, but his fierce love of privacy won no hearts. Reporters called him vain, tyrannical, imperious, brooding, moody. One wrote about the many well-wishers who "wait for hours sometimes" to have a personal glimpse or a word with DiMaggio, "waiting and knowing he may wish to be alone; but it does not seem to matter, they are endlessly awed by him, moved by the mystique, he is a kind of male Garbo." Another loner was Ted Williams, the Boston Red Sox hitter who won baseball's elite Triple Crown twice and was the American League MVP twice, in 1946 and 1949. Williams demonstrated a frank lack of interest in his fans, refusing, as a rule, to tip his cap to the crowds at Fenway Park. It made him fair game: One *New York Post* writer fumed that "when it comes to arrogant, ungrateful athletes, this one leads the league." Musing on Williams's death in 2002, an ESPN reporter asked, "What if he had been as determined to be liked as he was determined to be a great hitter?"

After hitting the home run that broke the all-time single-season record in 2001, the San Francisco Giants' Barry Bonds leaped onto home plate. History had just been made. Yet his teammates, rather than storm the plate to embrace him, stayed in the dugout and kept their distance. Bonds was not a hugging kind of guy. Arguably the greatest player of his generation, having hit his 600th home run in 2002, the San Francisco Giants left fielder remains one of pro sports' most talented and most admired athletes, but also one of its most definitive loners. He trains alone whenever possible, socializing with fellow players as little as possible. Nearly every article about him mentions it. Predictably, many also call him aloof, arrogant, hostile, and cold. "He seldom lets people inside his inner circle," *USA Today* noted in 2001. "Some call him combative and moody. Most of the time he's just unavailable."

What difference would it make, Bonds asked the *USA Today* reporter, "if I changed and started acting nicer to people? . . . I just wish people would accept me for who I am. Why should I change? . . . I don't care what people say or what the media portrays me to be, I'm proud of who I am. The Bible says you don't have to be nice, or not nice. Just speak the truth. Jesus always spoke the truth. Not everybody liked him, either."

When his team celebrates big victories in the locker room, Bonds stands off to the side—happy, but separate. In an ESPN interview, he acknowledged that the media would be much kinder to him "if I could just smile at everybody and wave." In 1993, during his first year with the Giants, he asked a reporter, "Why can't people just enjoy the show? And then let the entertainer go home and get his rest, so he can put on another show?" Asked how he felt as his team drew close to winning the

World Series in 2002, he told the *San Francisco Chronicle*, "It's hard enough for me to come in here and talk. I want to do my talking on the field. That's where it counts."

Bonds's problem is, he's real. It's his humanity, the fact that he lives and breathes. Because he is a human being, nonloners cannot quite bring themselves to fashion Bonds into a superhero, an icon whom they can wholeheartedly impersonate in their fantasies. He resembles them too much biologically to transcend the distrust and dislike they feel for the flesh-and-blood loner down the block. Bonds would have been better loved if he were a cartoon.

DURING THE SECOND World War, the BBC aired seemingly absurd lines of dialogue—*The dog barks at midnight* and such—during its daily programming. The vast majority of listeners never knew that these lines were secret coded messages for the Resistance, over the Channel in France. The messages announced actions and strategies, the comings and goings of paratroopers.

Like loners, Resistance fighters were outnumbered, unseen. They passed as ordinary citizens, but secretly they stood apart. In every home and army base, every shop and office, the BBC was popular culture. Only Resistance fighters, alone and in secret, could extract from that flow of comedies, concerts, and dramas seeds of meaning, blueprints they and only they knew how to use.

We neoloners are not likely to throw grenades onto Nazi transport trains. But, like Resistance fighters, we can prick up our ears for codes the mob does not know are there. Tricked out with coonskin caps and spider feet, the codes say *Hey, I'm here* and *This is possible* and *Watch what we can do*. Staticky though they might be, crowded out by other signals, the codes are still there. The mob doesn't know it. The mob is singing and dancing to our codes and does not know it.

3.

do you feel lucky?

[FILM]

Brave and bold and alone:
Where have all the cowboys gone?

I N *ONE HOUR PHOTO*, released in the summer of 2002, Robin Williams played Sy Parrish, a middle-aged man who works behind a SavMart photo-developing counter. Williams drew critical raves for his performance as what the *San Francisco Chronicle* called a "well-played loner" who becomes obsessed with a middle-class family whose snaps he develops, and whom he stalks with terrifying results.

"Sy is a typical disturbed loner," the *Northwest Herald* asserted. He is "a sinister loner," the Manchester *Guardian* offered—though another British paper called Parrish simply "a private man who very much keeps himself to himself."

The New York *Daily News* reflected that, given the film's allusions to hunting, "the camera here comes to symbolize the weapon a loner might use to describe and defend his territory."

A reviewer in *Knot* magazine mused that his generation, the eighteen-to-twenty-five-year-olds, is keenly familiar with "this type of social-misfit drama: Loner meets object of affection, loner tries to make connection, loner gets rejected, loner gets really violent. . . .

"Outside the movie theater and throughout our day, we see these loners everywhere and we try to ignore them because, frankly, who wants to be reminded of the failures lingering around our own lives?"

For effect, the film's production designer drained every scene featuring Sy of all color except white and gray blue. Writer/director Mark Romanek, a former music-video director, told one reporter that his inspiration for *One Hour Photo* was a type of film that emerged in the 1970s—dramas such as *Taxi Driver, The Passenger,* and *The Tenant,* in which isolated men inhabit worlds of their own: small, cramped, crazy worlds.

It was not always this way.

YOUNGER MOVIEGOERS WHO do not frequent revival theaters or video stores' vintage racks might never know that for a long, bright span in the middle of the twentieth century, loners were the undisputed heroes of the large screen. Saviors. Soldiers. Savvy characters, survivors who had lived and learned and could never be led. Their solitary nature—riding alone, fighting alone—highlighted not failure or neurosis, but strength. Self-reliance under pressure, against all odds, under fire. The evil in such films, which comprise genres that held the whole world in thrall, is not within the loner, but without. The loner is a force for good: all the stronger and purer for being concentrated in a single, solitary human being.

From a loner's point of view, of course, loner characters by definition provide filmmakers with ready-made material. No two of us are alike. And we live by our own codes. We combine big imaginations with an air of mystery, of the unknown. Our motivations are our own, thus unpredictable, thus interesting, in theory, to probe. As outsiders, we look and sound unique. Imagine how dull *Mad Max* would be if Max smiled and waved at everyone. As outsiders, we can have only one-of-a-kind adventures and misadventures. Charlie Chaplin knew this. Buster Keaton milked it.

IN THE GRITTY world of 1940s and early 1950s film noir, it is difficult to find a hero who *isn't* a loner. The classic noir protagonist lives alone in a cluttered bachelor apartment that appears never to have had a visitor. He drinks alone in bars, drives alone down mean city streets and empty country roads. He needs and trusts no one and nothing, and he tells us this in wisecracking, world-weary voice-over. Private eyes, falsely accused fugitives, morally complex hit men, saps suckered into mayhem and double-crossed; these knights in rumpled suits are disillusioned, disaffected, wracked by nightmares. Striving to right wrongs, escape or overturn injustice, or simply to score, the noir hero is a small man in a big, dark, incomprehensible world where he is brutally tested, battered, accused, and persecuted. In voice-over, he recounts his victories, but also his mistakes, explaining stoically the self-determined rules by which he plays. It gives these films an intimate first-person feel, accessing that private one-of-a-kind domain that is a loner's heart and mind.

Femmes fatales tempt him. Friends reveal themselves as enemies. Little is what it seems, we learn from this loner. And he emerges strong and uncorrupted—or else he dies trying.

AS THE HARD-BOILED detective Sam Spade in *The Maltese Falcon* and the hard-boiled detective Philip Marlowe in *The Big Sleep*, Humphrey Bogart played the classic noir loner: alienated, lean and hungry, cigarette always lit. Marlowe was the brainchild of loner novelist Raymond Chandler, who infused Marlowe and his other protagonists with poetic grit, their scowling masculinity affording, in certain lights, a hint of vulnerability that makes onscreen loners especially attractive. Aspects of these heroes were based on the author himself. A hard-drinking recluse, Chandler was dubbed by *Time* magazine "the poet laureate of the loner." He loved writing, but acknowledged that it was isolating work. He told interviewers it suited his true nature better than any other career ever could.

As a contract killer seeking retribution from a double-crossing client in *This Gun for Hire,* Alan Ladd is tender under a cold-blooded exterior. Taking refuge in a hideout after a murder, he cares for a stray cat, noting that he and the creature are both loners and thus kin under the skin.

Cinematic protagonists had never been so morally ambiguous before, nor so willfully alone. At first glance it seems odd that such dark films—*noir,* we cannot forget, is French for black— were so popular during wartime, when escapist comedies and fantasies are the more obvious cinematic fare. But films noirs served a psychological and emotional purpose for American viewers in that era. Noir protagonists with their disaffected, walking-wounded worldview were surrogates through which viewers could process their own wartime traumas. Even victory in a big war inspires guilt, horror, and shame, deep down: conflicting feelings of national success and personal loss, patriotism but also grief, conflicting desires to remember and forget—and the knowledge that millions have died, far away, *for my freedom, in my name.* These crises, universal yet scrupulously ignored over pot roast at the family dinner table, threw each American into a kind of isolation. In a bravely smiling, goody-two-shoes world, it would not do to break down and shriek *I have blood on my hands!* The ideal surrogate—outside, alone, questioning authority, finding the truth beneath surface appearances—was the noir hero. Quintessentially observant, revealing the evil that men and women do: only the loner.

As THE WAR faded from memory, becoming less of a tactile trauma and mercifully abstract, cinematic heroes changed. They doffed their suits and put on chaps. Still, they stayed loners.

By the mid-1950s, America's Wild West had emerged as the new arena in which heroes would be tested. Here in the wide-open spaces, under huge blue skies, searing deserts and majestic peaks were symbolic proving grounds for loners remote enough in dress and era to let viewers identify with them *only so much*. Safe amid the squeaky-clean hi-neighbor brightness of the times, Americans could ingest loner-lessons—rugged individualism, independence, claiming a domain—without having to take them quite as personally as they had taken noir films with their modern urban landscapes.

Exuding the wood-smoke whiff of nostalgia, Western-film loners lived by their own laws in a land owned by no one, their hearts as hard as their saddles but as unfailingly true as their aim.

Western films had been around since the beginning of cinema, but silent-era Westerns were black-and-white in both morals and film stock. The new arrivals set messy dilemmas amid Technicolor valleys, deserts, and plateaus—loner dilemmas that forced protagonists to choose between lives of companionship and loose-limbed, solitary freedom. In *The Searchers*, John Wayne plays a die-hard outsider, a Civil War vet on a mission to rescue a niece who has been kidnapped by Comanches. As the story draws to a close, the brave loner confronts the classic choice: settle down with a family or ride into the sunset alone? He rides.

In *High Noon*, Gary Cooper plays a town marshal whose isolation is portrayed as all the more righteous when his entire town—even his new bride—abandons him, leaving him to face a gang of professional killers on his own. Cooper won a Best Actor Oscar for his role in a film that is arguably the most important loner-Western ever made, and in the eyes of some cinema scholars the most important Western ever made.

High Noon's exaltation of the righteous loner is also a political parable. During the late 1940s and early 1950s, writers, actors, and directors were ruthlessly investigated by the U.S. House Un-American Activities Committee. Those suspected of having communist sympathies were blacklisted and denied the right to work or, if they worked in secret, to take credit for their work, often at the apex of their careers. The loner standing up for justice against an evil enemy outranking him in power and numbers was used frequently during that era to symbolize the victim of McCarthyism, often in films whose credits were riddled with pseudonyms of blacklisted artists. *High Noon*'s screenwriter Carl Foreman was one of these.

BUT TO TRACE the image of loners in cinema from that point onward is to trace a fall. From lovable tramps and noir knights and righteous riders it is a downward trajectory into madness, horror, ultraviolence. From hero to antihero to freak to scum of the earth.

Think *Psycho*. Think *Willard* and its ratboy. In *A Fistful of Dollars* and its spaghetti-Western sequels, Clint Eastwood created a solitary figure so far beyond the reaches of familiarity as to neither possess nor need a name. These films' Man With No Name is a renegade loner and sometime bounty hunter who says little and kills a lot. In 1971, Eastwood created yet another unforgettable loner, an iconoclastic San Francisco cop who, in *Dirty Harry* and its sequels, hunts down crooks however he damn well pleases, taunting one of them, *Do you feel lucky?* (The actor embodied both roles so convincingly that a 1993 biography of Eastwood is titled *Hollywood's Loner*.) Harry Callahan and The Man With No Name were edgy and enigmatic: ciphers neither as philosophical as noir heroes, nor as true-blue as traditional Western ones. They reflected a shift. The loner as main character was becoming less sympathetic, less a force for concentrated goodness, less identifiably human. Less an inhabitant of a recognizable world.

In *Mad Max* and its sequels, Mel Gibson's loner postnuclear cop takes on all comers with a vengeance after a biker gang murders his wife and child. In *Blade Runner*, Harrison Ford's Rick Deckard is a loner ex-cop on a mission to exterminate androids amid the plastic brutality of a futuristic Los Angeles.

Loners on film had become misfits, losers, marginalized and doomed. Consider Dustin Hoffman's limping, fringe-dwelling thief in *Midnight Cowboy*. Bud Cort's death-obsessed youth in *Harold and Maude*. Winona Ryder's misunderstood adolescent who communes with ghosts in *Beetlejuice.* Johnny Depp's tender, deformed freak in *Edward Scissorhands*. The leading genres of the post-Vietnam years were not loner genres. Buddy movies, family sagas, feel-good classroom dramas. *Fame.* The relentless friendliness of *Forrest Gump.* The fraternity of *Star Wars:* may the force be with you. And you. And you.

Loners went mad, lurking in basements. Their motives no longer made sense.

The prototype for cinema's latter-day loner was 1976's *Taxi Driver.* Twitching with rage and paranoia, Robert DeNiro's wanna-be assassin Travis Bickle terrifies. He stalks a pretty campaign worker, plots to kill a politician, likes pornography. *Are you talking to me?* he asks his own image in a mirror in his shabby flat, armed to the teeth. Leering, he adds a line that says everything about what loners meant to the world then. A landmark line:

I'm the only one here.

A violent act perpetrated near the end of the film turns him into an accidental hero. The sinister irony of this is hardly lost on viewers. Other loner psychos followed. Christian Slater's homicidal teen in *Heathers*. Michael Douglas's terrorist geek in *Falling Down*. *One Hour Photo*'s stalker Sy. Make your own list.

WHY SUCH A fall from grace?

As realism became more the fashion, as viewers began to take films more and more personally, cinematic protagonists and their morals became less allusive, less symbolic, less abstract. And so loner protagonists could no longer be heroes.

Another force has arguably hastened their descent. As corporations grow larger and advertising grows more sophisticated, culture in general glides more than ever into groupthink. Entertainment in the twenty-first century has more than ever to do with marketing strategies. What becomes popular now is increasingly determined by which manufacturer can spend the most money parading its product. And, increasingly, audiences are handed entertainment, prepackaged, with merchandising and mob behavior as not-very-well-hidden agendas. It is in the corporations' best interests to dissuade viewers from emulating loners, who tend not to adopt fads and to eschew to peer pressure, and thus who tend not to spend as much on entertainment's by-products, and on tickets to big-name blockbusters, as nonloners. Thus it is in corporations' best interests to make loners look bad.

Silly. Ugly. Crazy. Predatory. Lethal.

Oscar-winners *Shine* (1996) and *A Beautiful Mind* (2001) offered loner protagonists. Both were mentally ill, their separateness from others a symptom of their illness. In the latter, schizophrenic mathematician John Nash is urged to socialize, to become part of a group, as a strategy for combating his symptoms. One of the most celebrated cinematic loners of recent times appeared in 1991's *The Silence of the Lambs*: Hannibal Lecter, the elitist, misanthropic cannibal. In 2000's successful *The Grinch Who Stole Christmas*, holier-than-thou villagers torment a loner who, because of his unwillingness to share in their tradition, is marked as evil, only to be redeemed when he conforms. At the start of 2001's *Shrek*, its titular ogre is a mean, malodorous loner with low self-esteem. He becomes a sympathetic character only after the arrival of a donkey sidekick and a love interest who turn the film into a buddy picture whose moral is that loners can be nice and happy only when they stop acting like loners. The runaway success of *Spider-Man* in the summer of 2002 is an exception to the rule—but its character and story had already been around, and establishing loyalties, for forty years.

Kevin Costner's costly 1997 epic *The Postman* was a return to the old ways. Its do-gooding loner wandered a desecrated, postapocalyptic American West. Critics called it one of the year's worst films, not without reason. But intriguingly, they lambasted not just its slow pacing and wooden dialogue, but the loner archetype itself. A *New York Times* reviewer complained that Costner "has tried to turn [*The Postman*] into a classic 1950s-style western in which he is the revivified embodiment of that hoary movie archetype, the Man With No Name." The film's sensational failure seemed to puzzle Costner, who had believed in the picture so deeply that he not only starred in it but had also produced and directed it. "I loved making *The Postman*," he told the *New York Daily News* in 2000. "I understand they're showing it in school[s] now to illustrate mythic heroes."

Despite this film's intrinsic flaws, this is a terrifying fate. What does it mean when loner icons become classroom fodder, relics to be studied, like the Hundred Years' War and the cotton gin? The fact that the curriculum for such lessons is a film that was singled out as the worst in a year that also produced *Nemesis 4* and *Bleeders* adds insult to injury.

That solitary big-screen righter of wrongs—the vulnerable but attractive fringe-dweller—is not entirely obsolete but a severely endangered species. In his place have come repulsive loners, sympathetic only in the most perverse sense, and/or only when they stop being loners.

You may or may not subscribe to the conspiracy theory in which entertainment conglomerates are killing loner heroes in order to keep those outsiderish values from reaching the public. Maybe. Maybe not. Has the sun set on Mad Max? Is he an artifact? If loner role models are slipping out of sight, we have to catch them while we can. And if the theory is true, we must teach our descendants where to find their loner heritage: revival theaters and the vintage racks in video stores are our Louvre, our Forbidden City, our Smithsonian.

4.

marlboro country

*They want us to want what they're selling—but that would
mean wanting what everyone else wants.*

A TV COMMERCIAL for Smirnoff Ice begins with two pals
chugging malt beverages in a laundromat. Together, for
fun, the guys overload the washers with soap flakes and switch
them on. As the bubbles rise, other patrons jump into the act.
Exhilarating music plays as the crowd wiggles around, euphoric, in chest-high suds.

Loners bristle at being advertised to. We might not mean to
bristle, might not even see the bristle, but what else would loners do at being *told* to buy not just objects but lots of objects,
and for dubious reasons—because others buy them, because
someone who is being paid to say so says to? Objects doomed
to rapid obsolescence. Objects whose shimmer onscreen and in
magazines is the exact same kind that loners see in the real

world and realize is false, is cheap, is there only to trick the stupid and will disappoint. We know this on some level when the cheese melts on the pizza ad, but sudden hunger lunges out of nowhere and plucks *our* guts, too. We know we do not need a car, nasal spray, lipstick, life insurance, or at least not the specific brand or color being waved in front of us. *How dare you tell me what to do?* And yet we want.

Advertising is antithetical to the loner mentality. Yet it is masterful. It makes us clench. It turns us into accidental rebels: suffering the ache and labor of resisting strong-arm tactics, shunning the attractive, the seductive, the lavishly marketed. Resisting ads, insisting on buying what we want when we want and if we want, is radical. And failing to resist makes us feel, deep down, even just a bit, like Judas.

Or at least like idiots.

Time spent alone has a way of winnowing the inventory of what we need. It reveals that some of our best delights derive from the intangible—from actions, experiences, thoughts—rather than objects. Not that every loner is a miser or minimalist. I, for one, would not say no to a new lava lamp. But to decrease contact with others is to decrease the number of items that seem necessary. It is the presence of others and exposure to the mainstream media, the insecurity and camaraderie sparked by those kinds of contact, that also spark the impulse to buy. *Look what HE has. I want to impress HER.* Desiring and requiring stuff means casting your lot with others. Intrinsically we know this. Being a rebel is tiring. Especially when you are up against a great hypnotic army that looks like Naomi Campbell and whose battle cries are so catchy that you cannot get them out of your head.

ADVERTISING IS HARDLY a new idea. In one form or another, it has been around since the first vendor at the first marketplace hawked wares with provocative come-ons. It is any smart retailer's natural instinct. With the advent of printing, the idea of advertising to the masses took a great leap forward and never looked back. Early print ads focused naïvely but logically on the products' quality and their makers' efficiency. An ad posted in an Indiana newspaper in 1833 promises that chair maker and sign painter Samuel Rooker "will punctually attend to all orders with which he has been favored. He is prepared to do all kinds of turning (his lathe being propelled by steam) in the best manner and on the most favorable terms . . . executed with neatness and promptitude." A Victorian-era ad for Massachusetts's Worcester Corset Company declared simply, "This is by far the BEST corset and skirt supporter ever made."

But the process has become increasingly sophisticated over the years—especially the last fifty—as technology and wars and the rise of youth culture have spawned more jaded and over-stimulated consumers. Undisguised superlatives and boasting, *We're the best!* no longer do the trick. The modern advertisement is a product of scientific exactitude. Advertisers make informed and expensive use of art, psychology, and sociology. They draw on research, not just wishful thinking, to effect consensus and start fads. They rely on the masses' ready-made assumptions that certain things are beautiful, desirable, worth having. *Not* having them, advertisementthink goes, is to be uncool, a drag, left out, a fool. And that is a fate worse than death.

Advertising does not operate one-on-one but one-on-millions.

But loners cannot be unified. Our only shared feature is separateness, elusiveness, refusal to connect. We are the *absent* audience. We cannot be held because we are not even there. A clever ad for outboard motors in a sporting magazine might seize the attention of loners who own boats. But even then, we are hard sells. Because we do not feel as one with others or equate ourselves with others, we suspect whatever is popular. I am not the only loner who puts off seeing top-ten movies or reading top-ten books. That way our reading or seeing is not knee-jerk *responding*. Testimonials from others leave us cold. Gushing disgusts us. I think I might *never* read *Angela's Ashes*. We snicker and shudder at the presumption in phrases like "Happy Meal."

GIVEN THEIR WEALTH and the ferocity of their intent, advertisers buy top talent to serve their ends. It is no accident that brand logos and slogans are more famous worldwide than most national anthems and flags. The Nike swoosh. The golden arches. Levis' little red tag. Call them sellouts if you will, but some of the most talented artists, writers, musicians, and techies on earth work in advertising. And since so many creative people are loners, we have to face the fact that some of the minds behind advertising are lonerish minds. We have to hand it to them. Even as we shrink in horror at the gross manipulation of *Just Do It*, we nod in reluctant admiration for those loners—we know they are there—unseen, uncredited, cashing huge checks for hawking SUVs and cat food for the enemy.

It could have been me. After graduating from Berkeley with an English degree, I started looking for journalism jobs. My father felt this was a waste of my talent. Someone as clever as I should reach not just the residents of some city but of the whole world, he said. A woman in his car pool worked at a big L.A. advertising agency. Through her, he arranged for an interview. A sharp-suited executive leafed through my college-newspaper clippings. He smiled, nodding. *You've got something here*, he said. *You're good.*

Good at aiming to please. I had honed it all my life as an escape tactic. Make them laugh, then tiptoe away before they open their eyes. I had been poring over ads since I was three. We had *Sunset* and *Good Housekeeping* magazines in our house. I knew precisely how to call pesticide "magical" and margarine "golden." I knew why toucans should be used to sell fruit-flavored cereal.

After the sharp-suited executive suggested that I enter the firm's training program, I went home and watched TV. The ads glimmered and roared with new importance. *This is my new life*. Band-Aids for little ouches. A miniature man rowing a boat around a toilet bowl. Detergent sold by a knight on a snow-white horse.

A diet-soda ad.

It had been made especially for me, for my kind, nubile females not sure they should stop hating their stomachs. The actress lay on a beach towel, in a swimsuit, as the camera traced her silhouette, lingering at her tiny waist. Cinnamon skin, sleek with oil, so taut I could swear I saw her pulse. *One calorie,* the song went. The l-sound lingered on the tongue of the singer, promising beauty to smart girls who drank sugar-free soda, promising, from the sound of it, oral sex.

They knew exactly how to do it. Admiration soared inside me, mixed with the impulse the ad intended me to feel. *Drink me,* as the note on the bottle told Alice down the rabbit hole. And that mixture of admiration and impulse made a chemical reaction. It was the sizzle that makes you think *uh-oh* right before passing out. All of the implications did not penetrate my childish mind. Not the moral dubiousness of art being used to manipulate, and not the larger picture in which one creative person, me for instance, could be paid to make the masses jump in unison. I did not see it as a loner issue, then. I only saw it as a crime to sell women low self-esteem, of which I myself was a sufferer. I never went back to the agency.

I could have become an advertiser and seen it as some kind of revenge strategy: the loner getting back at the masses by treating them like the lemmings they are. Jerking their reflexes, draining their bank accounts, and laughing my solitary head off. I would have been rich now.

DAVID WOLLOCK WAS an ad copywriter for a national music retailer before leaving that job to write books on popular culture. Explaining to me the basic philosophy behind advertising, he is pragmatic.

"Advertising promotes the common ideal for everything," Wollock says. "If the common perception of beauty was fat women with no breasts, then all the ads would show fat women with no breasts. It's a numbers game: how to reach the largest number of people effectively." The formula by which companies' advertising budgets are calculated is based not on cost per individual viewer, reader, or listener, but on cost per *thousand* viewers, readers, or listeners.

"It's a mob mentality," Wollock says. "Most people like to think of themselves as part of a mob." Inclusiveness is king. When ads show people having fun, the implication is that the product is the source of that fun.

A Dr Pepper ad campaign that aired in the 1970s tapped into the loner mentality—sort of. Far overshadowed by Coke and Pepsi, Dr Pepper was a "loner" in the cola industry. Knowing this, and with no hopes of outselling its competitors, the company decided to capitalize on its own outsider image. In the commercial, a lone figure, quirky-looking but kookily cool, was shown drinking a Dr Pepper as the jingle began: "I'm a Pepper." One by one, other oddballs appeared, also drinking Dr Peppers, as the song asked, "Wouldn't you like to be a Pepper, too?" The implication was that all those lone oddballs out there are lively folks with minds of their own who use those singular minds to choose a singularly delicious drink. *These loners*, the company implied, *are having lots of fun! Wouldn't you love to join these loners?*

But even the Dr Pepper campaign proves that from an advertiser's standpoint, fun is portrayed most effectively by groups. The softball game, the pool party, the giggling clique—

"the message," Wollock says, "is, 'Hey, look what you're missing!'" Sometimes that message comes as a whisper, sometimes as a shout, teasing, or bullying. If a loner is looking, then the idea is to turn him: Tweak his lust or make him insecure or get him thinking *Hey, I'm lonely!* Failing that, Wollock explains, advertisers have no use for loners.

"Why would they want to approach you?" he asks. "If you're not impressionable, you're wasting their time."

They spend a fortune making us look as if we don't exist—or that if we do, we aren't having any fun.

CORPORATIONS BATTLE HARD to create brand loyalty, to make vast numbers of consumers prefer, for instance, one cola over another even though blind taste tests regularly show that there is little distinguishable difference between major brands of coffee, soda, beer, and cigarettes. Such items, dubbed "parity products" by industry insiders because, for all intents and purposes, the items are identical, must be hawked not on the basis of any tangible distinction. Instead, their success depends on the advertisers' claims that each has its own *personality*, individuality, its own message, and that certain brands speak for certain sectors of the population. Lifestyle, sport, gender—the bigger the sector, the better. Thus Virginia Slims were pressed on female smokers in the early 1970s, during the first big wave of feminism, as the "women's cigarette." Again, the lure and implications are all about inclusiveness. Clothes emblazoned with product logos are all, in a way, team uniforms. Wearing a Nike shirt or Red Bull hat is a declaration of membership. *I'm part of something big.* Such displays, replicated a hundred times over in any street scene or school hallway, reveal the nonloner bias. Brand loyalty means *Hey, I'm not a loner.*

Thus *portraying* loners as consumers in commercials is counterproductive. In liking to think of themselves as part of a mob, David Wollock says, "most people don't want to think of themselves as brooding and alone." An unrepentant nonloner himself, he muses: "Why would any ad show a depressed loner who masturbates five times a day? Well, okay, if you're marketing rubber blow-up dolls, sure."

Along those lines, the industry magazine *Advertising Age* used a 2002 Coca-Cola commercial to illustrate its lament that "the world's most iconic brand has lost its way." In the ad, a solitary hitchhiker on a deserted roadside in the Rocky Mountains waves a bottle of Coke at a passing big rig, whose thirsty driver stops and picks him up. That the trucker would be "sufficiently lured by $1.09 worth of cola to pick up a bearded loner" is so implausible, the article posits, as to be key "evidence that the company is at a loss to understand, in all its priceless dimensions, its own flagship brand." Or, at least, the company "sure doesn't understand how to advertise it."

THIS RULE HAS its exception. Cowboys sell.

And cowboys are, in the public imagination, loners. Independent. Inviolate. Like America. Rugged individuals who speak the truth, shoot from the hip.

The advertising cowboy, like the cinematic cowboy, eludes all those prejudices leveled against loners in the real world.

Behind the wheel of a Ford Bronco, he is not seen as a loser or a lonely pervert or a nerd. He is not seen as secretive. The opposite: without saying a word, he is meant to convey an openness like that of the big blue Western sky.

As such, the cars he hawks are not compacts, but behemoths with Wild-West names like Forester, Pathfinder, Rodeo, Range Rover. Sinewy hands gripping the wheel, he races across plateaus and down mountain roads. In his deadpan gaze is a look of quiet victory.

He sells cigarettes too, pimp that he is. *Real* cowboys smoke. Any day at a rodeo proves that. But tobacco is not *unique* to the Wild West. Faced with the challenge of promoting a parity product, Marlboro might just as easily have chosen any other archetype—a sailor or a hipster or an English lord. Yet the cowboy, the loner, was chosen. In the 1950s, just when the real Wild West was breathing its last, the Philip Morris company introduced its cowboy icon. Designed by the Leo Burnett advertising firm, the "Marlboro Man" was a ploy to broaden the appeal of a brand whose promotions, until then, had wimpily called the cigarettes "mild as May." Burnett's new ads, featuring the cowboy, promised that Marlboro "delivers the goods on flavor"—alluding to actual cowboys' work of delivering herds cross-country to slaughterhouses but also packing a subtle sexual punch. When the ads went national in 1955, sales skyrocketed, reaching $5 billion that year: an increase from just one year earlier of 3,241 percent.

Are the fragrant glowing leaves in every cigarette a small personal campfire, signifying the loner's dominion over all he surveys? In 1964, the ad agency gave a name to the mythical "Marlboro Country," whose sunsets mirrored the crimson in the brand's logo. After cigarette commercials were banned from TV in 1971, the solitary figure lent itself to print ads and billboards so perfectly that, one year later, Marlboro was the world's best-selling tobacco product.

How ironic that the Marlboro Man is, today, the most famous cowboy in the universe and practically the only one still in the public eye: a true loner, the sole survivor of his genre. (And how sad that he is held responsible for countless lung-cancer deaths—including, most famously and ironically, that of the male model who portrayed him for years: Wayne McLaren died in 1992 at age fifty-one. In his wake, Camel cigarettes' icon, "Joe Camel," has been similarly blamed for spawning a new generation of teenage smokers. Perhaps indicative of loners' ever-descending public image, Joe is a social animal, usually depicted amongst a clutch of cool camel pals.) Unlike the cinematic cowboy, the Marlboro Man is not a figure from the past, clad in a vintage costume. He is a contemporary cowboy, his prairies crisscrossed with paved superhighways. He brings those old values right into the present. As such, as the most famous cowboy in the universe, he represents for millions around the world America itself. Thus the arguably most famous aspect of America around the world is its loner aspect. America the individualist, the victorious and eternal loner.

As such, the cowboy has now been co-opted to sell cigarettes to Eastern Europe. Where better to press the macho loner into service than a place where, as Ayn Rand could have told you, individualism has for millions been only an uncatchable dream? Cowboys bow down to no authority. Cowboys do what the hell they want. Nobody spies on cowboys.

Eastern Europeans were already die-hard smokers by the time Philip Morris arrived. While nearly forty years of public-health campaigns in the United States had lowered the proportion of adult smokers here to some 25 percent by the mid-1990s, the World Health Organization determined that eastern and central Europe were at that time home to the world's highest proportion of adult smokers—some 60 percent of men and 30 percent of women. And that's not counting the kids. Offering higher-quality cigarettes than the locally produced ones to which Eastern Europe was long accustomed, Philip Morris leaped at the chance when restrictions were lifted on advertising in those countries. As Radio Free Europe reported in 1997, cinemagoers in Prague regularly saw the Marlboro Man in lengthy ads preceding films: "The mythic character's chiseled features are accompanied by displays of fine horsemanship, incredible scenery from the American West, and a soundtrack suggesting high adventure. . . . And in the Russian capital as throughout the East, the Marlboro Man stares down at passersby from innumerable billboards." Not only did "his" cigarettes taste better, they also symbolized the just-now-possible good things that come with being a loner: privacy, independence, discernment. It has been estimated that Philip Morris's exports to the region soared by more than 400 percent within four years in the mid- to late 1990s.

• • •

A CYNICAL OBSERVER might argue that today's youth is as ruggedly individualistic as the next Pepsi commercial tells it to be.

When ads trumpet our right to decide, they are strumming our cowboy consciousness. In creating brand loyalties, they brilliantly—if perversely—combine team spirit with our vision of ourselves as bold choosers, defiantly unique. "Have it *your* way," the classic Burger King commercial sings. "Be you," coaxes an updated Dr Pepper campaign. An ad for Vans sneakers that appeared in the summer of 2002 showed six styles of Vans side by side, differing from one another in color and, though only slightly, in style. The text read: "People make choices. Choices make people."

Real loners might well hiss at this deceit. We are not entirely sure we want to be a Pepper, too.

5.

i have to go now

We pick the cream of the crop,
then expect them to understand that
we want to be alone.

ON THE HOME page of a Web site for people seeking relationships, visitors are asked to sign "the following oath otherwise known as the Friendship Promise." Presented in petition form, the oath assures that the undersigned will "dry your tears . . . comfort your fears . . . give you hope" and "help you cope . . . we are here for you." Who, exactly, is meant by you and we is not entirely clear. Will these hundreds of signers really dry my tears? Are they really here for me?

The oath includes a preface:

"WHEREAS any healthy loving relationship is founded on friendship.

"WHEREAS no one should ever feel alone or friendless with so many caring people in the world. . . ."

And, most crucial of all:

"WHEREAS many violent crimes in our schools these days are commit[ted] by those others describe as 'A Friendless Loner.'. . ."

POSTMODERN NOVELIST Kathy Acker, whose angry works included such titles as *Blood and Guts in High School* and *My Mother: Demonology*, died in 1997. A mourner posted a lament on the Internet. Some eight years earlier, this mourner had accompanied Acker to an art show where "I met her friend Cindy Carr, who wore a woolen jacket on that summer afternoon. I recall that Carr was polite but very withdrawn. And now, reading the obituary [which Carr wrote for] the *Village Voice*, I discover that Carr portrayed Kathy as a loner. That description says far more about Carr than Kathy."

For this angry mourner, the word "loner" constitutes out-and-out slander. It is not merely a matter of using a less-than-accurate word. It is a matter of using a word whose connotations, in the mourner's mind, can only be negative. Thus the best strategy is to throw the insult back at Carr, to punish her for defaming the personable Acker with the l-word.

How, then, to mete out punishment? By citing as evidence Carr's "withdrawn" mien and unseasonable outfit—what kind of freak would wear wool in the New York summer?

As it happens, I once met Acker at a party. She was chatty with our hostess, who was a beautiful musician and radio personality. Acker kept her distance from most of the guests, a mixed crowd of struggling artists and unknowns. Why she kept her distance, I cannot know. A witness, that day, might have surmised that Acker was a loner. But another witness might have surmised that she was shy, stuck-up, aloof, having a bad day, feeling ill. What are loners to think of the angry mourner's insistence that Acker had *a lot* of friends? Similarly, after suicidal teen Charles Bishop crashed a plane into a Tampa office building in 2002, initial news reports called him a loner. Within days, the press was falling all over itself apologizing for having smeared Bishop in this manner. He had friends, the networks shouted. And we'll quote a few to prove it.

Is that what they think, then? That loners have no friends?

OF ALL THE ways in which loners are demonized, one of the most insidious regards our capacity for friendship. The crucial distinction fails to be made between a capacity for friendship, for relationship, and for *companionship*: the time actually spent in others' presence. Seeing us alone, the mainstream jumps to conclusions: that we have no friends, want no friends, are not capable of finding friends. They conclude that loners are either too mean for friends or too unlikable. Too misanthropic, too angry to entertain the possibility of kindred souls. Too spaced-out, too selfish, insane, inscrutable, withdrawn to attract any even if we wanted to.

Which of these scenarios is the worst? None is pretty, but which is worst? To have no friends because we are unlikable is human: pitiful, but human. Not to *want* friends renders loners beyond pity, beyond recognition, past humanity. It makes us monsters.

Of course loners have friends. Fewer than most nonloners have, maybe. But loners, with our extra capacity for concentration, focus, our fewer distractions, make excellent friends. To a few. One, maybe, but a real one.

But why do nonloners care? Why don't they cheer because the fewer friends we have, the more potential friends for them? They care because they need a universal currency by which to judge us. And friendship is something they all understand. A nonloner need not be smart, skilled, or in any way distinguished to have friends. Sometimes it seems the least distinguished acquire friends the easiest, giggling and jostling strings of chums. Instant collectives. All their lives, nonloners have dealt in this currency. They know its feel, its soft smoothness when old, its shine when new. Regarding friendship and its value, every nonloner is an assessor, an assayer, a professor.

And based on what they see, they say we lack friends. Thus we lack value. And by this standard alone, the friend standard, our characters are assassinated universally.

It is all a mistake.

FOR SOME LONERS, a paucity of friends is a matter of time. There is simply too much to do alone, no time to spare. Shared time, while not entirely wasted if the sharer is a true friend, must be parceled out with care, like rationed flour. And time shared, even with true friends, often requires loners to put in *extra* time alone, overtime, to recharge. It is a matter of energy: As a rule, loners have less for the social machinery, the talk and sympathy. Our fuel runs out. This is what nonloners don't understand about us, what they cannot see. We do not choose to have such tiny fuel tanks. These can be quite inconvenient. They are why we seem rude, when we do, why we seem bored and often are. Spaced-out and often are. Running on empty.

Not heartless. Not unappreciative. Not fools. We know the rest of the world has big tanks. We know they don't know.

I am hypoglycemic. I like sugar very much. Chocolate halvah, coconut cream pie. I know how little of it I can stand before the onset of sick, cotton-headed shock. But blood glucose can be measured in medical laboratories. Tolerance for company cannot. (Yet.)

No one wants to make himself sick. And if our vector is an overdose of chat regarding diaper brands or whom the Redskins might get as their third-round draft pick, we retract.

By contrast, the average nonloner seems able to stand hours and hours with almost anyone. Sometimes it seems they would rather have *anyone* around than no one. The absence of friends, at least companions, is by their lights an abomination. The result, from a loner's standpoint, is that many nonloner friendships are matters of default. Of convenience. Such high tolerance for company, we might argue, makes for much lower standards. To say loners must be choosy sounds stuck-up—the very charge nonloners always throw at us—but regarding friends, it is true.

NONLONERS HAVE A set of rules by which friendship is played. Dry your tears. End your fears. Give you hope. Help you cope. Loners play by a different set of rules. Ours is a smaller set. A simpler set. A purer set. Critics would call it rudimentary, unreasonable, skewed. They do not understand that what we have to give is not what always what others have to give.

We care. We feel. We think. We do not always miss the absent one. We cannot always come when called. Being friends with a loner requires patience and the wisdom that distance does not mean dislike.

Troubles always ensue when assumptions clash, when expectations do not match. Nonloners who wish to be our friends—and they do, it happens all the time—arrive assuming that their rule book is the only rule book. We are aware of their rules, just as immigrants come to recognize words in the languages of their adopted nations, yet speak their own languages at home. We are aware of *their* needs. Their idea of fun, their entreaties, their sense of time and how much is enough—these are all too familiar. Not sharing them makes us outlaws and, before we know it, we are being called *bad friends*.

A FEW YEARS ago, I met a very nice person. Nice and outgoing, so much so that people who knew I knew her told me I was lucky that she liked me. Like me she did: calling, coming over, planning outings.

How did I feel? Guilty. Any stirrings, warmth, affection lay under a guilty lid. Sure I liked her, though I saw differences between us that she seemed not to see or to think were unimportant. The aspect of me she called "the hermit" she thought charming—insofar as it was artistic, part of the mysterious charm of artists. The idea of me, her new friend, holed up in a room behind a locked door hunched over a manuscript was titillating—in the abstract, as long as it happened at those times when she did not happen to call and want to chat.

It came to pass—how could it not have?—that, in tears, she said I was rejecting her. She had a soft heart, she said, and it hurt because of me. I tried to say that she knew companionship only as an artesian well, always bubbling, being renewed constantly. She thrived on drinking from it, lived on it. She pouted, though she would not have called it a pout. Of course I thrive on friends, she said, friends are the most precious things to me in the world and you are one of those. You *were*.

I wondered whether holding back, saying *I have to go now* after long chats on the phone—they seemed long—was rejection. By her heart, it was. We both should have known sooner.

ONCE, ON THE other hand, I adored a friend so much that I made exceptions for her. We spent endless hours and days together and I never once looked at the clock. I told her everything, I let it all out. At the time, I thought I would have died for her.

She was my first friend. We were five. Until then I had met many children, kids at school and in Bluebirds and in the Jewish youth group and in the neighborhood and strangers to whom my parents made me introduce myself. They passed before my eyes like tadpoles in a stream. Then I met her. She was funny. One look sent me squealing, doubled over, not daring to catch her eye again for fear of bursting. She was smart. Wanted to be the first girl Sherlock Holmes, looking for clues on the streets of our tract, a playing card, a cigarette butt, and wishing they added up to something. She was daring and keenly observant.

I gave my friend objects. Any book or seashell in my bedroom she admired or even noticed—it was hers, no matter how hard I had worked to acquire it, no matter how much I treasured it. *Here, have it.* Every detail, every spark, we shared. Laughing all afternoon. Crying all night. The trillion secret jokes, secret names, secret codes.

She was not a loner. So could she be blamed for not always listening? For trying, sometimes, to escape?

But she always came back although sometimes not right away. I made a good choice. Fine investment, as an investment, for loners, friendship always is. We are still friends. We have a lot of laughs. She still wants to solve mysteries, to figure out who the Green River Killer is.

Even so, I do not seize the phone and call her, or anyone, when I feel miserable. This is one of those acid tests that separate the true loner from the person who is alone but would much rather not be: even in the gloomiest gloom, it is not my instinct to talk it over. Not that I am sufficiently brilliant as to console myself every time. It is more of a wallow. But instinct is instinct, and instinct will out.

FOR LONERS, FRIENDS are all the more essential because in many cases they are our sole conduits to the outside world. They are channels, filters, valves, rivers from the outback to the sea. When we find good ones, we pour ourselves into them.

Franz Kafka, the Czech author who explored his own experiences as a loner in such works as "The Metamorphosis"— whose protagonist awakens to discover that he has been transformed into a huge cockroach—had a best friend in whom he trusted implicitly. Kafka met Max Brod at university, and they remained close throughout Kafka's life; it was Brod who brought Kafka to his parents' home when Kafka was mortally ill. And it was Brod to whom Kafka gave his dying instruction: that all his unpublished manuscripts be burned. Instead, Brod published them. Does this make him a bad friend, or the best friend a writer ever had?

Emily Dickinson is infamous for her reclusiveness. Yet it might surprise many who are more familiar with her reputation than her actual writing that she was no stranger to friendship. Her sister-in-law, a family friend, a literary critic—each of these earned Dickinson's trust, her faith, and were the subjects of her poems as well as their rare early readers. Yes, for the last sixteen years of her life, from the age of forty onward, she never left her home and addressed visitors only through a partly closed door. But the idea that loners who *look* as if they have no friends know nothing of friendship are belied by lines such as "I should not dare to leave my friend," and poems such as this one:

Wild Nights—Wild Nights!
Were I with thee
Wild Nights should be
Our luxury!

Futile—the Winds—
To a Heart in port—
Done with the Compass—
Done with the Chart!

Rowing in Eden—
Ah! the sea!
Might I but moor—Tonight
In Thee!

It is all too easy for loners to forget how many of us there are, out there, somewhere. We generally will not meet each other, will not recognize each other and rush over, bubbling, urging each other to meet all of our other friends. Friends do not come easily to us. Too often we can be fooled into believing we do not have "enough" of them: that this reflects, as the outside world would have it, harshly on us. Or we can be fooled into believing that if we are too picky, we do not deserve for our search to end. It does. Or we can be misled into thinking that company, just a bit, betrays our true identity as loners. It does not. Not if she makes you laugh. Not if she always knows when it is time to go.

6.

just catch me

[LOVE & SEX]

They think we're eunuchs or compulsive masturbators.
Either way, we're fucked.

"ARE YOU A LOVER," asks a singles Web site in inch-high letters, "OR A LONER? Love means lots of things to lots of people. For some, it's a blissful overabundance of romance, passion, or friendship. To others . . . it's plain evil."

A quiz follows—"to find out whether you're a LOVER or a LONER." Its multiple-choice questions ask, for example, whether Valentine's Day means "(1.) spending time with my partner; (2.) nothing terribly special, just another day; or (3.) dressing up in an overcoat, going to a city park, and shouting 'Shame On You!' at anybody holding hands." Participants are asked to pick their favorite "romantic movie": "(1.) *Sleepless in Seattle*; (2.) *Casablanca*; or (3.) *Texas Chainsaw Massacre*."

Meanwhile, a list of official slogans for National Condom Week includes (along with *When in doubt, shroud your spout* and

Never deck her with an unwrapped pecker): Don't be a loner; cover your boner.

In the eyes of the outside world, loners' sex lives come in two varieties. Either the nonexistent type—we're atom-splicing nerds wearing unfashionable pants and mustering all the erotic drive of eunuchs. Or else we are raging perverts. Poring over porn—not even ordinary frat-boy porn but *creepy* porn—we masturbate compulsively. The attitude is revealed again and again in articles such as the *Denver Post* lifestyle-section story in which a psychotherapist cautions singles in the dating scene to make sure all their potential partners have oodles of friends: "Get to know who they hang out with," the therapist warns. "Many sexual predators are loners." San Francisco sex-advice columnist Isadora Allman regularly urges readers seeking partners to engage in as many social and communal activities as possible, from clubbing to staging charity carwashes—as if spending time alone was the short route to sexual misery.

It is in this realm, from romance to love to *making* love, that loners are perhaps the most grossly misunderstood. Love and sex are such personal pursuits, so intrinsically private that it seems impossible to make snap judgments about who wants what or with whom. Yet, private as they are, love and sex have been rendered public through the huge lens of the media. Gone are the days when one's choices were limited to friends, friends' friends, friends' siblings, siblings' friends, cousins, second cousins and, at most, the residents of a given community. The search has gone worldwide. So a process that begins with only two—two hands touching, two minds, two souls out of six billion—is presented to us as a mass movement, like track meets or college entrance exams, in which fierce competition and performance pressure shape the rules. Your opponents, your competition, comprises everyone besides yourself. Potential mates, too, could be anyone. Think of the mathematics: *anyone*. And you are locked into the race. It goes on constantly until you settle down, maybe forever, a heaven or hell depending on your point of view.

Meeting anyone at all is not a loner's long suit. Meeting an assembly line of maybes has as much appeal as severe sunburn. Opening lines, small talk, seem repulsive—and we haven't even mentioned *pursuit*. Spending any time even with those we know, even with old friends, can grate. For loners, spending time with strangers, again and again, a stream of strangers, not merely to get it over with but to discern whether someday you will put your tongue inside this person's mouth, is the definition of surreal.

As for sex, that level of intimacy lies at the end of a journey whose navigation no loner can take lightly. Social creatures, for whom saying hello is second nature and, it follows, can keep up light conversation in a crowded bar, have a knack for telescoping those stages between strangerhood and sex. Between them, it's just understood. And between them it seems easy to make casual arrangements of the sort that Benjamin Braddock, sleeping with a woman twice his age in *The Graduate*, likened to "shaking hands." At least it looks that way to loners, for whom every stage on the journey looms large. Just realizing that someone else is near, not even looking, sparks a loner's instinct to escape.

All this reality has little bearing on what outsiders presume. Prejudiced minds think in extremes, imagining that *all* loners want to be *all* alone at *all* times. That even die-hard loners might let someone else in, some*one*, just one but all the way in, simply messes up the stereotype. And that stereotype, so all-pervasive, makes us feel more self-conscious, more defensive. "You *said*, 'Leave me alone,'" the world argues. "Was that a lie?" Well . . . no. Even anchoresses, the reclusive medieval nuns who sealed themselves inside tiny cells for life, are known to have now and then relished meaningful relationships. The eleventh-century British nun known as Eve of Milton, for example, crossed the Channel to live near Angers in France, where she shared her seclusion and what one poet would soon afterward call "a wondrous love" with a male anchorite named Hervey. It has been said before, let's say it again: "loner" is not a synonym for "misanthrope." Nor is it one for "hermit," "celibate," or "outcast." It's just that we are very selective. *Verrry* selective.

Loners being as private as they are by nature and sex being as private as it is, what after all is the public to conclude about sex and loners? Where would it find its information? In the newspaper? The college dorm? All that jerking off, furtive yet not quite out of roommates' earshot, after long solitary nights at the lab fuels a modern archetype: loner as loser, without so much as a chance in hell of even losing his virginity—and, in the process, spoiling masturbation's reputation. In the first case, *sex* + *loner* equals unspeakable horror; in the second, belly laughs. Both sums make sexually satisfied loners into oxymorons. Even so, a *sexy loner* surfaces now and then, though more splashily in film à la *Bullitt* and *Pump Up the Volume* and *She's All That* than in real life. But more on sexy loners later.

• • •

I'M MARRIED. TO a loner. That makes two of us. Returning to the math-class metaphor, you might argue that *loner* + *loner* = *nonloners*, that being together obviates our loner status, cancels out our claim. Arguing back, I would say, "Look at us"—well, don't, we're in our pajamas, but I *swear* we're still loners, now as before. One of the public's biggest misconceptions is that loners care nothing for love: that we do not, cannot. Yet what drove Emily Dickinson's fieriest poems? Marie Curie, half of one of science's most famous and devoted couples, was a loner. Even Ted Kaczynski, the one figure with whom most modern loners would least like to be associated (and albeit who, in the final analysis, might not really be a loner at all), is said to have longed for love, sought instruction from a family friend in the writing of love letters, flirted in his own strange way with the town librarian who unwittingly helped him research recipes for explosive devices, and upon the marriage of his brother mourned his own singlehood.

My loner husband and I live in a house masked by green hedges from nonexistent passersby on a lane so obscure that it has no sidewalks, in a district remote from the flutter of life in town, the route from there to here a maze of switchbacks on heart-attack grades. People who have spent decades in our town have never heard of our street. We know no one will ever just drop in. We knew that when we found the place, hidden in plain view as if under an enchantment. That was one of its major attractions. The realtor suggested cutting down the hedge. We caught each other's eyes and smirked.

Putting two smelts together does not make them sharks. They stay smelts, so here we are, glad that the doorbell never rings, staring down at the phone in horror when it occasionally does, letting the machine answer. As writers, pursuing a solitary profession, we hole up silently in different corners of the house. Mean as it feels to admit, each of us secretly applauds when the other goes out on errands, leaving the whole house empty save one, though neither of us wants those errands to last long. On holidays it is just us. Weekends, just us. To extraverts, this might all seem so inhospitable, so isolationist. But we have gone to great lengths to make our lives this way, on purpose.

In meeting him, I was lucky. I was not looking. (Lucky!) We hit it off right away, and one of the likenesses we recognized in one another at once was that we were loners. When two loners meet in a potentially romantic situation, the relief surges like a tidal wave. We are so much more likely to meet nonloners. And say we bond with one, say attraction or intellect or a shared interest in *Sailor Moon* overcomes this fundamental difference. A shark and a smelt together will not both turn into sharks or smelts, and the difference will always loom. My father used this argument when telling me, while I was an eighth-grader wearing lots of eye shadow, why mixed marriages never work and why I must stop ogling the Catholic boys.

A FRIEND OF mine, a loner, is also married to a loner. They have three small children, and while they adore their children, a certain worry started when the eldest one was born: suddenly, my loner friend and her loner husband had company. And it would stay. And it seemed blasphemous, the worst depravity, for them to reel in shock at this. They *wanted* kids. They still do. They are very good parents. But even in a huge house with a huge backyard, having kids makes loners much less alone. Kids need things. They need attention. When they are small they do not know the meaning of the words *interrupt* or *private*.

This prospect has made many modern loners decide to stay childless, married or not. But such a decision is a luxury, like roller blades and ibuprofen, that only moderns can enjoy. Only recently did loners gain the ability to wed knowing confidently that, if they wish, they can remain childless. Before the advent of dependable birth control, walking up the aisle was walking straight into a tunnel that led directly to parenthood. Getting engaged, then, loners knew what they were in for. It makes you wonder how many stayed single before, say, the mid-twentieth century, simply because while they craved partnership they knew they ought not to be parents. Too many loners, through-out the ages, have become parents without wanting to, without having a choice, and have not had the talent for it. Too many loners have been bad parents boiling with resentment at their shattered privacy, blotting out anger and regret with mead or laudanum or gin or Valium and shouting from behind a locked door, *Leave Daddy alone!* Until recently, not being married meant not having sex, especially for women. Think of all those loners, down the millennia, who consigned themselves to celibacy, birth to death, and forsook partnership because, only because, the risk of giving birth to company—permanent company—was just too great.

. . .

LONERS WHO WANT partners are better off with loners. But if meeting strangers is difficult for loners, loners are also the most difficult strangers in the world to meet. Summon every dram of nerve and try a singles bar, a baseball game, a dance class—nonloners, nonloners everywhere. Scan the personal ads, and you will find phalanxes of nonloners for whom reaching out is the natural impulse. At parties, spy the loner lurking in the kitchen pretending to look for ice or napkins, or hovering by the door eager to leave. The loner at the party tries to appear occupied, peering with sham absorption at the liquid in her wineglass or the Erté poster next to his solitary post in a stiff chair no one else wants in the corner farthest from the sound system. Then again, sometimes it is he who mans the system, changing CDs and adjusting the volume with such busy efficiency that nobody would think to interrupt him. When the dancing starts, she freezes. Not a single tendon betrays the fact that she hears a beat. Not one thumb lifts. As couples rise and swirl and pound the floor, she vanishes. One way or another, she does.

Loners, if you can catch them, are well worth the trouble. Not dulled by excess human contact, not blasé or focused on your crotch while jabbering about themselves, loners are curious, vigilant, full of surprises. They do not cling. Separate wherever they go, awake or asleep, they shimmer with the iridescence of hidden things seldom seen. The pearl, the swallow's egg, the lost doubloon, the jewel in the lotus, membrane. You don't need to be told this. You know.

· · ·

SOUTHERN CALIFORNIA RELATIONSHIP-seminar leader Dr. Alexander Ávila specializes in counseling shy clients. Not all shy people—and around 40 percent of all Americans identify themselves as such—are loners. Nor are all loners shy. My loner husband, for example, regularly gives breezy, rousing speeches to roomfuls of potential investors, and has spoken calmly and wittily to TV reporters. He doesn't do these things unless they're necessary, but he does them.

But in truth, there is significant overlap between shy people and loners. Ávila's "new definition of shyness" as "a life-enhancing state of extraordinary sensitivity and profound self-reflection" also offers food for thought to loners who don't mind a bit of self-help jargon. In his book *The Gift of Shyness*, Ávila touts the virtues of shy partners in relationships. Empathic, never predatory, they share many of the selling points that loners boast, and for good reason. "Those who date a shy person can be fairly certain that their partner won't cheat on them," Ávila promises, adding that shy partners "are the deepest of thinkers" who "excel in the one thing many people lack: the gift of listening."

Turning his attention directly to "the stay-at-home intro-vert" who yearns for a relationship, he warns that reluctance to spend extended time in crowded public places reduces our chances, statistically, of meeting anyone at all. Thus, after mus-tering the first few words of dialogue with an attractive stranger, this individual will arrange a date recklessly, desper-ately, jumping at the chance to get it over with. But a scarcity of past experience and limited energy for prolonged cruising leaves loners lacking what Ávila calls "a mental measuring stick" with which to judge potential partners. Thus, he warns, we too often make snap decisions—wrong ones.

"Regardless of how limited your dating opportunities . . . the worst thing you can do is settle for someone who is not your ideal," he writes. When we spoke, Ávila told me how those "worst things" sometimes play out. Aggressive women sometimes "go after the shy introverted guys," picking them as prime partners precisely because such guys, whom Ávila calls "more tender and good-hearted" than standard-issue men, seem easier to manipulate. And a number of such guys have found their way into Ávila's office with black eyes, having been physically abused by their partners.

That's an extreme situation. But it's also an image that lingers in the mind. Ávila has concrete advice for loners seeking relationships: all we need is just "one really good partner." How to find him or her? *Join,* he insists. In a way it's the same dreaded refrain: games, clubs, teams, fraternities.

For loners, "most of the time it's them against the world," says Ávila, who describes himself as shy, but not a loner. If a man's before-dinner grocery run "is the one time he goes out of the house all day," then the entire pressure of meeting a potential mate must be borne by those twenty minutes at the local Piggly Wiggly. As a "grown-up introvert, you may have a natural aversion to group activities." He proposes a program in which loners keep track of how many hours they spend each day engaged in "introvert activities (writing, reading, meditating, eating alone, and relaxing)" and how many in "extravert activities (going to a dinner party, window-shopping at the mall with a friend)." Those seeking partners should alter the ratio on the program, ratcheting up the latter type of activities by joining a group that provides an ongoing social structure larded with lots of available singles.

As any angler knows, fish are most easily caught in stocked ponds, or aquariums. But loners are not the sort of fish that travel in schools, and we dislike stocked ponds. Joining is more or less anathema to us. Will all those dinner parties and trips to the mall with friends make us feel like impostors? Acting in a way so alien to our true impulses means presenting a false face to the world—and to whichever possible partners we meet in those surroundings. *Pleased to meet you, I'm not really like this.* Is this any way to start?

STANFORD UNIVERSITY'S Dr. Lynne Henderson agrees that joining is the best way to meet possible partners. She also agrees that, for us, it is also one of the hardest. To her clients at the Shyness Clinic, she recommends thinking of joining as a means to an end, which she likens to daily bouts with the Stairmaster.

I can make myself do things I don't want to do, Henderson urges her clients to tell themselves, *in the service of meeting a partner.* "I don't like to work out, either," she concedes, comparing what she calls "social fitness" to physical fitness. "But I make myself do it." And while physical fitness requires a lifetime commitment, social fitness needs to last only until that "one good match" is made. "The search is not forever," Henderson promises. "Sure, it's a chore." But everyone does chores, so why should loners be excused?

Reaching goals—such as finding someone who understands your fetish for wristwatches and bondage—is all about "maximizing your strengths and minimizing your weaknesses," Henderson says. "People aren't born with social skills any more than they are born with Ph.D.s in math." Both take brains and diligence. "If you want something badly enough," Henderson reasons, "you can be strategic about it."

Sometimes this means just asking for help. "Introverts often have very good friends. And good friends tend to be good matchmakers. Do your friends know anyone you might like? Just ask."

Returning to the exercise metaphor, she notes that "not everybody's a tennis player." Others are squash players or water-polo players, so to speak. Thus relationship-seeking loners ought to choose groups very selectively, she advises, based on activities or principles they already enjoy—"even if you've never thought of them as group activities." This helps to squelch that self-betraying, false-face sensation. If you like hiking but usually hike alone, Henderson says, it wouldn't kill you to join the local hiking club. If you've always wanted to learn Hindi, enroll in a class rather than buying a set of learn-at-home cassettes. Readers' and writers' groups offer unique forums, she says, for members whose hobbies are all about being alone. She calls this process "niche-picking." It makes being in a group bearable—even if only just—by making the group structure a by-product of the main action. Being already well-versed in that action before you join the group "can be so advantageous," she adds, "because then you're the expert, and everyone will come to you. And if you're willing to help them, even just a little"—well, that makes you all the more attractive, Henderson says. And it's less of a workout.

BUT THE INTERNET makes that workout even easier. All comprising the written word, all in the privacy of your own home, on your own time—it creates a comfort level for which loners attempting to meet one another in an earlier era would have given their left arms. For those who, no matter what the shrinks advise, would rather die than join Toastmasters, the touch of a keyboard and the soft glow of a screen are magic and power beyond imagining. The bedroom light goes off. Taptaptaptaptap. Countless matches, emotional and erotic, have been made online—and even if many of these bonds simmer in cyberspace forever and never progress to the skin stage, that's fine with some of the loners involved. ("It's *in person* that the *real* issues come out," Alexander Avila warns.) Being able to speak from the heart or, okay, from a bit farther down without being seen lends loners a directness that standard social games deny us. Our voices, which in times past would perforce have been confined to diaries or silence, now shout and whisper and croon across the blue. A host of electronic angels, the Internet lifts away our shame and hesitance, the smiley or blank masks we wear in public, all the fear and boredom small talk forces us to feel. Stripped of our gags, wrists untied, we relax into natural postures and start signaling to one another at the speed of light.

In chat rooms and on-line bulletin boards, the subculture emerges, defining itself and its preferences as it could never do in a public sphere. "I pick men who are very comfortable being loners," one young woman confides on a girl-talk bulletin board. "I don't mind the separation between our moments together." "Single, attractive male seeks sexy, loner hippie chick," reads a personals ad in the Missoula, Montana *Independent*'s online edition, "who thinks it's cool to live and be free." "Cynical queer loner, thirty-two, recently committed to polygamy," reads a posting on a gay Web site from a man who seeks a new partner and really means polyandry, but warns, "I will not be willing to spend every waking minute of my life with you." At a heavy-metal Web site, a woman seeks "long-haired guys . . . loners. No Christians." Another listing on the same site specifies a desire for "goths, loners." At a Web site seeking male pen-pals, "Sandra" calls herself "a loner, a bit shy, but very open-minded. I have a high sex drive and I enjoy all sports and I'm extremely athletic." So many sites are dedicated to special interests—from *Lord of the Rings* to Indonesian lepidoptera to yaws, not to mention autocastration—that like minds are only ever a click or two away.

On-line dating services direct special appeals to loners in general. The home-page text of a French one begins with: "Attention, senior managers, stressed-out fortysomethings and loners tired of being alone." Another site, called Solo for Singles, welcomes new users by reasoning that "true loners often seek safety by staying away from people. If they don't even work with numerous people, they will have a hard time sharing experiences with someone who is attractive to them and vice versa."

Even the word "cybersex" has the self-consciously sci-fi shiver of something from a Philip K. Dick novel. Yet the future is here. Unsolicited porn—sexual spam—accounted for as much as 8 percent of all email traffic in the summer of 2002. Hooking up with a live human being, albeit unseen, to spin on-line fantasies is easy and costs nothing. Whether those fantasies are the garden-variety touch-me-lick-me type or travel down some fetish corridor, they make it possible for raving, heaving ecstasy between two—or more—partners to remain a technically solitary pursuit, performed in the utmost privacy, the small closed circle of the self. A lot of loners can tolerate only this. It seems, in one sense, simple. *And so clean.* You're home. You aren't hurting anyone. You're only looking.

Cybersex is masturbation with a twist. Porn sites and sexual chat rooms have done more for loners than any of us want to admit.

It is here that the public's fear of loners—that primal *what-is-he-doing-in-there* fear—breeds at its hottest and smears the most poison. The *worst* he could be "doing in there," after all, is something that blends sex with the bizarre, sex with what must at all costs remain hidden. The world waits, outside the room of every loner, to break down the door and catch him in the act.

A Web site aimed at helping parents protect their kids from cyberstalkers explains patiently that even "before the advent of the Internet, pedophiles were essentially loners"—thus, now, shielded from easy detection by the Net's anonymity, they can pursue their prey with impunity. In a 2000 UPI article, a psychologist calls the Net "a trap for people seeking sex." It is "the crack cocaine of sex addiction," Dr. Alyson Nerenberg goes on to explain. Having "treated people who spend 10 to 15 hours with their computers daily seeking sex partners," Nerenberg declares that "these people are often loners who have drifted away from all other human contact" and thus "have to have more and more" cybersex. An S/M Web site warns its users against "predators. . . . They come in all shapes, sizes, and ethnic backgrounds . . . although the majority are white males between the ages of 18 and 35. They are usually loners."

IT IS HARDLY possible to even think of cybersex without imagining the solitary onanist angling his body slightly so as to avoid spraying the screen, the keyboard, the mouse and mousepad. The rise of cybersex electrifies the masturbating-loner archetype, but the archetype was already set in stone by the time Edison— a loner—invented the lightbulb. It's so obvious. The image of the loner as compulsive masturbator is a projection born of the public's bafflement at how we could possibly be spending so much time alone. What else could we possibly be doing?

Masturbation, like the loners with whom it is so ubiquitously associated, has a bad rap. In films from *Being There* to *There's Something About Mary*, masturbation is joke fodder. This, of course, is because it is a solitary practice. Things done alone are mysterious, dangerous, wrong, shameful, incomplete. In the eyes of the world, they do not count. On the sexual-options coolness scale, it ranks pretty much at the bottom, barely above bestiality.

"Masturbation has never been highly regarded," laments Joani Blank, who founded Good Vibrations, San Francisco's innovative sex-toy store, in 1977. Her own string of books, including *I Am My Lover* and *First Person Sexual*, have established Blank as self-pleasuring's most passionate pioneer. Most people, she explains, do not see it as an end in itself, or anything to boast about or even as "having sex." (Woody Allen, to his credit, has called it "sex with someone you love.")

"If there is only one 'right' way to have an orgasm," says Blank, who is a longtime sex educator but not a loner herself, "please let me know what the 'wrong' way is. I believe there is no such thing." For her anthology *First Person Sexual*, she asked a wide variety of men and women to write about their own experiences: not about the fantasies that got them off, but the acts themselves. Out came tales of lubricant and candles. But many contributors were unable to write about this except in the third person—à la "*his* hand flew up and down" and "*she* reached for the photograph of Ewan McGregor." Blank went through and changed all those pronouns to "me," "I," and "my"—hence the book's title—"and in every case it made the writer feel much better."

IN ITS PREMIER issue, the alternative-lifestyle journal *To-Do List* introduced a whole new typology, and a tongue-twisting brand name for it: the quirkyalone.

"We are the puzzle pieces who seldom fit with other puzzle pieces," wrote the magazine's editor, Sasha Cagen, in the

issue's lead article. "We inhabit singledom as our natural rest-
ing state. . . . Secretly, we are romantics, romantics of the highest order. We want a miracle. Out of millions we have to find
the one who will understand.

"For the quirkyalone, there is no patience for dating just for
the sake of not being alone. On a fine but by no means transcendent date we dream of going home to watch television. We
would prefer to be alone with our own thoughts than with a less
than perfect fit. We are almost constitutionally incapable of
casual relationships." As for whether "being a quirkyalone is a
life sentence, I say yes, at the core, one is always quirkyalone.
But when the quirkyalone collides with another, ooh la la. The
earth quakes." After the article was reprinted in *The Utne Reader,*
Cagen became a sought-after media pundit, interviewed widely on the subject of "deeply single" singles—seekers of love
who aren't desperate to date merely for the sake of dating.

The speed with which her concept was understood and
absorbed dispels once again the stereotype of unsexy loners.
Dispels it, at least, for alternative-lifestyle types. The masses
whose flesh crawls at the word *alternative* are still happy with
their conviction that anything done alone is at best not worth
doing, at worst a sin. The Church reveals its antiloner bias by
reviling masturbation. An old boyfriend of a friend of mine
used to call her—they lived hundreds of miles apart—to confess, crying, that he had jerked off. *I did it again,* he moaned. She
would yawn. It was three in the morning, her time. *So?*

So tell me it was wrong, he wept.

No, my friend said. *Hang up and do it again.*

He would get furious. He wanted her to help him correct what he could see only as a flaw in himself, wash the sin from himself. She would not help. He broke up with her and started sleeping with other girls. A sin, too, but one he could brag about. A sin that drew him out of solitude, which was a greater sin, and brought his penis out into the world, where it could proudly join the crowd.

before leaving her limp again. Insisting that her appetite had vanished, she firmly refused food. The former star student and skilled horsewoman would stay in bed for fifty years, the rest of her life. Fancher would never join the outside world again.

Dubbed "The Brooklyn Enigma," Fancher made headlines. Reporters marveled at her ability to read, embroider, write in a fine, tiny penmanship, and fashion intricate wax flowers, although blind. They marveled, too, as years went by, over her claim that she no longer needed to eat. Widely admired for having the good grace to unhinge her young fiancé from his obligation, Fancher welcomed visitors to her dark bedroom. She had become a lifelong recluse, never going out into daylight again.

MOLLIE FANCHER WAS a celebrity, but she was far from unique. In the latter half of the nineteenth century, middle-class young female invalids were so numerous in Britain and America that there was a collective term for them: "bed cases." Doctors were all too familiar with the range of complaints that included headaches, feebleness, paralysis, contortions, trances, fainting spells, blindness, deafness, and muteness—and which resolutely eluded any diagnosis, any evident cause. Confined to their bedrooms for life, arguably by choice, these celibate odalisques comprised a veritable subculture. Writing in 1883, physician G. L. Austin called such patients duplicitous and "unreasonable." Speaking up for many in his profession, Austin accused these women of exaggerating their symptoms and of exhibiting an inability to perform certain tasks only when it suited them. As

Michelle Stacey reports in her book *The Fasting Girl,* one classic bed case of the period was Alice James, sister of the writers Henry and William James. In 1866, at eighteen, Alice first began complaining of headaches and eventually, Stacey writes, "ended up devoting her life to her illnesses."

James herself called her illnesses "nervous crises." It is a telling description. The ideas of "nervous disease," neurosis and hysteria had been in circulation for some time; and while nineteenth-century doctors no longer believed, as their ancient Greek forebears did, that such ailments sprang from a misplaced uterus (*hystera*), they speculated widely on the likelihood that these patients' symptoms had deeper emotional roots than physical ones.

In the ensuing years, the debate has been joined by sociologists, feminist scholars, and others. Why, they wonder, did debilitation and thus—and this is what matters to loners—seclusion become fashionable? It seems a sad fashion, denying its practitioners freedom and fun. Yet it also freed them from adult responsibilities. Becoming an invalid was one way to escape the marriage market or, if wed, the nuptial bed. Mollie Fancher's case is an example of this. But why would sex and marriage suddenly seem unendurable? Neither of them were all that different in the nineteenth century than they had ever been before.

Other things *were,* though. Other aspects of young ladies' lives were speeding futureward at such unprecedented warp-speed that they resembled a Jules Verne novel. Sparking this change was technology.

Like mushrooms under a tree, innovations appeared one by one to instantly, and forever, change the once-familiar structure of human society. Between 1840 and 1879 alone, these included the electric telegraph, the telephone, the lightbulb, the transcontinental railroad, and the passenger elevator. Tasks that had been taken for granted since the dawn of civilization were suddenly no longer required, or were performed in utterly new ways. Tasks that had always been performed by human flesh were taken over by machines. Motion and light and time and space and talk, and thus reality itself, morphed radically within a single generation: Mollie Fancher's generation. Thrust over a threshold more dazzling—but also more disorienting—than had ever been crossed before, some were thrilled. But some were frightened. And for the frightened, coping with those changes meant hiding from them.

That Fancher met her fate while riding public transportation seems a plot point worthy of a novelist: the future rushing to meet a bright young woman and knocking her, literally, off her feet. The accident and Fancher's chosen response to it allowed her to dodge those aspects of the new world that seemed beyond handling. Slipping away, bed cases refused to grow up, choosing instead the finite, low-tech landscapes of their vanished childhoods—and of the world's vanished childhood. In a buzzers-and-bells era too new to have any points of reference, they found refuge under the covers, in their own rooms, alone.

At first glance it seems only too appropriate to include a discussion of Victorian invalids in a book about loners. Bed cases were the ultimate loners—right?

Well, no. They adopted the habits of loners, the guise of loners, as it suited them. Mollie Fancher was by all accounts sociable. Even bundled up in bed she entertained a stream of visitors. Look closely. In retreat, hiding from the plugged-in world, a bed case was the vortex in a whirl of doctors, relatives, well-wishers, all fluttering around the helpless shut-in. Faces always hovered over the bed facilitating therapies, feedings, entertainment, hygiene. This was a flight not into independence, as true loners might make, but into dependence. To call bed cases loners, as seems customary now, is to insult loners. It misses the point entirely.

TECHNOLOGY ITSELF IS neutral. Whether it works for evil or good, distinctions which themselves are in the eye of the beholder, depends on who is flicking the switch. Its very impartiality is its most terrifying aspect, but also its best.

Technology has existed, in some form or another, since humans first used rocks to brain their prey. That the Industrial Revolution is called a revolution is only because it saw the birth of *so much* industry—technology—all at one time. It changed the paradigms of speed and distance, manufacture and communication. In changing life, it changed work.

And what does work mean for loners? For some, the smart and lucky ones who work alone, it means accomplishing things without being made to suffer. Simple as it should be, no loner can take this point for granted. Along with whatever other hardships work brings—difficulty, danger, dullness, unfair pay—loners who labor any way besides alone endure one more. It is a hardship nonloners don't even know exists, cannot conceive of.

How much time spent with others is too much? Side by side, within their sight, in earshot—forty minutes? Two hours, tops. Yet today's standard work shift lasts eight. Putting loners in busy workplaces all day is like making albinos pick cotton without sunscreen. The Industrial Revolution turned work into more of a crowd scene than it had ever been before. Loners needed to make a living like everyone else. It was presumed that they must join the mob that was the workforce. A presumption, yet a punishment.

A preindustrial village is a kind of fishbowl: small and confined, its occupants few and familiar. Even the least solitary jobs in that almost-entirely-vanished world demand contact only with relatives and friends, not hordes of strangers. Jesus worked in Joseph's carpenter shop.

With the rise of industry, farms gave way to meatpacking plants. Smithies gave way to steelworks. In so doing, the average workplace expanded exponentially. In factories, the average worker was surrounded by row on row of other workers, often for brutally long shifts. In 1836, one British cotton manufacturer lamented: "Since Lord Althorp's Act was passed in 1833, we have reduced the time of adults to sixty-seven and a half hours a week, and that of children under thirteen years of age to forty-eight hours in the week, though to do this latter has, I must admit, subjected us to much inconvenience."

As economic centers shifted from countryside to city, crowding became status quo. Dickens was not the only writer who railed against the misery that came with the brand-new metropolis: infectious disease, dirty air, accidents, murder, madness. The very technology that made life faster, brighter, and better in general made the lives of those who ran its machines hell. But writers decrying slums and factories do not mourn the special misery, the added agony, that such conditions visited on loners. Who, lamenting typhoid, smog, and amputations, would add to those ills *too much company?*

TECHNOLOGY CREATED CITIES. Some had flourished for thousands of years; some sprang from the land like Athena from her father's head, fully formed. Social critics have always blasted urban anonymity. And in those days about which Dickens wrote, living in cities meant sharing rooms, sharing beds—not with lovers but with siblings, strangers, coworkers because a shared room might have just one mattress. Privacy was not an option.

But as cities developed and society learned to accommodate itself around the industries that fueled them, living standards changed. With the twentieth century, it became possible for the average worker to live alone—men at first, later women as well. Previously, living solo had been the province only of rich lords and pariahs. But metropolises spawned the perfectly respectable studio apartment, ubiquitous and cheap, with room enough for only one. With this change, cities became their own kind of paradise for loners. In the very anonymity critics derided lay the privacy loners have always craved. In cities, unlike villages, the never-ending swarm of souls and wheels and sounds renders residents circumspect. City people are as a rule less curious about strangers than country folk. They do not strike up conversations so quickly. Knowing few of their neighbors, if any, city people are simply not all that interested in whoever lives down the hall or downstairs. Anonymity makes people stick to their own business. Thus, thanks to technology, the urban loner has emerged and flourished over the last hundred years. Toting our groceries and daily mail in and out of Apartment 2C unwatched, free, we have slipped out of the fishbowl into the sea.

HOME LIFE IS one thing. But the workplace, even as it diversified from factory to office and to the other urban fixtures, banks and big stores, remained crowded. The twentieth century firmly established offices as the mainstay of middle-class work. Replicated endlessly around the world with numbing regularity, cubicle upon cubicle, floor upon floor of tower upon tower, the corporate world works like the beehive it resembles. In the corporate system, teamwork wins.

On my first day at one of the two offices where I have worked, a cake was brought into the kitchenette for the birthday of a woman in a different department. An announcement was made on the PA system. All around me, my new colleagues rose and headed for the kitchenette. I stayed right where I was, wanting to appear dedicated and complete my project for that day. Down the hall I could hear singing and laughter, the clink of a knife. One of my officemates, having noticed I wasn't in the kitchenette, came back to fetch me.

"Office rule," she said. "We always make a showing when it's someone's birthday. *Everybody. Always.*"

Taking a solitary tray to a quiet corner of the employee canteen is not quite cricket. Interviewed for *Newsday*, a loner who worked for a public-relations firm, a highly sociable office in a highly sociable field, lamented that "being in such an environment has caused me to be deeply depressed. Much of this has to do with extroverts' feelings toward quiet types and their tendency to ostracize."

For outgoing types such as Joani Blank, founder of the San Francisco sex-toy store Good Vibrations, no office environment can be busy or social enough. Blank told me she adores meetings, even those that go on for hours with everyone talking at once. For her, this is the very definition of work well done.

"When someone wants to end the meeting and says, 'Let's just go home and sleep on it,'" Blank told me, "I feel completely shut down. I feel rejected. Turning my key in the lock of my door at home, I already feel lonely."

DESPITE THE FRIENDSHIPS that sometimes sprout there, offices are artificial societies. Millions of these false societies, self-governing short-term civilizations with their own rules and hierarchies, are in constant flux at any given time. They shift in both dynamics and population with every new hire, every layoff. They end abruptly, crashing down in a hail of pink slips. Yet as liquid as they are, as potentially loveless, these are the surroundings in which a great many working adults spend a great majority of their waking hours. Imagine a white-collar worker on his deathbed. Looking back at images of his life unspooling before his inner eye, he realizes how much of his time, what a huge percentage, has been spent alongside people he would never have chosen to know. He hears thirty years' worth of trivialities, *How about those Seahawks?* against the remembered bloop of the watercooler. How awful to think of deathbed scenes at all. But, for loners, instructional.

Formulas for creating a successful twentieth-century workplace have no room for the loner. Exemplifying this, an article in *Business Solutions* magazine is subtitled "Loners Beware." In the article, a CEO explains her company's hiring policy: "We look for employees who have been involved in group activities (be it church events or intramural sports teams) in their personal lives." The office's ambience, the CEO adds happily, "would drive a loner crazy. We encourage teamwork and brainstorming." To further ensure a sociable staff, "we hire mostly on personal references . . . our star performers were hired because they're friends of friends."

In an on-line interview, the CEO of a Web applications development company declares that his strategy is to "avoid admitted loners. Singles or workers with few friends, little family nearby and no social life . . . while it's illegal to ask about family or personal issues," he says he gets around this by asking applicants about their hobbies or what they do for fun. "The fact that they have some sort of support group outside work is good," he explains. "It gives us some measure if they're sociable or not."

An article in an industry journal by a Canadian orthodontist offers tips on maximizing a clinic's profitability by enforcing a vigorous team mentality. He compares good workers to squirrels who scurry around together stashing nuts in summer as preparation for winter. "Everyone is working toward a shared goal. . . . [Thus] I would much rather hire an inexperienced team player than a super-competent and experienced loner. The lone squirrel may provide for itself but won't do much toward the good of the group. Ironically, the competent loner can mess up the whole team."

Applying another animal metaphor, he encourages what he calls "goose behavior": "Geese are noisy. How come? They're cheering each other on! . . . How about naming an 'employee of the moment' for a particularly positive or outrageous act of caring? Such recognition can be just as motivating and satisfying to a team member as a raise in salary." A worker's best reward, he writes, is "a sense of belonging."

With this in mind, he advises other employers, "Keep score."

SAVVY NONLONERS START networking during their college days, honing the social skills that loners often find ridiculous. For not having a clue, loners pay a price and keep on paying. My father learned this firsthand. He had dreamed as a boy of becoming a veterinarian or oceanographer, both relatively solitary scientific professions demanding only a bare minimum of human contact. But World War II derailed his plans. In the army as a member of the Signal Corps, he learned enough about electronics to feel, when the war ended, that he would be better off with an engineering degree in a year or so than starting from square one in veterinary school or oceanography. He became a cog in the vast cold war aerospace industry. It meant working in a busy office, consulting constantly with fellow engineers, and traveling nationwide to other complexes, consulting with *their* engineers. He liked the science, liked the instruments, the satellites on which he worked. Hated the Christmas parties and obligatory cocktails with coworkers. During a business trip to Cape Canaveral in 1986, he spent that cocktail hour longing to get away from his officemates and the astronaut they had invited along. As they drank and chatted, showing one another snapshots of their families, my father could barely contain his desire to flee. Later, after the astronaut died aboard the doomed space shuttle *Challenger,* my father would always remember with a guilty shudder that evening's desire, a loner's wish.

By being a man on the cutting edge of technology who began his career precisely in the middle of the twentieth century, he was destined to have, in spades, both what he loved and hated most. Solar cells, satellites, and fifty years of being sandwiched between other people's desks.

Generations of loners like him have endured this agony and irony: adoring the work but despising the workplace.

Yet—at the end of the twentieth century—something happened. Loners found a way to make technology rescue them from the cage it had created.

THE INTERNET IS, for loners, an absolute and total miracle. It is, for us, the best invention of the last millennium. It educates. It entertains. It transforms. It facilitates a kind of dialogue in which we need not be seen, so it suits us perfectly. It validates.

It makes being alone seem normal. It makes being alone fun for everyone.

And so it has its critics. They claim it keeps kids from playing healthy games outdoors. They say it is a procurer for perverts, a weapon in hate crimes. Underlying all this, of course, is the real reason for their dismay: the Internet legitimizes solitude. The *real* problem is not that kids don't play outdoors, but that they do not play with other kids.

Terror is afoot of a sci-fi world in which machines have rendered social contact undesirable and, desired or not, obsolete. In 2000, the Stanford Institute for the Quantitative Study of Society released the results of a newly completed research project. It revealed that one fourth of those interviewed for the project who used the Internet more than five hours a week (and thus were, by SIQSS's definition, "regular users") reported that they spent less time socializing outside the house or being with family or friends than they had done before discovering the Net. This percentage led the researchers to conclude that the Internet is an isolating technology that separates users from the "real world." Subsequently, a study conducted at UCLA found that a majority of its participants did *not* spend less time with others.

The Stanford study made Internet users look bad, backing up that assessment by saying *See? They spend more time ALONE.* Its UCLA counterpart made loners look bad, too, by saying *Hooray! Internet users still spend time with others.* Both studies sparked heated commentary. Either we should all panic because Internet use is creating a world of hermits, the commentators seemed to say in the first case, or, in the second, that we should all celebrate because Internet use is not creating a world of hermits. *Global Reach* magazine, for one, was dismayed that the mainstream media "favored the UCLA study over Stanford's, discarding the notion that Net use creates loners and workaholics."

That this issue attained such a high profile at all is troubling. Who cares whether Net users behave like loners? Commentators never spew fire over the fact that offices force loners to act like nonloners. It is the specter of loner behavior, like a plague, that strikes terror across the land. Our friend the Internet, neutral as all technology, has done—not of its own volition, as it has none—the same thing that crime reporters have, and profilers, and witch-hunters. It has kindled that age-old panic which shows itself at every chance it gets: *fear of loners.*

THE NET HAS turned hanging around the house into a wild adventure, has made school a snap. But, most radically of all, it has changed work.

Whether or not the Net has rendered socializing obsolete—and so what if it has?—no one can deny that millions of jobs around the world need no longer be performed in offices but anywhere a laptop goes. In other words, at long last, the worker can work alone. This is a giant leap in evolution, an Emancipation Proclamation for loners. We call it paradise, they call it telecommuting.

On average, American telecommuters in 1997 worked at home some fifteen hours per week. Nearly 20 percent worked at home full-time. In 1999, the workforce reportedly included 20 million telecommuters. In 2002—at a time when over 51 percent of North American companies offered their workers telecommuting as an option—a study by the Cahners In-Stat market research group revealed that about 24 percent of the American workforce, more than 30 million employees, spent at least part of every workweek telecommuting from home. The study predicted that this number would grow to nearly 30 percent of the workforce—nearly 40 million workers—by 2004.

Thirty million, the 2002 figure, is a significant increase over the 20 million American telecommuters reported in 1999. It is nearly ten times the 3.6 million telecommuters identified in a 1997 U.S. Bureau of Labor Statistics survey. (Another survey, also completed that year, reported 11.1 million telecommuters.) The Internet can take major credit for this increase, in which the 1997 figure represented a growth of almost *90 percent* over the findings in a comparable 1991 survey.

As for its efficacy, studies show increased productivity among telecommuting employees ranging from 8 percent to as much as 30 percent. Among loners, increased productivity is all well and good. But it's the advent of work situations that don't require us to sell our souls that really matters.

NOT ALL LONERS are creative, nor are all creative people loners. But the overlap between the two is too large to be mere coincidence. Much has been written about the fact that children who spend a great deal of time alone tend to be more imaginative than their socially active peers. And while Freud dismissed imagination as escapist and infantile, he would hardly have enjoyed a world devoid of art, music, theater, and books. As artists know, the creative process is consummately singular. It is a sojourn whose signposts are legible only to the sojourner, and are often cryptic even to him: a trip whose personal nature is its point. Those born creative tend either to be born loners or to become loners, early, knowing it will fuel the flame that is their raison d'être. Down the years, how many loners have been called upon to be creative in cramped cubicles, coworkers on all sides, phones jingling and shoes scuffling a partition away? Thinking of them means thinking of how many masterpieces were *not* written, how much cleverness or discovery died before it could ever see the light of day.

Not having to be in any given place at any given time, to perform under watchful eyes, allows for a shift of staggering proportions. Demands having been removed from the body, the mind breaks free.

The eventual implications of such a shift are hard to anticipate and even to imagine, in terms of ideas and achievement and personal happiness and, not inconsequently, fortunes. Carnegie Mellon University economics professor Richard Florida sees these massive changes coalescing with the rise of what he calls the "Creative Class." Numbering some 38 million members in 2002, by Florida's calculations, this class represents a full third of the nation's workforce. And what Florida calls "the creative ethos" has, unsurprisingly, much in common with the loner ethos.

In the emerging "Creative Age," as he puts it, creative output is the most highly prized commodity. It is "the *decisive* source of competitive advantage . . . the winners in the long run are those who can create and keep creating." Thus, Florida writes, "schedules, rules, and dress codes have become more flexible to cater to how the creative process works."

Members of the Creative Class "do not want to conform to organizational or institutional directives and resist traditional group-oriented norms." "Creative Class Values" include individuality, self-statement, self-determination, and meritocracy—in which producing good work is more important than making a particularly good impression. All of these are loner territory. The Creative Class's lifestyle is experiential, its achievements fueled and inspirations sparked by being out of the office and in the world, observing it. Nice work if a loner can get it.

FLORIDA CITES A study showing that the amount of free time Americans spent socializing with others dropped from 8.2 hours per week in 1965 to 7.3 in 1995—a shift of nearly 20 percent. Given the years in question, this change was clearly fueled not only by the Internet but also other diversions, most of them technological. TV and videos along with computers are relentlessly blamed for dissembling society.

What are loners to make of the presumption—the message in all that fretting—that a less sociable world is automatically a worse one? That free time spent socializing with others is automatically superior to time spent in other ways? When headlines say *Internet Users Spend More Time Alone* it is not just a comment but a wail, a banshee heralding a death. What if a certain girl spends her time on-line studying the life cycle of luna moths while the girl next door spends her social time sharing a crack pipe with the boarder? Or even, say, sitting on the porch with Kate and Morgan talking about nothing for hours? Is socializing all that great? Riots are socializing. Arguably, more damage is done and time wasted in company with others than alone.

Technology has merely made this obvious. The fact that loners and nonloners alike would rather plug in than talk or touch suggests that everyone is finally getting wise to how nice it can feel to be alone. How much they can achieve or, even the most passive of them, see. How many realities lie a click away. It is dangerous wisdom.

Whether or not technology entices nonloners to act like loners is, for loners, less important than what it can do for *us*. It makes possible work, play, even relationships that would never have happened otherwise.

Our loner ancestors lived in forest cottages, were woodsmen, shepherds, solitary seamstresses, fur trappers. Some, chasing heaven, were hermits. Now the world is too full—of buildings and people, buildings full of people—for us to finesse those kinds of refuge. History is like this. Having led us to the city, having made the city swell and swarm, making us stay, technology offers a latter-day escape. An escape from itself: a sort of Chinese-puzzle irony. Cars are caves on wheels. And the keyboard is a forest, is a meadow, is the open sea, a habitable planet, a pot of gold, an island, the palace where the prince is looking for a princess, Shangri-la, the Serengeti, Swedish lessons twenty-four hours a day.

8.

the diving bell

[ART]

Inspiration comes to those who know how to be silent,
how to wait, how to translate the ineffable.
Sound like anyone you know?

ON VALENTINE'S DAY in 1937, the *New York Times* ran an article about the Norwegian painter Edvard Munch.

Munch "was recently persuaded, with great difficulty, to exhibit his work in London," ran the article, explaining that the painter "considered by many to be Norway's greatest artist . . . lives the life of a recluse near Oslo."

"The large country house in which the artist lives his secluded life has only two residential rooms. The rest of the building is given over to workshops and storerooms filled with packing cases and pictures that Mr. Munch declines to sell. The old artist paints in a roofless barn, with long grass instead of a floor, underfoot. Only two persons may intrude upon him, one a shipping agent, and the other Pola Gaugin, son of the famous painter. Some time ago, however, Professor Dorner, head of the Landesmuseum in Hanover and an admirer of Munch's work, managed to pay a call.

" 'Mr. Munch hates all contact with the outside world,' Professor Dorner relates. 'It took several days trying to get in touch with him, but at last I managed to coax him not only to consent to see me but also to show his pictures at the London Gallery.

"'He is old and ill but paints all the time. He never answers letter; piles of correspondence are heaped on a desk in one of the rooms.'"

Munch is most famous for his 1893 work *The Scream*, in which a figure standing on a bridge, head in hands, fixes the viewer with a wide-eyed, openmouthed gaze at once imploring and anguished as two top-hatted pedestrians stroll nearby with apparent unconcern. In Munch's own words, it was inspired by "a breath of melancholy" that swept through the artist one day at sunset when the sky turned blood red "and I sensed a great, infinite scream pass through nature." That preternatural scream, of course, was one which no one else on earth could hear.

ARTISTS HEAR WHAT no one else hears. They see what no one else sees. They say what no one else says. They must. And to do this, they traffic in the slippery yield of their own souls. They bring to earth the wrack and lode of depths that only they can reach and still come back alive.

Inspiration is a flash. A momentary flicker that—if the would-be recipient is mired in mindless chatter—might easily die unseen. It cannot be repeated, duplicated, slowed down, cached for viewing at some more convenient time. The mind awaiting inspiration must be primed, ever awake, aware. For this it is best off alone.

She is gifted, they say. *She has the gift.* A gift with hard labor attached. After inspiration must come the plunge down inner passages, the search which suffocates but liberates: the spelunking where no one could help even if you wanted them to. Instead, plucking souvenirs from those depths, you must keep asking yourself, in a tongue only you can speak, *What next? But how?* while shapes and colors swirl out of control. A gift, but a subpoena.

Which can take weeks to fulfill. Years. Your whole life.

Which requires initiative. Commitment. Loner values, loner aptitudes. Conviction that something so personal is worth doing no matter what. No matter if they try to talk you out of it. No matter if they call you self-indulgent, talentless. They will. No matter—all the better—that it is best done alone, some would say *only* done alone. No matter if they do not understand. Deluded, they think you are doing this for them. Sillies. Edvard Munch refused for many years to sell or even show his paintings anywhere. He saw no cause to share.

Art breeds loners. Loners breed art.

IN A LETTER TO his brother, Michelangelo is said to have written, "I have no friends of any sort and I don't want any." Leonardo da Vinci swore by solitude as the road to wisdom and artistic perfection. In company, he is said to have once declared, "only half of you will belong to yourself." Paul Cézanne was a recluse in his hometown, Aix, where he devoted himself to painting studies of nearby Mont Sainte-Victoire. Pierre Bonnard was a contemporary of Matisse and Monet but, loner that he was, honed a style wholly apart from the popular movements of his time as he painted his beloved wife, Marthe, in luminous tones again and again. Edgar Degas painted pretty ballerinas but always went home alone; he is said never to have had a love affair all his life. Pablo Picasso, despite his numerous love affairs and several marriages, was a self-described loner as well. Gustav Klimt rendered pairs of lovers with a whimsical sensitivity far ahead of his time; his sister wrote of him that "like all artists, he also needed a lot of love . . . he was not naturally gregarious but a loner, and it therefore had to be the duty of his brothers and sisters to eliminate all the little things in his daily life that were inconvenient. . . . We understood his silent coming and going. . . . Once he had gathered strength, he would plunge into his work with such vehemence that we often thought the flames of his genius might consume him alive." The list goes on: Jean Dubuffet. Ford Madox Brown. Charles Schulz. Georgia O'Keeffe lived in isolation in New Mexico, far from artistic and intellectual circles, and drove Southwestern backroads solo in a Model A Ford with its backseat removed so that she could paint in the car. A biography of Andy Warhol is tellingly titled *Loner at the Ball.*

EVIDENCE SAYS ARTISTIC talent is inborn, a genetic trait. Any kindergarten teacher can see that some five-year-olds draw and paint and sculpt better than the rest of the class—that they love it and apply themselves to it. It matters to them. Whether those five-year-olds grow up to be professional artists or even adopt art as a hobby depends largely on environment: whether adults encourage them, whether they have access to art supplies, whether they exist in a time and place that let them pursue art. The *skill* is inborn—my old boyfriend Jan was a brilliant cartoonist, drawing at a professional level even in tenth grade. He soared through every art class at school. He won prizes. But Jan's parents did everything they could to discourage him. They told him art was unimportant. They ignored his awards. Worst of all, in his senior year of high school, when he should have been applying to colleges, his parents refused to pay for his education if he studied art. He joined the air force instead after a recruiter told him he could earn an art degree in the service and join a mural-painting outfit at the base. That recruiter tricked Jan. He was shunted into clerical work.

After finishing the service, he became a hospital clerk, his dreams of becoming the next Robert Crumb long since shattered. Yet Jan still drew. He did not have the fight in him to go against his parents, apply for an art-school scholarship, a student loan. Years in the military crushed part of him, and he did not draw as much as he might have done in happier days, when he had hope. Yet still he drew. He draws now. That was never wrested from him, could not be.

Artistic temperament is not a choice. Jan suffered for his. And it means being aware, from the time one discovers that other people exist, that other people do not see things as one does. Sometimes it seems that other people all see things alike, and that however everyone else sees things it is not as one does.

It startles the young artist at first—the first few times he is told walls are not for drawing on, that mashed potatoes are not clay, that horses are not blue. In time he realizes, Oh, I'm on my own with this. My visions can't be shared or discussed in mixed company. And if I try to talk about them, someone might laugh or shake her head uncomprehendingly or try to make me stop.

Someone might hurt me.

With that epiphany comes the shock of realizing that there is an inside and an outside, and the artist is outside. Not by will. By blood. By a force beyond understanding, no more mutable than the fact that one breathes. A shock. The knowledge that one is alone in the world. Alone in mind, in mission if not in flesh. All alone, neither able to answer to any boss besides oneself nor willing. Forever alone, a thrill and an awesome responsibility. And life from then on is a party of one.

THE PARTY SOMETIMES gets out of hand. It makes artists keep odd hours, have odd habits, keep no company, attract pity and usually poverty and stares. Being stationed permanently on the outside, summoned to the depths—*Drop everything, just jump into your diving bell and dive*—requires constant access to the self. Artifice cannot be afforded, nor can subterfuge. Small talk, politesse are troublesome barriers when the message must break the surface. The most horrifying thing about art is its honesty, the truth lashed to the mast. This, too, makes artists loners and loners artists. It is the tendency of the recipient to kill the messenger.

As a strategy, some artists hide. Some go mad. Some get

angry. Some cut the traces and construct for themselves a world within the world: its design and environment chosen carefully to best serve the art. To serve *only* the art. A world for one.

Piet Mondrian is known for the angularity of his style—bold opaque squares factory-perfect, outlined in inorganic black. In his Paris apartment and later in a New York studio, Mondrian worked in an isolation so steadfast that both his colleagues and the press marveled at it. While early in his career he produced expressionistic landscapes, distinguishable trees and flowers in subtle colors, the style he later created and which made him world-famous was starkly minimalistic, geometric, dispensing with any reference to actual objects in the natural world. Accordingly, the titles of his works changed from the likes of *Tiger Lily* and *The Red Tree* to *Composition No. 3* and *Composition in Blue, Grey and Pink*.

Just as Mondrian's paintings are frequently misjudged as lifeless and cold, the artist himself was misjudged. Ascetic, given to meditation and frugal meals, he arranged his studio to embody his style. Nothing natural was permitted inside—not even light; the window in his Paris apartment was perpetually covered. A rare visitor later recounted how Mondrian's workspace reflected "the same monastic simplicity which he always preferred. The walls . . . are carefully painted white. The only things that stand out are the famous squares of cardboard painted in the three primary colors" and which were judiciously placed here and there amid all that stark whiteness. His dishes were bright yellow, his table bright red. "He could have lived equally easily in any town in the world, so long as he had a room arranged according to these laws," the visitor noted. "His studio was like one of his pictures, just as each one of his pictures was drawn in his own image. He lived in it just as he lived in his work. It was the dwelling of a *grand solitaire*."

By all accounts, Mondrian was a contented man. He was not a crazy man or a lonely man or a suicidal man or a failure or a man who lived in squalor. He had social graces, knew his manners, but chose not to be in situations where these would be called upon. Fully functional, he published an art magazine and achieved great renown in his own time. For his troubles this quiet figure was lambasted by one art critic as a "cold, ruthless Dutchman." Like any loner whose openness to others goes only this far and no farther, Mondrian would of course be called ruthless. Selfish. Envy lurks in these accusations, wistful envy for the visionary, for the herald, for the one whose master, archive, palette is always himself.

THE BRITISH PAINTER William Roberts first became famous for his powerful renderings of WWI battles, then was a founding member of the Vorticists—avant-garde abstract artists whose name was devised by Ezra Pound. In his memoirs, Roberts recalled how a *London Observer* reporter "describes me as a 'recluse,' an 'eccentric,' and a 'loner.'" An *Evening Standard* art critic "adds some important touches of his own to my 'Public Caricature,'" Roberts wrote. "He finds Roberts to be 'a notorious recluse,' 'a hermit,' 'accused of outright misanthropy,' is 'waspish and angry.'" This kind of art criticism "has its proper place," the artist wrote, among the *Standard's* "accounts of Rapes,

Dope Peddling, Muggings, Kidnappings, and the like. This recluse accusation was first made in 1971 after a visit my wife and I received from an *Observer* newspaper reporter named Barrie Sturt-Penrose. We entertained him with coffee and homemade cake; in return, he went back to his paper and named me recluse. It was repeated and enlarged upon in a catalogue introduction" in which an art dealer took up the chorus.

"Very little is published concerning the characters and tastes of . . . art dealers and critics," Roberts noted. "Their 'Public Images' are practically nonexistent. It would be helpful to know how they came to be art dealers or art critics, whether they are 'Playboys' of the art world, or just solitary figures, 'Loners,' as it were."

Roberts seethed at being called a loner. The word was an "accusation" tantamount to "kidnapper" or "rapist." Just as many loners would not call themselves eccentric but are called that anyway, artists might not call themselves loners, but the public will jump in and do it for them, thank you very much. Artists cannot escape the one-off spark of inspiration, whose translation and transmutation demands solo dives. And all the cake and coffee in the world will never vault them from the outside to the inside, make them safe from that place loners know so well, where great, infinite screams are heard.

9.

singular glamour

Writers' closest companions are inside their heads.

A RELATIVE OF mine does not read my books. A stack of them stands obelisklike on a dresser, rising in height as years pass but never budging, as the sun fades the varnish around them in a neatly damning oblong. Their titles and my name gleam on bindings virgin with that sleek, never-cracked crispness. The books make sticky sounds when parted from each other, like cries of protest.

The person whose dresser it is makes a point of buying my books when they come out, and of mentioning buying them. *I bought it!* Yet during the months and years when I am writing one, the person with the dresser forgets what it is about. I tell the owner of the dresser at the outset, then again when asked—say, a week later. Then all is forgotten and the asking stops.

The person with the dresser can remember many things that have nothing to do with me and books. Details of conversations with the postal carrier, with shop clerks, with strangers at Bargain Barn. The person with the dresser asks me how I am, what are my weekend plans. The neighbor's nephew had his fourth birthday and got a wind-up dog. My books might as well not exist.

PAINTERS AND SCULPTORS now and then hire models. Writers, on the other hand, have no use even for hired company while writing. Even the *hint* of human beings distracts—a doorbell, a phone, shouting in the street. Appointments scribbled in a day-book. And distraction *kills*. It slices the heads off fictional characters just as they open their mouths and begin to speak. It lops their limbs off as they try to walk. It pours acid on poems in utero.

Painters and sculptors have the company of paint and clay and stone. Musicians have the company of instruments. Writers have nothing so beautiful, just utensils and dumb machines. And their own minds, which makes this the most solitary profession of all.

Only a brain. A three-pound organ the size of an eggplant produced *Moby Dick*—another one Shakespeare's collected works. Yet another, Barbara Cartland's 723 romances. A brain working like a ticker-tape machine, processing constantly, reporting, disgorging. And ironically, as alone as writers must be, writing is all about communication.

Written works do not produce fast reactions as pictures and sculptures and music do. It takes no effort to see or hear. But to

read—to grasp what the writer has done—requires commitment. Engagement. As is the case with most art, the relationship between maker and audience is remote in time and space.
The writer is nowhere to be seen when the reader takes up the
book, or even dead. But most often, books go unread. The fiction shelves in any library are heavy with novels—look at their
checkout slips—that have not been lent for years. Thus the
writer, knowing this as writers do, is even more alone. Who will
deem my work worth his time to read? The few. Yet writers
write. And knowing what they know makes their isolation
almost a sacrament.

WHEN MY FRIEND Marie was in her twenties, she lived alone
in a Berkeley apartment writing fiction. Some of her work won
literary prizes, but, even more than that, she loved writing. She
loved it so fiercely that she would not consider having a roommate. She let her answering machine collect incoming calls,
and she went out very seldom, usually alone.

"I enjoyed the solitude," she recalls, "because I didn't like
being interrupted." And yet "this life alone was considered self-
ishness by others, who noted that I did not share my time, my
thoughts, or my possessions with anyone."

Angry people acted as if she was wresting herself away from
them: stealing herself. They told her to forget the M.A. in creative writing which she had earned with honors and to get a real
job. In her apartment, Marie was not actually alone. Her stories, full of love and roads and music, were the only company
she sought, more than enough.

She wanted to sustain this for a lifetime. The odds were against her. They always are, when loners say *I am serious about this. My life and my art are one. This sitting-at-the-keyboard-all-by-myself-all-day thing is not a hobby.* This is what writing demands of writers: time. Energy. Courage. The fury of many and the rudeness of the rest.

YOU COULD WRITE a whole book about writers who were and are loners. J. D. Salinger. Thomas Pynchon. Harold Pinter. J. K. Rowling. Jack Kerouac. John Steinbeck. Anne Rice. Yasunari Kawabata. H. P. Lovecraft. Paul Bowles. Charles Bukowski, buried in my home town. Henry David Thoreau. Sam Shepard. Nathaniel Hawthorne spent a secluded childhood with virtually no company but his mother, a widowed recluse. Hawthorne read profusely and would later write to his friend Henry Wadsworth Longfellow about his isolation, "I have locked myself in a dungeon and I can't find the key to get out." As a boy at boarding school, Eugene O'Neill had already established himself as a loner and spent most of his time reading and writing. Stephen King—who wrote twenty books in ten years and was rumored at one point to produce some 5,000 words a day, 365 days a year—scrupulously avoids interviews. When King announced in 2002 that he planned to stop publishing, *Entertainment Weekly* predicted he'd become the new Salinger. Virginia Woolf, whose writing captures humankind so accurately, desperately needed the "room of one's own" of which she wrote. James Dickey lived fast and hard, his loner nature and his passion for his craft making him a much less than ideal husband

and father. American Book Award–winner Sandra Cisneros, the only daughter in a constantly mobile family of nine, felt closer to characters in the books she read—such as the heroine of *Island of the Blue Dolphins*, who lived alone on a desert island for eighteen years—than to her flesh-and-blood peers.

Before being killed in the First World War, H. H. Munro wrote savagely funny short stories under the pen name Saki. Having spent his childhood almost entirely alone under the harsh care of a hated aunt, Munro mocked convention and hypocrisy in macabre tales such as "Sredni Vashtar," whose small-boy protagonist establishes a religion-of-one with a polecat-ferret as its god. Less bitter but just as keenly aware of her own isolation, Munro's contemporary, Beatrix Potter, also spent a great deal of her childhood alone. She did not attend school and devoted her days to collecting specimens on solitary countryside rambles and drawing them in the nursery. The rabbits, mice, and squirrels that were her only childhood friends inspired the illustrated storybooks for which Potter later became famous.

Vladimir Nabokov devoted much of his youth to collecting butterflies and composing chess problems—a pursuit which he would later say demanded "glacial solitude." At school, other students considered Nabokov aloof. He relished being a goalie during soccer games, set apart from the rest of the team and, as he later recalled, "surrounded with a halo of singular glamour."

Nor can writers resist writing about being alone. This, too, could be the subject of a book. In "Childe Harold," Lord Byron writes of "the feeling infinite, so felt / In solitude, where we are least alone." Andrew Marvell noted aptly, "Society is all but rude / To this delicious solitude." In "The Crystal Gazer," reclusive Pulitzer Prize–winner Sara Teasdale vows to "gather myself into myself again":

> I shall sit like a sibyl, hour after hour intent,
>> Watching the future come and the present go,
> And the little shifting pictures of people rushing
>> In restless self-importance to and fro.

Alexander Pope, more famous by far for "The Rape of the Lock," devoted an ode to solitude. A childhood illness had so severely deformed Pope's spine that he never grew taller than 4´6˝. This—and the fact that British universities would not admit him because his parents were Catholic—surely fueled the sense of separateness that inspired Pope's "Solitude: An Ode":

> How happy he, who free from care
> The rage of courts, and noise of towns;
> Contented breathes his native air,
>> In his own grounds. . . .

> Blest! who can unconcern'dly find
> Hours, days, and years slide swift away,
> In health of body, peace of mind,
>> Quiet by day.

> Sound sleep by night; study and ease
> Together mix'd; sweet recreation,

And innocence, which most does please,
    With meditation.

Thus let me live, unheard, unknown;
Thus unlamented let me die;
Steal from the world, and not a stone
    Tell where I lie.

Never marrying, Pope lived throughout his adulthood with his mother on an estate beside the river Thames. Now hailed as one of his era's greatest poets, he was known during his lifetime for being irascible, hypersensitive, hypercritical, and viciously hilarious. In 1728 he produced a satire lambasting his own critics and the dullness of people in general. Later expanded to four volumes, it was called *The Dunciad*.

William Wordsworth wrote worshipfully of solo travelers he encountered while wandering his beloved Lake District. The narrator of Wordsworth's famous poem "Lines Composed a Few Miles Above Tintern Abbey" draws on memories of rural solitude to soothe his city-weary soul. Recalling "a wild secluded scene" leads to "[t]houghts of more deep seclusion." He remembers smoke rising from "some Hermit's cave, where by his fire / The Hermit sits alone."

Now far away in time and space, "'mid the din / Of towns and cities," the poet's "purer mind" seeks to flee "the heavy and the weary weight / Of all this unintelligible world." To this end, he makes himself remember a wonderful day when "I wandered lonely as a cloud / That floats on high o'er vales and hills." The only "crowd" he saw that day, he tells us, was a field of daffodils. And now those flowers "flash upon that inward eye / Which is the bliss of solitude."

AS MUCH HAS been written about the reclusive habits of Emily Dickinson as about her nearly two thousand short, sharp, elliptical, and passionate poems. The passion in these poems, their frank casual diction, puts them a hundred years ahead of their time and makes the poet's hermitlike existence all the more mysterious. And her hermitlike existence has made the poems all the more famous: objects of titillated scrutiny, like a bustier found in the closet of a nun.

Brought up in a Massachusetts household by a devout father who coaxed her *not* to read and a mother who believed her to be thoroughly uninterested in literature, this unassuming figure never married. As far as anyone knows for certain, she never engaged in a romance at all. As a young woman, she began retreating from the public eye. By the age of forty, she refused to leave the family home and would not greet visitors face to face, talking with them only through a half-closed door. Her relationships with those she loved best—a handful of friends and relatives—were conducted almost exclusively by mail.

Fewer than a dozen of her poems were published during her lifetime. When more appeared posthumously, their wit and frank longing shocked those who had known her. Not so surprising were those numerous verses about isolation in which, for instance, Dickinson writes of the soul that "selects her own society" and then quietly "shuts the door"—or of the soul as "an imperial friend" to itself, secure in self-sovereignty.

THE PRAGUE-BORN poet Rainer Maria Rilke kept up a running correspondence with a young neophyte in which he offered an accurate picture of the professional writer's life. In one letter, Rilke notes: What is necessary, after all, is only this: solitude, vast inner solitude. To walk inside yourself and meet no one for hours—that is what you must be able to attain. To be solitary as you were when you were a child, when the grownups walked around involved with matters that seemed large and important because they looked so busy and because you didn't understand a thing about what they were doing.

"And when you realize that their activities are shabby, that their vocations are petrified and no longer connected with life, why not then continue to look upon it all as a child would, as if you were looking at something unfamiliar, out of the depths of your own solitude, which is itself work and status and vocation? Why should you want to give up a child's wise not-understanding. . . .

"Think, dear Sir, of the world that you carry inside you, and call this thinking whatever you want . . . only be attentive to what is arising within you, and place that above everything you perceive around you. What is happening in your innermost self is worthy of your entire love; somehow you must find a way to work at it, and not lose too much time or too much courage in clarifying your attitude toward people. . . . Only the individual who is solitary is placed under the deepest laws . . . and when he walks out into the rising dawn or looks out into the event-filled evening and when he feels what is happening there, all situations drop from him as if from a dead man, though he stands in the midst of pure life . . . if there is nothing you can share with other people, try to be close to Things; they will not abandon you; and the nights are still there, and the winds that move through the trees and across many lands; everything in the world of Things and animals is still filled with happening, which you can take part in."

As he is writing this letter at Christmastime, Rilke draws a connection between solitude and faith, noting that "with work and with the repose that comes afterward, with a silence or with a small solitary joy, with everything that we do alone, without anyone to join or help us, we start Him whom we will not live to see, as our ancestors did not live to see us."

WRITING NOVELS TAKES the longest. Someone I knew spent thirteen years on hers. It earned fine reviews, then quickly went out of print. If novelists were in it for the money or praise, all but one in a million would be out of luck. Those thirteen years—the prime of that writer's life—are past. But are they wasted? Well, she was doing just as she pleased. Sandra Cisneros, mentioned earlier, spent nine years writing her multi-generational novel *Caramelo*.

Writers are advised to write about what is familiar to them. Aloneness is familiar. If not physical isolation, then spiritual. Thus Thomas Mann's solo traveler, eyeing the boy whose heart he will not win, in *Death in Venice*. Thus Kobo Abe's determined *Woman in the Dunes*. Herman Melville's Captain Ahab in *Moby Dick*. Knut Hamsun's starving writer in *Hunger*. Harper Lee's Boo Radley, the town bogeyman and mysterious recluse in *To Kill a Mockingbird*. Reclusive chocolatier Willy Wonka in Roald Dahl's *Charlie and the Chocolate Factory*. Ernest Hemingway's eponymous fisherman in *The Old Man and the Sea*. Raymond Chandler's cool, intuitive gumshoe, Philip Marlowe. Maria, driving the freeways in Joan Didion's *Play It as It Lays*. Richard Wright's desperado in *Native Son*. Patricia Highsmith's canny opportunist, Tom Ripley.

Reading literature means reading, again and again, about ourselves. Maybe projections of ourselves. Fantasy blowups of ourselves. Ourselves *in extremis*, ourselves *if only*. Ourselves swept away. Ourselves disguised in chain mail, space suits, codpieces.

Few protagonists come right out and announce themselves as loners so forthrightly as Captain Nemo in Jules Verne's *Twenty Thousand Leagues Under the Sea*. Nemo—his name is Latin for "no man"—helms the *Nautilus,* a sci-fi submarine whose absolute self-sufficiency is his lifework. When a trio of ship-wrecked sailors is rescued and brought aboard, Nemo demonstrates to these unwanted visitors the marvels of agriculture, cuisine, even medicine he has mastered aboard the sub. His collections of art and scientific specimens and books are "my last souvenirs of that world which is dead to me." His is "a secret which no man in the world must know," Nemo says solemnly, "the secret of my whole existence.

"I am not what you call a civilized man. . . . I have done with civilization entirely, for reasons which I alone know. I do not therefore obey its laws," he says, "and I ask you never to speak of them again."

Having fled some unexplained tragedy or travesty on land, Nemo declares: "The sea does not belong to despots. Upon its surface men can still exercise unjust laws, fight, tear one another to pieces and be carried away with terrestrial horrors. But at thirty feet below its level, their reign ceases, their influence is quenched, and their power disappears. Ah, sir, live in the depths of the waters. There only is independence. There I recognize no masters. There I am free." The sea provides all he needs. "Where could one find greater solitude or silence?"

In *Steppenwolf*, Hermann Hesse presents the isolationist urbanite Harry Haller. That author and hero share initials is no accident.

An observer at the start of the novel notes that Haller "was not a sociable man. Indeed, he was unsociable to a degree I had never before experienced in anybody. He was, in fact . . . a real wolf of the steppes." As alienated as he is intelligent, Haller declares his distaste for "the world of men and of so-called culture," which "grins back at us with the lying, vulgar, brazen glamour of a Fair and dogs us with the persistence of an emetic." Instead, he allies himself with wolves whose habit is "to trot alone over the steppes and now and then to gorge . . . with blood or to pursue a female wolf."

"How could I fail to be a lone wolf," Haller demands, when he shares none of the workaday world's "aims nor understand[s] one of its pleasures?"

New in town, he spends long hours alone in his room. "Solitude is independence. It had been my wish and with the years I had attained it. It was cold" in the room. "But it was also still, wonderfully still and vast like the cold stillness of space in which the stars revolve." A chance meeting with a former professor provokes an invitation to dinner at the latter's home. Haller accepts reluctantly, overruling, as loners often do, "my genuine desire of staying at home." Later, "I dress and go out to visit . . . without wanting to at all, so it is with the majority of men day by day and hour by hour." More people are loners than realize it or admit it, Haller asserts: "Without wanting to at all, they pay calls and carry on conversations." Haller's hyperawareness is the kind that comes to those who accept "no reality except the one contained within us. That is why so many people live such an unreal life. They take the images outside them for reality and never allow the world within to assert itself."

It is a loner named Gregor Samsa, a traveling salesman, who awakens one day to discover that he has turned into a huge cockroach in Franz Kafka's "The Metamorphosis." In "The Hunger Artist," Kafka created another loner, a circus freak whose act comprises the deliberate "art" of starving to death. Separateness has seldom been expressed so effectively.

Kafka himself was a lifelong loner. Keenly aware of his emotional distance from others, he poured himself into his writing. The written word forged strong relationships for writers, he maintained, albeit at a distance and with strangers or, as he called readers, "ghosts." Kafka's extensive correspondence with

Felice Bauer, whom he met in 1912 and with whom he fell instantly and wildly in love, is a study in lonerish reticence. Marriage plans flare up, then fall through. "The possibility of our being together for any length of time doesn't even exist," Kafka explained finally, as "my attitude to my writing and my attitude to people is unchangeable; it is a part of my nature, and not due to temporary circumstances. What I need for my writing is seclusion, not 'like a hermit,' that would not be enough, but like the dead. . . . I have always had this fear of people, not actually of the people themselves, but of their intrusion."

HARUKI MURAKAMI BECAME one of Japan's all-time best-selling novelists with big, surrealistic, pop-culture-flavored books like *A Wild Sheep Chase,* which features a talking sheep, and *The Wind-Up Bird Chronicle,* whose hero spends a great deal of time at the bottom of a well. Overnight celebrity did not rest well with the reclusive Murakami, whom many peg as a future Nobelist. When his books started selling well, he left Japan to spend several years in self-imposed exile in Europe and America. He once told an interviewer that his writings return again and again to "the figure of the loner . . . because it isn't easy to live in Japan as an individualist or as a loner. I'm always thinking about this. I'm a novelist and I'm a loner, an individualist."

The novelist-as-recluse is a cliché. The public kind of *expects* novelists, especially very literary ones, to be reclusive. Titillation throbs in articles that allude, for instance, to "the elusive Annie Proulx" or to the latest rumor of a Thomas Pynchon sighting. When Pynchon leaped through the window of a Mexico City hotel room to avoid being cornered by a reporter, it made news-papers. (That and other reports about Pynchon often refer to his friendship with the late Richard Brautigan, another literary recluse.) In that titillation is deference. Awe. That such great works sprang from—who? That not-so-special-looking little man or woman in the cheap shoes? As a recluse, the novelist is part magician, Rumplestiltskin, alchemist.

But as such he is also suspect. No one *saw* him do it. Did he do it? How?

In *The Catcher in the Rye*, J. D. Salinger created the disaffected yet tender teenager Holden Caulfield, whose narrative on post-Second World War America exposed the hypocrisy and con-formism that loners cannot stand. Caulfield, who has since comforted generations of outsiders, made the young Salinger instantly famous.

He appeared before an audience only once. Fame and its trappings, small talk and hordes of sycophants, disgusted him. He went into recluse mode, turning down interview requests and refusing to allow his photograph to appear on the jackets of all subsequent books.

There *was* a string of books, popular with audiences, but these were all his fans could hope to get from him. It perplexed Salinger, as it perplexed the similarly lionized Jack Kerouac, why fans felt they had the *right* to want more of a writer. He stopped publishing new works in 1965.

In his New Hampshire home, Salinger practiced yoga and Zen meditation, solitary pursuits that primed him for the days he spent in a cement-block bunker on the property, writing. His wife and children were forbidden to interrupt him. The divorce papers filed by Claire Salinger in 1966 state that "the libelee . . . has for long periods of time refused to communicate with her." A neighbor who came around canvassing for a charity later recalled how the author "met us at the driveway with a gun in his hands saying, 'Just go away.'"

Rumors surfaced in 1997 that Salinger was planning to publish a novella through an arrangement with a tiny Virginia publishing house. Titled *Hapworth 16, 1928,* the work had previously appeared, many years before, in the *New Yorker.* In the *New York Times,* critic Michiko Kakutani reflected on Salinger's "withdrawal from the public world: withdrawal feeding self-absorption and self-absorption feeding tetchy disdain." When Salinger subsequently withdrew *Hapworth* from the publisher, it was rumored that Kakutani's jab was the reason.

His absence and silence continue to generate buzz. A memoir published in 1998 by a woman who had had a brief affair with the author several decades earlier was followed two years later by the memoir of Salinger's daughter, Margaret, which claimed he drank his own urine, spoke in tongues, and was once married to a Nazi.

In 1999, London's *Sunday Times* reported that reliable sources were claiming Salinger had written no less than fifteen novels which he was hoarding in a safe at his home. Had he never become a recluse, had he simply died or produced a dwindling stream of mediocre books—for career-minded novelists, those fates are pretty much the same—he would have slipped into humdrum obscurity. His name might be remembered today. Or it might not.

THAT THE PERSON whose dresser has a stack of my books on it has never read them—not one, not even a single line by means of subterfuge, *I loved the part about the cannibals!*—might shock you. Would it shock you if I said nearly everyone else I know is that way, too?

Granted, I do not know so many people, but nearly none of them ever ask me about writing. Not a word. How would they feel if I never mentioned their pregnancies, their children? Writing is practically all I do all day, every day, yet they talk about daycare and holidays and the assholes in the accounting department. Like the person whose dresser it is, they ask how I am but the question is general. *As if how I am could be any other way than how I write.* They ask how is my husband.

What they talk about is people and activities involving people.

Writing is done alone. People do not talk about the things they do alone. Do they talk about bathing, masturbating, emptying the litter box? Based on his research about casual human conversation, University of Liverpool psychology professor Robin Dunbar concluded that at least two-thirds of it "is taken up with matters of social import." These include "who is doing what with whom and whether it's a good or a bad thing; who is in and who is out, and why." No other subject than these occupies more than ten percent of all conversation, most subjects no more than two or three." Even on campus, where he conducted much of his study, "it's the tittle-tattle of life that makes the world go round, not the pearls of wisdom that fall from the lips of the Aristotles and the Einsteins. We are social beings."

In their world, it is not safe to talk about things done alone. Unsafe or boring. Nearly everything a loner does is done alone—at least, the things that matter. So that when we loners are in company, those sparse occasions, with those lucky few, what matters to us is not mentioned. Writing—the physical part of it—evades description. *I just sat there.* But one writes about topics, and nothing is more interesting in the world.

Why don't you ask me? If you fail to, I will be a cipher to you, as scrutable as a whiffleball and not as interesting. These hours, these days, this screen, this is my life. They do not ask. It will not come up if I do not bring it up. And I do not. I think I should not have to. I am testing them—not that they know.

10.

jesus, mary, and jennifer lopez

[RELIGION]

They gather together to ask the Lord's blessing.
The problem with organized religion is, it's organized.

TO SEE RELIGION in action is to see mobs. Swarming. Seething. Singing. Swooning. Studying. Marching. Slaughtering, slaughtered.

Church mobs chant, lit in the spumoni hues of stained glass. Buddhist temple mobs file down mountain paths, all saffron robes and sandalwood. Mobs immerse in the Ganges; never mind the microbes and the floating ashes of the dead. Medieval mobs stampeded the unwary as they rushed to venerate the preserved flesh of saints. Other medieval mobs on horseback massacred Moors. The Moors, in turn, turned their Christian captives into slaves and sold them. Mobs in town squares watched witches burn in the name of the Inquisition. Mobs clash now, each asking its god to make it win, the blood of both mingling as it spills. Backwoods mobs. Cults. Militias.

Mobs who title themselves grandly—the Salvation Army, the Moral Majority. Promise Keepers.

They want us to think faith is a collective thing.

They want us to think faith has a lot to do with fellowship. That an electrical charge links believer to believer, giving them the right to call each other brother, sister, father.

Sure, faith is a jolt. And nonloners respond to jolts with a yearning for validation. *Did I feel that? Whoa, you felt it, too?!* By sharing, by comparing notes, nonloners decide what is true. It is telling that in at least two major religions an important milestone in spiritual progress is called Confirmation.

Loners react differently to jolts. Since loners are often alone, jolts tend to strike when loners are alone. So there is no one near to whom one might exclaim, *Did you feel that?* But would we anyway? We keep things to ourselves. The most profound things we keep the most to ourselves. We nurse jolts. Saying nothing. For loners, discussing the mystical deflates it like air escaping a balloon. Faith is a private matter—at least, by loner logic it is. Praying in public, worshiping while rubbing elbows, seems uncouth, like French kissing on a commuter bus.

For some loners, the structure of mainstream religion feels like a straitjacket. Having to appear in the same crowded place at the same day and time each week—in school it could barely be borne. Does the divine run on a schedule, too, with penalties for tardies? Nor can we force ourselves into feeling brotherly about a mob of strangers just because they use the same names to summon the supernatural as we do, just because they have read the same holy book, or because we light candles at the feet of the same statues.

We are chary of consensus, and spirituality is so subjective. To a loner it hardly seems possible—not even *plausible*—that millions could agree on what God likes and dislikes and whether pork or beef is verboten. How, we muse, can millions nod in unison approving the validity of liturgy? How can the unseen move so many strangers in exactly the same way? Those millions—nonloners, of course—would say it moves them alike because it is real. They would say the unanimity by which it moves them *proves* it is real. Loners cannot help but suspect something else afoot, something pedestrian. We know nonloners learn by imitation. We know they shore up their self-esteem through imitation, through securing a sense of belonging. Nonloners thrive on this, so why would it not tint their view of heaven? Among nonloners, religion fends off loneliness, one of their greatest fears, both within the soul and without. Fellowship itself is a mark of faith. And it is fellowship, the heat of shouting brethren, that spurs movements—call it civilization, call it fanaticism—by which mainstream religions make history.

Within most organized religions is a built-in drive to multiply, to proselytize, to breed. This is how they become monolithic. It is the same survival instinct by which primitive societies laud joiners and detest outsiders. Terror of extinction still haunts the major religions: an old habit, unlikely given their numbers. Holy wars reveal those fears in action, as do systematic forced conversions such as those the Christian Church performed on

Vikings, Aztecs, and Pacific Islanders, often at swordpoint. Violence, or rumors of it—the specter of holocaust, obsolescence or both—make the faithful want to swell their ranks. Their martial paradigms, which are nonloner paradigms, have survived for thousands of years.

> *Onward, Christian Soldiers!*
> *Marching as to war,*
> *With the cross of Jesus*
> *Going on before;*

> *Christ, the royal master,*
> *Leads against the foe;*
> *Forward into battle,*
> *See His banners go. . . .*

> *Like a mighty army*
> *Moves the Church of God:*
> *Brothers, we are treading*
> *Where the saints have trod.*

> *We are not divided;*
> *All one body we,*
> *One in hope, in doctrine,*
> *One in charity. . . .*

Onward then, ye people!
Join our happy throng,
Blend with ours your voices
In the triumph song.

For loners, fellowship is not a factor in the faith equation. The *organized* in organized religion is a problem sometimes so intractable—a boulder in the road—that many loners come to think of ourselves as spiritually dead. We slink away feeling like failures, calling ourselves lapsed. Because we cannot bear a crowd, we say—blithely or bitterly, resignedly—that we are not religious.

It is a common conceit that only shrines as big as stadiums are shrines at all.

The crusaders have fooled us.

Shouldn't the divine hear a lone voice as clearly as it hears a chorus? If, in fact, it *is* divine, its ears ought to be good.

What is a loner to do who *is* religious? Who loves the same god a mob does, observes the same feast days, prays the same? Who has no quibbles with—take your pick—*kaddish* or the rosary or Ramadan? Loners though they are, they can make themselves accept that it might just be possible to share a deity. Yet the one thing they cannot share is public worship, praying where the crowds are.

Such loners have launched traditions of their own: small separate entrances. Underground passages. Within earshot of the flock but, like all good loners, out of sight.

. . .

CHRIST HAS BEEN called a loner. It is noted that he spent forty days alone in the wilderness. He urged the severing of social ties when he said, in the Book of Luke: "If anyone comes to me and does not hate his own father and mother and wife and children and brothers and sisters . . . he cannot be my disciple." (Luke 14:26) Matthew, too, reflects on that statement, noting how Jesus promised spiritual riches to "everyone who has left houses or brothers or sisters or father or mother or children or lands, for my name's sake." (Matt. 19:29) Matthew goes on to describe Jesus' denunciation of "the hypocrites [who] love to stand and pray in the synagogues and at the street corners, that they may be seen." Instead of praying in a crowd, Jesus urged, "when you pray, go into your room and shut the door and pray to your Father who is in secret; and your Father who sees in secret will reward you." (Matt. 6:5-7)

That sounds like loner talk. Yet consider the source. Christ was too good at guiding crowds to have been one of us. Christ coaxed, convened, convinced. Those who shunned their loved ones on his advice did so in order to join a throng of disciples. Christ had followers. He needed followers. His closeness even to the Twelve Apostles keeps him firmly out of the loner camp. These twelve comprised a prototype for all later fraternities, sharing and caring, Judas notwithstanding. As the Last Supper ended, Jesus declared: "I give to you a new commandment, that you love one another, even as I have loved you, that you also love one another." (John 13:33–35)

He had the multitudes eating out of his hand. His forty days in the wilderness were likely motivated by sheer exhaustion: a need to flee, for respite from his fans, as some film stars today buy their own private islands. Maybe Christ went off alone as a test, knowing he would be hungry, thirsty, lonely, tormented by Satan. True enough, he was.

In practice, Christianity came to be a very public not private religion. As it grew in popularity, as it superseded ancient Roman paganism and spread throughout Europe and beyond, it has become boldly visible. As such, its most visible practices are shared practices: pilgrimages and revivals, masses, campus crusades, televangelism, phenomena such as the Crystal Cathedral in Orange County, whose televised services beam out to millions of viewers. But from those crowds, loner iconoclasts have hewn solitary lives in huts and holes and aeries, perched atop poles or buried alive.

Born around the year 251 in Koma, Egypt, the man now known as Saint Anthony was a wealthy young Copt. It is said that one day at a church service he heard those words of the Gospel in which Jesus urges his listeners to "come and follow me." Interpreting this as a personal directive to enter the wilderness, Anthony felt profoundly moved. Selling his property, he moved first into a hermitage near Koma, then into the desert, where he set up housekeeping alone in an abandoned tomb. There, in solitude, he stayed for more than twenty years. He made it harsh: eating but once a day, and even then only bread and water, sleeping only two or three hours every night, wearing a hair shirt which the desert heat made itchier. Hagiographers and such painters as Hieronymus Bosch bring us images of demons tempting Anthony, to no avail.

Word got out. Soon a wave of followers fanned out across the sands, seeking a life of consecrated solitude, like Anthony's. It was that rarest of phenomena: a fad that entailed acting like a loner.

Chroniclers counted ten thousand hermits' cells between Cairo and upper Egypt during the fourth century. Many of these lodgings were chiseled out of rocky precipices along the Nile, accessible only by slender wooden bridges which the hermits would remove at will. On a branch of the river southwest of Cairo, the writer Rufinus of Aquiloa noted that "there is not a door, a tower or a corner which does not house a solitary." Those among the hermits who became saints, and there are many, are known collectively as the Desert Fathers.

IN *THE DECLINE and Fall of the Roman Empire*, Edward Gibbon called Anthony "a hideous, distorted, and emaciated maniac . . . spending his life in a long routine of useless and atrocious self-torture." (This is a striking assessment from an eighteenth-century British historian who, a loner himself, once called solitude "the school of genius.") Other early hermit saints sealed themselves inside hollow trees, immobilized, viewing the world through knotholes. Others bound themselves in chains and lived that way, alone, for years. Simeon Stylites dwelled on a platform, alone, atop a pillar.

As their legends have it, these saints met their own highly personalized demons. Of one fourth-century recluse, it has been written that "like a horde of barbarians his thoughts came crawling in upon him from all sides, raining down as it were a shower of arrows." Mary the Egyptian, an ex-prostitute, was seized in solitude with urges to sing dirty songs. Pachon had a vision of an Ethiopian girl he had desired long before, as a teenager. The apparition drew close and sat on Pachon's lap, looking and feeling exactly like the real thing. Lust inflamed him, and it was all Pachon could do to slap the image until it disappeared. His hands, legends say, smelled like the girl for two years afterward.

Loners know about those demons. Even the least spiritual and least neurotic has known solitude so deep that you can hear a pin drop at the bottom of your soul. The brave let it bounce and abide, rather than run to the corner bar or seize the remote control. It happens when doubts, regrets, choices made, and chances missed swoop out of the crannies into which we have stuffed them. Even the most secular of us has said, "I wrestled with my demons."

THE DESERT-HERMIT craze began to ebb as many nonloners, marooned in the sand and miserable, realized their mistake. A kind of compromise arose: monasteries and convents. These were *semi*hermitages, set off from the outside world and shared by groups of men and women. These were communities after all, but a few orders were truly isolationist. The Camaldolite order, named after the Camaldoli monastery near Arezzo in Italy, was founded around 1012 by the man who would later be canonized as Saint Romuald. Inspired by the Desert Fathers,

Romuald established a routine for his monks in which each man occupied his own austere cell, joining his brethren only in chapel. Nothing but dry bread and water were to be eaten every day except Thursday and Sunday, when fruit and vegetables might be added; garments shorter than the usual monastic costume were worn to make the brothers feel more vulnerable. Saint Peter Damian would later write that Romuald wanted *totum mundum in eremum convertere:* to turn the whole world into a hermitage.

Another staunchly eremitic tradition, dating back to Byzantine times, is the community of monks on Mount Athos in Greece. In the eleventh century, as many as 180 separate monasteries clung to this steep, nearly 7,000-foot limestone precipice. Today only about twenty remain, with *kathismata* (tiny houses) and *hesychasteria* (more austere structures or rough caves for the most extreme hermits) clinging to the sheer rockface like swallows' nests.

RELIGIOUS LONERS IN medieval France and England had another option. It is surreal to modern eyes. Those were surreal years.

Plagues swept through towns, felling entire populations. War and disease were endemic. Christians fought their fears with passion plays and paranoia, melees and belief in miracles. God and the Devil loomed vivid and vindictive. They were held responsible for sun, storms, stillbirths, everything, watching souls like surveillance cameras. Is it so strange, then, that many a church had its resident anchorite or anchoress living there in a tiny cell, sealed into its walls for life?

These recluses could be found in most cathedral towns, silent behind the ventilation slots cut into the church walls into which their cells were built. Inside, a recluse had only a cross, a chamber pot, the clothes she wore and, if she chose, a cat. The faithful brought food and water and carried off slops.

It was a sanctioned way of dying to the world. The anchorhold, as the cell was called, was considered a half-grave. The *Ancrene Wisse*, a manual for anchoresses, called an anchorhold a "burinesse." A nun choosing this kind of life would undergo a ceremony whose scripture and ritual were almost the same as those for funerals. One anchoress's ceremony, recorded near Canterbury in the latter half of the twelfth century, features the woman lying corpselike on the church floor as a portion of Isaiah was recited: "Go into your rooms . . . shut your doors behind you. Hide yourselves a little while." Holy water is sprinkled on the nun; then a censer is drawn over her body. Mass is celebrated, a choir sings the funeral antiphon, urging, "May angels lead you into paradise." Last rites are given. Then the nun enters the cell that has been prepared for her, singing, "Here I will stay forever; this is the home I have chosen." Further prayers, those traditionally said over corpses, are recited as the cell's door is shut with the recluse inside— once and for all.

IT WAS A solitude totally absolute yet utterly dependent on the aid of outsiders. Ignored, an anchoress would die of thirst or starve to death in conditions feculent even by medieval standards. To this end, Aelred of Rievaulx, the author of a twelfth-century anchoresses' manual called *De Vita Eremetica,* urges the reader to post an old woman outside her cell to keep unwanted visitors away and to secure the services of a strong young girl to carry all the heavy pots and jugs.

Aelred's tone, as he advises on how best to be buried alive, is pragmatic and in places even chatty. His intended readers were not considered mad. Not freaks. Strolling past anchorholds while going about their daily rounds, townspeople took for granted the unseen figures within and, in a way, relied on them as symbols of calm in a time of crisis. As the *Ancrene Wisse* explains: "It is for this reason that an anchoress is called an anchoress, and anchored under a church like an anchor under the side of a ship, to hold it, so that the waves and storms do not pitch it over. . . . She shall hold it secure so that the puffing and blowing of the Devil, that is, temptations, do not pitch it over."

Theirs was a permanent privacy but in medieval times, for women, asking for any privacy at all was nearly asking for the impossible. The average life included teenage marriage, constant pregnancy and motherhood from nuptial bed to tomb. Solitude as we know it was out of the question.

And then, as now, sometimes the world seemed too crazy to bear.

Italian novelist Toni Maraini based her novel *Sealed in Stone* on the true story of Alix Bourgotte, a French novice who renounced the world in 1418 to enter an anchorhold where she spent fifty years. In her cell, out of which she could see only through a hole the size of a brick, the fictional Alix considers her decision:

"During the insurrection in which my father was killed, I lived as a complete recluse in order not to see the dead with their insides hanging out, without hands . . . I had glimpsed something so dreadful that it violated reality and made it unbearable . . . I had to escape reality." After seeing a young man drawn and quartered in a public square and discovering that portions of the corpse are to be displayed citywide, she vows, "so I'll never go again to Porte Saint-Martin, or to the gardens, or any other place because even the pebbles conspire with this world of evil."

"I wanted to escape completely from the city," Alix declares, "from everything that stole my space." Mourning a figurative loss of space, she resolves to confine herself to a *literally* tiny space, comforting herself with the thought that upon her immurement "now everything must stop."

Her solitude is both refuge and protest, her cell a well of controlled sanity in a world insane. "I could not crack life from without . . . I could subdue reality only by turning it inside out," Alix surmises. Less sensitive souls might take public disembowelings at face value, one pool of bile at a time. But, watching a crowd making merry at a May fair, Alix sees the outside world for the unendurable cataclysm it is: a spiritual rupture, a rot at the heart of what passes for civilization. Neither willing nor able to bear any longer the dissolution of the beauty of the world, she makes her choice. Cataclysmic days call for cataclysmic measures. At first glance, modern loners might shrug off any resemblance between Alix and ourselves. But who among us has not shrieked while reading the newspaper, *What a fucked-up world!* and wished to ditch it? Our luck is that to escape dictators and carjackers we could possibly emigrate or retreat to the woods or, almost like Captain Nemo, live aboard a boat. We can, if not protect ourselves decisively, at least study our options, which are many, and find part-time refuges or partial ones. We are mobile. We do not live in a theocracy. This is our luck.

How did these creatures spend their buried lives? If options were few outside the walls, inside they were fewer. And yet "of little," the *Ancrene Wisse* promises—advice every loner knows is true—"much waxeth." The manual instructs its readers to pray, eat, drink, and sleep, though the schedule and extent of these activities were up to the recluse herself, as was her manner of dress. The outer life having been abandoned, the inner life was expected to grow unimaginably vivid: a never-ending meditation session. To heighten her inward focus, a recluse was ordered to consider nothing that would *utword drahe hir heorte*, "draw her heart outward."

Warned that extreme solitude would render whatever she saw through her tiny window almost unbearably intense, the anchoress was warned to keep her eyes and hands well inside that opening through which they were wont to leap, as the *Ancrene Wisse* put it, "like wild beasts." Talk with passersby was not totally out of the question. Yet too much talk "grows into a vast flood which drowns the soul, for as the words flow, the heart becomes dissipated, so that for a long time afterwards it cannot be truly recollected."

Desire ached. When lust teased them, anchoresses were advised to visualize their parents "drowned, or slain . . . or that your sisters had been burned in their houses. Such thoughts as these will often root out carnal temptations."

But desire for fleshly lovers and a heavenly one were different things entirely. An anchorhold was an astoundingly private place. "With burning love embrace your Beloved," the *Ancrene Wisse* directed, "who has come down from heaven to your heart's bower, and hold Him fast until He has granted all that you ask . . . stretch out your love to Jesus Christ; you have won Him. Touch Him with as much love as you sometimes feel for a man. He is yours to do with all that you will."

THE ANCHORITIC LIFE was long out of style in the 1960s, when Columbia-educated Kentucky monk Thomas Merton decided to become a hermit. Merton's requests to move out of the main house of Gethsemani Monastery and into an isolated cottage on the property were denied for years before his superiors finally granted permission. There, in what he happily called his hermitage, Merton blossomed into one of America's most prolific religious writers. Producing book after book of his own, he also published English renditions of the works of Lao Tzu and kept up a lively correspondence with celebrity pen pals ranging from Georgia O'Keeffe to the Dalai Lama.

Merton became America's most famous monk and its most famous hermit. To an eager outside world, which read about him in lifestyle magazines and bought his books, he was an interpreter of the solo life, producing journals that stand today as some of the most extensive and accessible accounts ever written of living alone. "In the hermitage," Merton wrote in his journal soon after taking up occupancy there, "one must pray or go to seed. The pretense of prayer will not suffice. Just sitting will not suffice. . . . Solitude puts you with your back to the wall (or your face to it!) and this is good."

In "the hermitage: quiet and cool," where "I talk to myself, I dance around . . . I sing," he noted with delight what he saw. "A few birds. And nothing. Who would want to live in any other way?" With jazz-edged rhythm and ringing imagery, Merton exulted: "I am a solitary and that's that. . . . I am telling you: this life in the woods is IT. It is the only way. It is the way everybody has lost. They have all lost their way and ended up in Coney Island, with the distorting mirrors and the clowns with cattle prods that sting them up the tail and make them run to their shame." Pretense, he noted, "is easy in the community, for one can have the support of a common illusion or a common agreement in forms that take the place of truth." But alone, "one is reduced to nothing, and compelled to begin laboriously the long return to truth."

Yet the cottage was no anchorhold. For all the derision with which Merton blasted society, and for all his gloating about his hard-won solitude, still his deluge of mail included invitations and requests from fans who wished to visit. He accepted some. Joan Baez came to the cottage. Like Thoreau, Merton entertained more guests than you might think. He was a hermit *and* a host. He was having it both ways.

"I become anxious to keep up with all that is being said and done, and I want in my turn to be 'in there,' to play my own part," he wrote. "I think I will need to go out to Europe to see Trungpa Rinpoche's place in Scotland, and the Tibetan monastery in Switzerland." Like Elvis Presley, Merton basked in the benefits of a charisma fueled largely by his loner status. Good as his books are, Merton was a bit of an impostor. A famous recluse is an oxymoron. *I'm a hermit, look at me!*

He was not unaware of his hypocrisy. "Once in a while I get a glimpse," he wrote bitterly of the super-hermit profile he was cultivating, "of the folly that is really at the heart of this 'zeal'!"

The ultimate test came in 1966. Shortly after declaring in his journal, "The one thing for which I am most grateful [is] this hermitage," Merton fell in love with a nurse at the local hospital where he underwent surgery. It was the real thing. After returning to the cottage he spent hours on the phone in impassioned conversations with this woman who, in his journal, he calls only "M." Soul-wrenching letters flew back and forth between them, and M. paid several visits to the cottage, giving Merton good reason to rue his vow of celibacy. But in the end they parted. "Sure, I love M., but it can never interfere with my main purpose in life," he wrote, "and that is that."

Ironically it was when Merton left his hermitage and went out into the world—to Asia, where he convened with important figures including the Dalai Lama—that he died in a busy Bangkok hotel, electrocuted by the faulty wiring on a fan. To the end, he was torn between extremes.

IN RENDERING INTO contemporary English the works of Lao Tzu, whose collected epigrams are called the *Tao Te Ching* and comprise the Taoist spiritual text, Merton was working with the words of a consummate loner. Whether or not Lao Tzu actually ever lived—his name means only "Old Fellow"—is up for debate. If he did, he was born between the sixth and fourth centuries B.C.E., but almost nothing else is known of him. The writings attributed to Lao Tzu are cryptic, concerning the *tao,* which means "the way," the path, the ceaseless process of change. Every aspect of life, Taoists believe, is either bright solid forceful *yang* or dark moist passive *yin,* and everything is always changing, so the balance between *yin* and *yang* is in constant flux. Since the *tao* is in everything and *is* everything, it makes everything at once sacred and secular. To ride the *tao* is to go with the flow.

Certain Chinese mountain ranges are honeycombed with old pavilions, paths and caves used by Taoist recluses present and past. Amid the roar of streams and storms, the smell of grass, such hermits can truly live by the *Tao Te Ching*'s famous proviso, *Those who know don't talk.* As spontaneous as sunshine, as flexible as bamboo, as free as a twig drifting downstream, the Taoist hermit is a classic icon in Chinese art and literature. In Song Dynasty ink-wash paintings, hermits appear as isolated specks on soaring cliffs and in tiny boats, ready for anything. They get drunk, admire the moon, and elude visitors in dozens of Tang Dynasty poems such as Liu Chang-ch'ing's "Looking for Ch'ang, the Taoist Recluse of South Stream":

Everywhere along the way where you had been,
In the grass, I saw the depressions of your soles.

White clouds obscured the islet where you live,
Fragrant grass veiled your empty doorway.
After the rain, the pines were radiant;
Searching for you, I followed the stream to its source.
The blossoms, the stream, my meditation
Came together—there was no need of speech.

Like the unseen hermit, the narrator, too, is alone. Find the
path, he says. Follow the stream. Savor the flowers, the flow.
Find the islet. Be like the hermit.

In traditional Chinese culture, Confucian traditions form a
tight net of interpersonal hierarchies. It is from the fifth-century
B.C.E. teachings of Confucius, the philosopher known in Chinese
as *Kongzi*, that China adopted many of its age-old standards for
filial piety and obedience to elders. With its Confucian backbone
and overlays of other strong social structures, the Chinese mainstream frowns on living alone, being alone. Communism is nothing if not social. Woe betide the loner assigned a lifelong job at
the commune. Amid this ambience, Taoism has always presented a respite, a refuge from a system defined by personal obligations. During the Cultural Revolution, many Taoist shrines were
smashed, looted, and burned, and Taoists imprisoned and killed
as part of a policy to stamp out religion. This did not in fact
crush Taoism altogether, though it stanched to a trickle the number of hermits heading off into the crags. Even so, some are still
up there. A Manchurian man I know met some and even stayed
with one while on a hiking holiday. While researching his book
Road to Heaven, the American author Bill Porter tracked down

hermits so remote in space and spirit from the world below that they knew virtually nothing of the events that had shaken its foundations for the last thirty years.

BUDDHISM ENDORSES A strong sense of community—not just among the *sangha,* the monastic fellowship that is one of the "three jewels" for which devout Buddhists give thanks daily, but also between all sentient beings everywhere on earth, for which devout Buddhists are taught to cultivate compassion. The man now known as the Buddha was a Nepali prince, Siddhartha Gautama, and like Christ he was a born leader. As Christ would do some 500 years later, Siddhartha entered solitude as the means to an end. (Hermann Hesse, the loner novelist, wrote a book based on this.) Long meditation under the famous bo tree brought the prince *satori*—enlightenment—much of which involved discerning the tragic but inevitable link between desire and pain.

Neither as socially oppressive as Confucianism nor as free-wheelingly mystical as Taoism, Buddhism rests between the two. Aspects of the practice appeal to loners: the inward sojourn of meditation, the bright one-off flash of *satori*. From deep observation flows acceptance and, from this, serenity: the mindfulness by which each moment, as the Vietnamese Buddhist master Thich Nhat Hanh likes to say, is a precious moment.

Loners do some of this anyway. Spending a lot of time alone is like an accidental meditation. A casual mindfulness. We do not have to work at this, at observation or serenity. Any loner is halfway to Buddhism without knowing it. So it should not surprise loners that Buddhist hermits have produced some of Asia's most immortal poetry.

One of these hermits was Han Shan, an eighth-century Chinese monk known in English as Cold Mountain. In his Zhejiang Province hermitage, on a mountain that is also called Cold Mountain, Han Shan wrote bold loner-friendly verses studded with directives about trusting one's own true nature. He calls his departure to the hermitage an "escape," and boasts that his solitary life gives him no worries.

It was Han Shan's Zen-flavored works that captivated the American poet Gary Snyder while he was a student at UC Berkeley. And it was Snyder's fascination with Han Shan that, in turn, fascinated Jack Kerouac when he arrived in Berkeley. Kerouac's 1958 novel, *The Dharma Bums*, launched a Buddhist craze in the West almost single-handedly. Forever the observer, traveling solo and watching from the sidelines, the beat writer felt especially moved by the solitude celebrated by Han Shan and his kind. Kerouac's 1965 book, *Desolation Angels*, recounts a euphoric stint as a fire lookout—a modern hermit—on Washington State's Desolation Peak.

The twelfth-century Japanese Buddhist monk Saigyo abandoned his wealthy family for the hermit's life, settling alone into a little dwelling deep in cherry-blossom country. There he wrote his three-volume *Sankashu*, or "Collection from a Mountain Hut," whose verses compare his departure from the world to a game of hide-and-seek, noting happily that "the path has vanished / To this mountain hut." In one poem, Saigyo vows: "Leaving no trace, / Deeper into the mountains/ I'll go."

At the close of that century, another Japanese Buddhist hermit, Kamo-no-Chomei, wrote his epic poem *Hojoki,* or "Visions of a Torn World" after a series of natural disasters laid waste to Kyoto. In the wake of an earthquake and fire, the poet explains, "I retired from the world." His remote hermitage was ten feet square, collapsible so that it could be disassembled and moved to an even more remote spot if need be: "I hide myself away, deep in the hills." With a bamboo mat and bracken bedding, lulled by the perfume of wisteria tassels nodding outside, "I can be lazy if I like—no one here to hinder me, no one in whose eyes to feel ashamed." Picking up a musical instrument, "I do not play to please another's ear. I play just for myself." When tasks need doing, the poet reasons with a loner's logic, performing them oneself "is hard, yet simpler than using someone else."

"I realize how far I am from the world," the poet writes:

The hermit crab prefers a tiny shell,
Aware of its needs
And so with me.
I know my needs
And I know the world.

I wish for nothing

Quiet is my only wish

People in the world
Do not build houses

To suit their real needs

I love my lonely dwelling,
This one-room hut.
Sometimes I go to the capital
But when I return
I pity those who seek
The dross of the world.

As ONE OF the world's most populous nations, India has in its major faith a complex pantheon of gods. But even this divine crowd has its loner.

Shiva is hailed as the master of both creation and destruction. The river Ganges is said to flow from his long hair. He is one of the faith's reigning deities and an acknowledged loner. In contrast to social-butterfly Krishna, Shiva is a solitary ascetic, a recluse who meditates nude while seated alone on a tiger skin in a cremation ground. This spooky setting represents his domain: the verge between death and birth.

His devotees, holy men known as *sadhus,* have for thousands of years lived austere lives and practiced extreme physical discipline far from the hurly-burly of Indian family life. Their wildly painted faces and ash-smeared bodies—pierced with spikes, posed in yogic knots, lifting bricks with their penises— appear regularly in documentaries about "outrageous Asia." These reclusive followers of a reclusive god take lifelong vows of silence. Some wear metal chastity belts, others sit with one arm raised for years on end, atrophied to the width of a stick.

Like Shiva, some *sadhus* go nude to demonstrate nonattachment to worldly goods. In the past, *sadhus* were more numerous, but even today it is estimated that they number as many as four to five million. They are an age-old fixture on the crowded landscape, a counterpoint to the crowds.

So standard is the archetype of the recluse in India that it characterizes not just one but two of the four *ashramas*, or stages through which all Hindu men—though not women—are ideally expected to progress. The first *ashrama* is *Brahmacharya*, the student stage, in which a youth undergoes his formal education, preparing for the social and spiritual life of the second, *Grihastha*, the householder stage. At this point, as a family man, he pursues wealth and enjoys sex until he reaches age fifty or so. Then comes the third stage, *Vanaprastha*, the hermit stage, which leads in turn to the fourth: *Sannyasa*, the wandering-ascetic stage. The third stage demands such a sharp break—the renunciation of home and family, work and society for a life of prayer in a secluded hut—as to have become nearly obsolete in modern times.

Those who manage to reach the fourth stage are called *sannyasis*. While those at the third stage can call a hut home, those in the fourth have no home but the road.

JUDAISM IS A very social faith. While no less a personage than the Old Testament prophet Elijah did a solitary stint in a mountain cave, emerging to hear the "still small voice" of God, it is the patriarchs, soldiers, and sovereigns who get nearly all the applause. Holiday celebrations rally around such heroes as Judah Maccabee and Queen Esther, whose mission was to save their people. As the author Jay Michaelson, a devout follower of *halachah* (Jewish law), puts it: "Judaism does not generally venerate the hermit who retreats to the forest to commune with God; it venerates the individual who leads a community, or commits acts of loving kindness, or is hospitable."

Social intercourse is written into the Torah, which tells Jews that the best way to worship God is to perform *mitzvot:* acts of love and kindness. Typical *mitzvot* include "love the stranger," a command that appears in the Torah not once, but three dozen times.

This is only logical, as the Jewish people have been under attack for nearly three thousand years. Jews have more reason than the followers of nearly any other faith today to feel vulnerable. The Babylonians and ancient Egyptians held Jews as slaves. The Nazi Holocaust, outmarriage, anti-Semitism, and Islamic extremists vowing to wipe Israel off the map have all posed significant threats to Jewish survival. News reports of suicide bombers willing to die in order to slaughter Jews mandates cohesiveness.

Thus the path that religious Jewish loners have hewn for themselves is obscure, a tortuous byway fraught with secrets and signs.

During the renaissance, an unprecedented number of European Jews took an interest in studying the cabala, a mystical tradition that had begun with the Gnostics in Hellenistic Egypt. Using intricate formulas, numerology and scrambled biblical passages, cabalists trace the bonds between finite and infinite, between fathomless God and flawed humankind. In a realm too esoteric for any but the most rarefied minds, they also explore horrors rivaling those of the real world: demons, the evil eye, zombielike *dybbuks*. Tackling these concepts in their search for, among other answers, the "true" name of God, the most famous cabalists were known for isolation: for holing up in their houses and avoiding idle conversation.

One of these was Rabbi Isaac Luria (1533–1571), nick-named Ha'Ari or "The Lion." This hermit, a legend in his own time, spent some thirteen years in solitude on the banks of the Nile studying the cabala, and bequeathed to the world a cabal-istic doctrine now known as the Lurianic system. His teachings were embodied in the *Etz Hayim* or Tree of Life, a book whose premise many compare to the Big Bang theory. In Luria's cos-mogony, the universe was shattered at the moment of creation into countless "holy sparks," which flew off in all directions and settled into all things, rendering all things in today's world holy.

Luria's teachings inspired Israel ben Eliezer, born a century later, to study the cabala and to eventually found Hasidism, a branch of Orthodox Judaism whose followers adhere to a dis-tinctive lifestyle with its own practices, rites, and look—the male Hasid's instantly recognizable black suit, stiff hat, and long forelocks. Eliezer, now known as the Bal Shem Tov or "Master of the Good Name," was orphaned at five near the Ukrainian-Polish border. Even as a small child, he was attract-ed to solitude. As he would later recall, "I was drawn to walk the fields and the great, deep forest near our village. . . . Often I would sleep overnight in the field or the forest." Found there once by a wise man who asked what Eliezer was doing, the lit-tle loner replied: "I like the field and the forest, because there are no people—the great majority of whom are arrogant and dishonest. I am not afraid of anything."

He lived a wandering life with the wise man for three years. Then one day, in a small village, his mentor directed Eliezer to the remote hut of a devout hermit, who would become his new teacher. There in the forest, boy and man lived apart from the world for four years, studying the cabala.

The Bal Shem Tov set a precedent for Hasidic solitude. Even so, it is not for everyone. But the Polish Hasid Rabbi Nahman advised his disciples: "Find a day for yourself—better yet, late at night. Go to the forest or to the field, or lock yourself in a room. . . .You will meet solitude there. There you will be able to listen attentively to the noise of the wind first, to birds singing, to see wonderful nature and to notice yourself in it . . . and to come back to harmonic connection with the world and its Creator."

In Nahman's view, solitude is only for the brave, only for those able "to study the mysteries of silence . . . his inner voice, the voice of the World."

ONE NIGHT A while ago, I bumped into a woman whom I knew to be a witch. A follower of Wicca, whose million or so adherents worldwide see themselves as upholders of the ancient European pagan faith, she had been chanting—the last time I saw her, which was years before—with a hundred other witches in a park to celebrate the summer solstice. But she had stopped attending such events. She left the coven to which she had belonged. She works her rituals alone.

She had become, she said, a solitary. Not just "solitary" but "*a* solitary." In her faith, there is a word for it: a name she knows and others recognize. Wicca is as much a crowd scene as any other religion, its full-moon rites as fellowship-happy as Sunday services in church: maybe more so, since most covens work nude. Even so, there are profuse Web sites for solitaries, books for solitaries, packed with instructions for working spells alone and celebrating holidays—sabbats—alone.

Perhaps Wicca makes such allowances for loners because, while neopaganism is one of the world's fastest-growing faiths, it is still not exactly mainstream. Well aware of the prejudice against them, witches are quite secretive: staying inside the "broom closet," as they say. So as organized religions go—and Wicca with its discrete traditions and Books of Shadows is extremely organized—this is the outsider, the one other faiths call a freak, just as Hasidism is collectively a lonerish branch of Judaism. Their growing numbers notwithstanding, modern witches have good reason to empathize with us.

IF THE CHRISTIAN eremitic tradition was already passé in Thomas Merton's time, it has by now faded even farther into the realm of the archaic, the arcane, the artifact. In a few medieval English churches today, empty anchorholds are open for viewing. One such cell, at All Saints Church in King's Lynn, is a high-ceilinged, white stone space scarcely wider than a walk-in closet. A list of names evinces the succession of anchoresses who lived here between the twelfth and sixteenth centuries: Isabella,

Katherine, Margaret. Their names make these women seem real, immediate. Yet the cell's tiny size and starkness ranks it alongside all those other British tourist attractions—reconstructed torture chambers and grisly waxworks evoking medieval illness and medicine—aimed at making us all realize how grim those times were, and how far gone. In other faiths, too, the hermit archetype has been mostly eclipsed, no longer vital and no longer all that well-regarded. Fewer and fewer Hindus today progress beyond the second *ashrama*. An increasingly populous world—a world less convinced, at least in a general sense, of the presence of devils and angels—has rendered lifestyles such as those chosen by Saint Anthony and Han Shan impractical and nearly impossible. Now and then we read of "modern hermits" such as the New York Episcopalian brother who, it was reported in the summer of 2002, was directing an addiction-recovery center for HIV-positive men.

"Life as a hermit doesn't mean holing up in a remote cave," begins an article in a local paper about fifty-year-old Randall Horton, a recovered alcoholic and former Silicon Valley computer whiz who took holy vows in 1980 and, in accordance with Episcopal law, is officially a hermit, a solitary, "but not," the reporter hastens to note, "a recluse." In a recovery center "decorated with religious symbols," the gold-earringed Horton oversees residents and prays with them, though his "short noon and night prayers are normally done alone." The implication is that hermits are newsworthy novelties—freakish by definition but not totally repulsive if, like Horton, they make like normal human beings and interact and do not insist on being alone.

FROM THE LOOKS of things it is all too easy to assume that religion has nothing to offer us. Squinting up at monoliths, dogmas blasting in our ears, we have good reason to shove our hands in our pockets, shrug, and walk away. To some loners, the very premise of two people, much less two million, agreeing on anything, much less on which type of headgear will catch God's eye, is so principally flawed as to make every mainstream faith seem hilariously funny. What would loners' religions be like, religions-of-one, if we were permitted to have them? Tantric yoga on golf courses at midnight? Surfing and plainsong? Jesus, Mary, and Jennifer Lopez for this loner. Twenty-foot-high flaming effigies for that. Amen.

II.

new disorder

[SANITY]

They say isolation drives you crazy.
Sure it does—when you can't get enough of it.

"CRAZY" IS ONE of those words. We play around with it; we use it in a less-than-accurate way. Everyone does. We say it when we mean something else. When we say something was a crazy coincidence or that something is driving us crazy, we do not mean, precisely, outside the realm of the sane. Not certifiable. Not crazy, really. No more than we really mean love when we say we love the Houston Astros or onion rings. It is one of those words.

But.

"Crazy" is a dangerous word. Loners have more reason than most to fear it, even if we say it now and then ourselves. We have heard it too much—about ourselves.

It is bad enough in casual conversation. And on the news: *Let's hope they catch that crazy loner.* One of the quickest and surest insults, larded as it is with implicit science, is to call someone crazy: to interpret his behavior or his stance as the results of mental illness. It is a handy insult, too, because it invokes proof and implies that this proof is evident to all. In this sense to call someone crazy—someone who, say, is a loner—is to employ the old witch-hunt technique. Declaring certain individuals unfit, offenders, thus deserving death. *Ladies and gentlemen, observe this birthmark proving that this woman is a witch. Ladies and gentlemen, observe this man spending Saturday night alone, smiling over a comic book. Insane!*

It is a way in which majorities assume authority. A way of saying *in* or *out.*

As if it were not bad enough that loners must deflect all those other accusations—friendless, sexless—we must also face, like a dark cloud boiling constantly on a nearby hill, the taunt, the threat: *You're crazy.*

Sticks and stones. Bad enough when average joes say so. But what of highly paid professionals?

Therapists hold their clients' psychological well-being in their hands: that throbbing baby-bird softness of hopes and sorrows. *They* can see into hearts, can they not? And so they know loners are just the way we are; that we might have trouble sometimes, but being a loner is not the trouble. That loners are by nature no more or less likely to be crazy than anyone. That being a loner itself is not a sign of being sick. They know that.

Right?

During the fifty-minute therapy session, amid those smooth sofas and soothing carpets, clients seeking solace lay their souls bare. Whether fully functional or barely getting by, the client proffers confidences, terrors, problems to be probed like viscera in the hands of a haruspex. Truth must be told. If not, what is the point?

In client-therapist dialogue, social interaction is one of the first topics raised. Do you socialize? With whom? Doing what? When? How does it make you feel? Discerning the nature of a client's relationships gives the professional a view of the client's place in an inarguably crowded world. Fiery relationships suggest—what? Insufficient boundaries? Low tolerance, high aggression, being surrounded by bitches and assholes? Stress? Client and therapist work together to separate the fibers by which the former is strung, like a spider in a web, into his position. One by one—is this a strong thread or a weak one? Snarled or straight? It gives clients and therapists something to do.

Clients without relationships raise warning flags. It is a rare condition, after all, and thus a likely danger sign. Psychologists have seen plenty of real-life evidence that clients without social webs around them are in trouble. "Social isolation" is a "fertile breeding ground for depression," asserts the Aetna health-insurance company, voicing the commonly held view.

But it behooves professionals to ask whether the client *wants* a web. Maybe he does. Maybe he wishes everyone adored him. Maybe he longs for a wife and kids but breaks out in a panic every time he tries to strike up conversations with attractive strangers. Maybe he's lonely. Maybe he's just new in town. Maybe he *had* friends and a family, but they fled because he hit them and said Jesus made him do it. In which case, yes, the absence of social ties is problematic. It is so because to him it is a problem. In the last scenario it is also a problem for the ones he hurt. He feels isolated, and he feels bad.

But isolation is in the eye of the beholder.

The word, like alone and apart, has taken on a nasty tinge in common usage. Its root is the Latin *insula*, meaning "island." Yet islands are nice. They have an air of hedonism, sweet fruit, laissez-faire—at least the hot ones do. The cold ones evoke bracing air, bold nerves, uncommon strength. To be islandlike, isolated, insular, is to be at rest in the middle of the sea, contented, self-sufficient, singular—you would think. You *do* think. And yet no man, as John Donne wrote, voicing the view of the mob, is an island. His words echo down the halls of clinics all around the world, to this day, where isolation is considered a symptom of illness and thus must be cured.

IF THEY ASK whether we are alone by choice, they are doing their job. If they do not try to dissuade us, fine. If they move on from there to praise our self-awareness, our skill at choosing and living as we choose, they are doing their job. If they show us how to handle the slander, censure, jokes, and misapprehension, how to toss all of that off like orange peels, or weeds, or flimsy baffles set in place to hide the real road—if they do that, then they are doing their job.

Some of the most lonerish loners are resonantly sound of mind. Mondrian was not depressed. The solo sailors discussed in another chapter of this book are prime examples, too.

Loners know that. But we are the minority. It was not so long ago that homosexuals were considered mentally ill, even by psychological professionals who subjected them to humiliating therapies aimed at rooting out their "problem" and making them straight. Today such ideas and practices have been discredited, though the evangelical Christian community sustains a movement devoted to changing the orientation of gay churchmembers.

Being gay, like being a loner, is in this respect a nature-or-nurture question. Those on the "nurture" side might say I was born gregarious—that every baby is, because humans are social animals, because in such a populous world anything else is maladaptive. According to this logic, I and other loners "had a chance" to grow up sociable, but blew it. Or our parents blew it for us. They kept us away from other children. They abused us, thus filled us with shame and made us misanthropes. Or we experienced trauma in, say, third grade when the whole class ganged up on us, calling us Fatso or Gimp or Kike. It soured our naturally friendly natures permanently and forever.

Since the mid-twentieth century, the nurture side of the argument has been the popular one throughout the West, and has dominated discussions of childrearing, social welfare, education, and other issues involving human development. Does it matter? To some. Individuals who are happy see little benefit in spending their time trying to decide how they got the way they are. Those who are sad, however, make much of it.

MIT psychology professor Steven Pinker comes down on the "nature" side. Behavioral geneticists, he argues in his book, *The Blank Slate*, have assembled prodigious research proving that human tendencies, talents, and the like are determined biologically. Thus, he believes, our tendencies and talents are ours before birth. Newborns are fully fledged beings with personalities already intact, he maintains, and not "blank slates" to be inscribed by their culture, their companions, their experiences. Among the piles of evidence that support his view, he cites the results of 2001's human genome project, as well as many cases of identical twins separated at birth and raised apart as strangers, but who are found, as adults, to share a remarkable array of characteristics in common. Research has uncovered that these shared traits include political views, mathematical aptitude, amiability, and tendencies to giggle, gamble, get divorced, have accidents, and commit crimes. A famous pair of such twins is Ann Landers and Abigail van Buren, who became the top advice columnists of the twentieth century. Pinker writes that the five major ways in which human personality can vary are all "heritable"—that is, inborn. They include "openness to experience, conscientiousness, extroversion-introversion, antagonism-agreeableness, and neuroticism."

Pinker has had his critics, including such notables as Noam Chomsky and Stephen Jay Gould. Liberal commentators, religious leaders, and others across a wide spectrum have attacked the validity of Pinker's evolutionary psychology.

But if Pinker is right, his research indicates what many loners have always suspected: that we were born this way. It is intrinsic and immutable, as preprogrammed as whether we are good at math or languages. It is more *us* than blood or bone, both of which are replaceable, or hair color and curl, which can be changed. Of trying to reverse what is essential—trying to talk us out of it or train it out of us, deriding it as bad or ugly or evil or pathological—only disaster can come. I am not crazy now, but forced to act like a nonloner for an extended period, I might *go* crazy. Forced to deny their orientation, cut off that way from reality, loners could lose their minds. As deep-sea fish die in a shallow tank. They are fine at the bottom of the sea, strange as it might look down there, inhospitable though it might be to whales and jellyfish and skin divers. As deep-sea fish that is where they have to be. Dead in shallow tanks. In the deep sea, not dead. Loners left alone, sane. Loners manipulated, loners not allowed to be alone, perhaps insane. And we are forced to live in their world, aren't we? Their shallow tank. Made just for them.

What the mob requires for its sanity is what whittles away relentlessly at ours. Because nonloners far outnumber us, their prescription for soundness of mind stands as good medicine. Contact! Chat! Cell phones! Spending as few hours as possible alone! To us it is not medicine but a dangerous drug at best—it numbs, it drains, it blinds, it depresses, it requires extensive recovery. At worst, it is poison. If loners comprised the majority, we would decree our own prescription. Work at home! Turn off the ringer on the phone! Cross the street to avoid someone you know! It's good for you!

In which case, if it were that way, we could decree our loner standard for insanity. That talking to others all day is symptomatic of failure to individuate. That it indicates an unhealthy fear of thinking. That being unable to entertain oneself is surefire proof of being sick. There would be new disorders if we were in charge.

THAT SAID, WE would do well to think of being loners as what makes us hale, whole, not in need of fixing unless that part of us is denied. Garden-variety loners are not *de facto* insane any more than garden-variety gays are insane. Or garden-variety nuclear physicists. But *that* said, there *are* mental illnesses whose symptoms include acting like a loner. One of these is ADD/ADHD, Attention Deficit Disorder/Attention Deficit Hyperactivity Disorder. Kids who a few generations ago would have been called spazzes, bullies, juvenile delinquents, lazy, crazy, stupid—kids who can't sit still in class, who space out or start throwing things—are now often suspected of being ADD/ADHD candidates. Some say the disorder constitutes a new epidemic: between 1985 and 2001, the number of ADD/ADHD diagnoses in America soared from about half a million to between five and seven million. Symptoms include restlessness, inability to pay attention, and what the Learning Disability Forum calls an "inability to play well in a group." In the American Psychiatric Association's *Diagnostic and Statistical Manual for Mental Disorders IV* (*DSM4*), a list of characteristics and personality types that typically apply to ADD/ADHD sufferers includes "social loner." No definitive cause has been found, though neurological sources have been suggested.

Because they can be aggressive and cannot concentrate— and thus cannot concentrate on what other people are saying and doing—ADD/ADHD patients are often alone. No one wants to keep company with those who cannot acknowledge the presence of others.

Another syndrome that isolates its sufferers is social phobia. Terrified of social contact, seized by panic attacks and severe self-consciousness when meeting others—often just when *anticipating* meeting others—social phobics keep to themselves. They dread the prospect of being scrutinized, judged, or embarrassed in public. Physical symptoms sometimes accompany and exacerbate the emotional ones: heavy perspiration, tremors, nausea.

Not all social phobics are loners by nature. Some wish they could get back into the game. Blaming themselves for the problem, they feel even worse. Another relevant syndrome is avoidance personality disorder, characterized by depression, extreme social anxiety and a feeling of personal inadequacy. Another is schizoid personality disorder—a syndrome, not to be confused with schizophrenia, whose sufferers are notably withdrawn, experience few emotional extremes either positive or negative, and display a marked lack of feelings for people in general.

WHEN NATURAL-BORN loners do experience difficulty, psychological professionals face unusual challenges. What would bring this client happiness? Given the dominant paradigm, how is a therapist to advise a patient who actively dislikes being around people, whose peace and happiness depends on not being with people? How difficult is it to tell the client that this is okay?

My friend Marie is a loner. "I have always needed the freedom to be alone," she says, capturing in one word—freedom—

the key to what it is we all want. Who could argue with free-dom? Is this not the land of the free? In her twenties and thir-ties, Marie lived alone. She was writing fiction at the time and saw her solitude "as good because it fostered independence, while others considered it bad because it was 'isolation'—the term used by therapists."

Marie has been seeing therapists for more than fifteen years now, largely because "the result of this independence/isolation is overreaction to any social contact. I brood about a single non-hello from a store clerk for weeks. I go through great lengths to avoid people; for example, I will walk around an entire city block rather than pass someone I know even slightly. No one is allowed in my apartment other than my boyfriend, and I won't get in situations involving more than one other person. Human contact is painful and I have a very low tolerance for pain. It is painful because no two people can interact without conflict. Social contact and the resulting emotions overwhelm me. I am extremely reactive in a tearful way and feel 'done to' by others. I also feel rage when anyone invades the careful boundaries I have erected around me. Paradoxically, even though my solitude is by choice, I feel hurt when people dislike me or ignore me. Their behavior makes me hate them even more."

Marie reads a lot and, ironically, as she notes, "the books are about people. Also, I am comfortable at a racetrack crowded with hundreds or thousands of racing fans. Many of them are lowlifes or misfits like me. At the track I can be anyone I want to be, and I can also disappear into the crowds so no one can find me. The racing fans and I share a common interest about which I am able to talk with a fair amount of knowledge. Off-track, people talk too fast about subjects I can't understand, such as world events. I feel that there is a socially acceptable way to be, and I am not that way."

Marie's counselors have coaxed her to enter group therapy, which proved of no use to her, and have given her "homework assignments" aimed at forcing contact with others—enter a certain store this week, speak to the clerk, ask a stranger a question.

Still, Marie continued to feel distressed around others. Working in an office proved untenable. Being a loner by nature was one thing. The panic and hostility she had come to feel so frequently were becoming insufferable.

She agreed to try medication. Selective serotonin reuptake inhibitors—SSRIs—became very popular treatments for anxiety disorders after psychiatrist Peter Kramer's book *Listening to Prozac* became a national bestseller in 1993. Coining the term "cosmetic psychopharmacology," Kramer claimed that Prozac had made many of his patients "better than well," and declared that the drug "seemed to give social confidence to the habitually timid, to make the sensitive brash, to lend the introvert the social skills of a salesman." After the FDA approved another SSRI, Paxil, which is now used widely to treat social phobia, newspapers ran a flood of stories calling it the new "shyness drug."

As has been discussed elsewhere in this book, not all shy people are loners and not all loners are shy. But the idea of altering personalities chemically is science-fiction scary. Imagine a film, or maybe a future, in which those qualities the masses deemed sick were "cured" with a system of forced medication. Could loners be medicated out of being loners? Medicated right out of the world?

AFTER SEVERAL YEARS on medication, Marie says, "Prozac has helped me speak up more, so I am able to order food or drink in public places. However, medication has made things worse because it causes severe tremor, so I quake violently when trying to talk to anyone. This increases others' perception of me as a disturbed person. One of my psychiatrists labeled me with a medical term: sociopath."

In the late 1990s, especially in high-tech hubs such as California's Silicon Valley, diagnosis rates began soaring for a form of autism known as Asperger's Syndrome. Usually first identified in childhood, it is characterized by a lack of basic social skills and an apparent inability to anticipate or comprehend the emotions of others—leading the sufferer, as a result, to inhabit a world of his or her own.

No definitive cause has been found for autism, whose name derives from the Greek *autos*, meaning self. As autistics go, those with Asperger's are relatively functional. They do not find life in this crowded world easy, but with the aid of behavioral and other therapies, most can grow up to hold jobs and care for themselves.

Asperger's was first included in the American Psychiatric Association's *Diagnostic and Statistical Manual of Mental Disorders* as recently as 1994. Curiously, while about 70 percent of autistics are to some degree mentally retarded, this does not apply to those with Asperger's. Many Asperger's patients are extremely intelligent, revealing an aptitude for computers and other technical pursuits very early in life. Kids with Asperger's tend to fixate on computer games and video games with a repetitive relentlessness called, in clinical circles, "perseveration." Because of its prevalence in tech-industry hot spots, some researchers have suggested that children are inheriting the syndrome from parents in whom it was never diagnosed—but who grew up being pegged as geeks and computer nerds.

Wired magazine's Steve Silberman has speculated on the gifted/autistic/loner link and its genetic ramifications. It is just possible, Silberman has written, that "slightly autistic adults—[with] the very abilities that have made them dreamers and architects of our technological future—are capable of bringing a plague down on the best minds of the next generation. . . .

"High-tech hot spots like [Silicon] Valley, and Route 128 outside of Boston, are a curious oxymoron: They're fraternal associations of loners. In these places, if you're a geek living in the high-functioning regions of the [autism] spectrum, your chances of meeting someone who shares your perseverating obsession (think Linux or *Star Trek*) are greatly expanded. As more women enter the IT workplace, guys who might never have had a prayer of finding a kindred spirit suddenly discover that she's hacking Perl scripts in the next cubicle."

The increased media attention has led to a kind of Asperger's Syndrome solidarity movement. Adults—many of them loners—who have been diagnosed with the syndrome or who, undiagnosed, are convinced that it fits them are airing relief at its being identified and explored. One typical Web site offers a list of "probable aspies" throughout history. It includes noted loners Albert Einstein, Stanley Kubrick, Erik Satie, Michelangelo, and the playwright Alfred Jarry, who lived alone in a crawl space with a stuffed owl. Also, there is the best-selling nature writer Gerald Durell, who wrote amusingly about his loathing for social occasions. Bill Gates is widely vaunted as an Asperger's candidate. So are Jane Austen, H. P. Lovecraft, Thomas Edison, Wassily Kandinsky, Alfred Hitchcock, Mark Twain, Isaac Newton, Gustav Mahler, George Bernard Shaw, Michael Palin, and Al Gore.

HOW DO SHRINKS really feel about us? In an essay titled "One Hundred Tears of Solitude," British therapist Dr. Raj Persaud charges that rising divorce rates and other woes have turned the West into "a society of the socially withdrawn—hermits, even. Are serial killers and mass murderers simply expressing a common wish: People get in the way of life, so please leave me alone?

"We gaze in horror at images from the Third World of whole families living in one room; here, we can barely cope with sharing the same roads," Persaud declares on his personal Web site, decrying the idea that it is "fashionable to be independent and therefore alone.

"Some psychologists have even argued that the capacity to be alone, without experiencing loneliness, hence the capacity to enjoy your own company, is a sign of personal maturity and perhaps the acid test of mental health," Persaud marvels. Grudgingly, he allows that "practically all creative people, and certainly most geniuses, have preferred to be alone for long periods, especially when producing their best work"—and cites Michael Jackson as an example of this. Eyeing "the loners in the deserted corner," Persaud explains that it is common practice in his profession to offer unsociable clients special social-skills training to help them integrate more easily at work and school. But some clients "reject this, preferring to be alone. They have never really enjoyed company and don't want to be changed." Perhaps, he reasons, loners are stunted in their development. After all, "sustaining genuine fellowship requires a certain maturity."

On the playground, at the watercooler, the loner is observed, held up to standard templates, and assessed. *That dude is bonkers.* It's so easy, so comforting, in a way, for our observers to offer that explanation for what they find difficult to understand. *He's crazy, see?* It is a weapon. Do not mistake that fact for a second.

12.

the l-word

[C R I M E]

*Criminal profilers, the press, and law enforcement are really
scaring our next-door neighbors.*

ONE WINTER DAY in 2002, fifteen-year-old Charles Bishop
flew a single-engine Cessna into a Tampa office building.
Luckily, no workers were in that part of the building that day,
so no one was killed in the crash—except Bishop himself. The
boy had left a suicide note lauding Osama bin Laden, whose
followers had destroyed New York's World Trade Center just a
few months before. Right before crashing into the office building, Bishop had veered menacingly over a nearby U.S. Air
Force base. The WTC attack and mass murder were clearly on
his mind.

Newspapers around the world promptly dubbed the boy a
loner.

The *St. Petersburg Times* and India's *Deccan Herald,* along with
many others, quoted Tampa Police Chief Bennie Holder calling

Bishop "very much a loner." Within two days, CBS News was calling him "a 'troubled' boy and a loner." Joining the chorus, the BBC declared: "Plane Crash Boy 'Shunned Others.' " To support that label, the BBC quoted a neighbor of Bishop's declaring that the teen "never talked to anybody."

A few days later, the news coverage did a dizzying about-face. "Friends Say Teen Suicide Pilot No Loner," announced ABC News. "Loner label fails to describe teen suicide pilot in Tampa," echoed the *Detroit News*. Bishop's extracurricular activities were cited as evidence: the boy had "played basketball and flag football, tutored first-graders and was a flag-bearer." One paper after another chimed in, declaring that Bishop was not, in fact, a loner after all. He'd had friends, some of whom were quoted and photographed as proof. Others who had known the teen came forth, or were conjured, to recast his public image. Bishop's former English teacher told *Good Morning America* viewers that "Charles got along beautifully with the other students." He had "worked well in groups." Bishop's middle-school headmaster told the *St. Petersburg Times*: "Hopefully, it has become apparent that he was not a loner."

As the dead boy's public image seemed to grow more newsworthy than his crime, ABC News summarized the turn-around. "The bright, patriotic Charles Bishop described by teachers and classmates," it reported, "sounds nothing like the outcast loner . . . making the questions about the incident all the more baffling."

So, we are told, it's *baffling* when someone who pilots a plane into an office building *isn't* a loner.

· · ·

IT IS A word crime writers love. *He was a loner* is a crime-story cliché. A quick look lasting no more than ten minutes yielded the following headlines, all found in major papers: " 'Loner' charged in killing." "Police-shooting suspect described as loner." "Loner jailed for downloading child pornography." "A loner with a deadly secret." "Jury hears portrait of a loner." "Loner announced his plot to murder six."

"Killer was top student, yet still a loner," marvels a headline in the *Indianapolis News*. "Loner's obsession with occult led to fatal stabbing," notes Britain's *Guardian*. "A gypsy-hating loner who shot to kill," offers the same paper. Delving beneath headlines into stories themselves yields more. A child-killer "was a loner with few friends, the jury in the Sarah Payne murder trial heard today." "A 'classic loner' just fired from his job at a machine tool company returned the next day with a rifle," another story begins. "A student described as a brilliant loner went on a shooting rampage at the University of Iowa after being passed over for an academic honor," runs another. A piece about a racist, homophobic bomber explains how "a twisted loner whose only friend was a rat dreamed of fame, power and the establishment of a master race—as had his hero, Adolf Hitler." The story goes on to add that he "spent hours" in the solitude of his rented flat, secretly constructing bombs. "He ignored his fellow tenants," we are told. Aha. Of course. We should have known.

Like the bogeyman and the witches and ogres in fairy tales, the criminal-as-loner serves a social function. It sets the criminal apart from ordinary people, from the masses, designating him as a freak, a demon, and an alien. This ties up matters neatly. It explains things. No "normal" person—one with friends and family, who says hello to his neighbors, who is recognizable as one of the mainstream tribe—would rape a toddler or feed his murdered wife's corpse to a wood chipper. (The weirder and more perverse the crime, the more rapidly the press starts calling the perpetrator a loner. In even that lamebrained condemnation is a brutish compliment: they admit loners are creative.) Declaring criminals loners—especially the sickest criminals—is a form of primitive self-defense. It sets crime and the criminal mind safely outside the familiar realm of the majority. It is a way of saying *This could never happen here. The kind of person who does THAT could never possibly be one of us.* The creep whose deeds render him horrible by any standards must be further demonized. Must be farther removed, set off farther than jail or the status of *killer* and *condemned man*. To ensure his separateness, to quarantine him, fling him beyond recognizability, sympathy, and even humanity, call him a loner.

While serving this purpose, the neutral word "loner" acquires a hideous coating.

Even as this scares the masses, it consoles them. At some level, the idea of the homicidal monster lurking out there somewhere titillates, like the idea of sharks. This demonization lends the l-word a certain power. It purges.

BUT LEARNING THE true stories of criminals who are called loners in the press reveals, with striking frequency, that these are not genuine loners. At first glance, they look or act like loners, but they are not. *They do not wish to be alone. Their dislike of being alone is what drives them to violence.* But more on that later.

Journalists are clever, but they did not come up with the loner/killer thing all on their own. They take their cue from law enforcement. In the ranks, the antiloner prejudice is taken for granted—not as prejudice, though, but as fact. Typical is the poster an Illinois police department issued after the murder of a local man in 2000. In an effort to locate the unknown assailant, the poster advised its readers to look out for anyone who "may be a loner." This "loner" was also, the poster added, likely to exhibit "paranoid, nervous, agitated, or apprehensive behavior, boasts or brags about getting away with something" and may have recently repainted his or her car. The fact that loners are about the least likely people in the world to boast or brag seems to have escaped the cops.

In the autumn of 2001, after anthrax spores sent through the mail killed several Americans, the FBI issued an official profile of the sender. "Loner Likely Sent Anthrax, FBI Says," ran the *Los Angeles Times* headline. "FBI looking for a loner," declared Taiwan's *Taipei Times*. Other papers and networks worldwide joined the chorus. The profile also suggested that the killer was a twentysomething American male scientist, familiar with New Jersey, who tended to hold grudges. While these details were mentioned in the articles, they did not make it into the headlines. Front pages did not scream, "Garden State grudge-holder sought" or "FBI pegs chemists." Of all the possible earmarks, "loner" took the hit.

If "driving while black" is cause for suspicion, then driving while a loner is none too safe, either. Imagine the uproar if all the articles cited so far in this chapter had used the words "Canadian" or "CPA" instead of "loner."

IN THE SUMMER of 2002, a California man was charged with attempted murder after spraying Raid on his ex-girlfriend's lipstick and allergy medication believing it would poison her. Years before, this man had warned this woman that if she ever left him for another, he would kill her. When she finally broke up with him, he put his plan into action. His intended victim discovered the insecticide on her belongings before any harm was done, and the man was promptly arrested. The couple's neighbor told the *San Francisco Chronicle* that the allegations surprised her because the accused man was "outgoing and friendly."

"I didn't believe it," she told the reporter. "You'd see him more than you'd see her, and he'd wave. I thought he was a great guy. . . . My son and his friends used to ride their bikes and stop and shake his hand and talk to him."

This would-be killer seemed unkillerlike because he shook hands. The premise is absurd, and all the more compelling for its absurdity. Does it take a genius to see that it takes a *social* man to become so possessive, so enmeshed with others, that his rage and jealousy over a breakup make him want to kill? *These* are the motives that ignite most violence. Anger. Envy. Desire. Betrayal. Resentment. Rejection. Love. These are social motives, the concerns of those wrapped up in the thoughts and actions of others. These are the motives of those who cannot stand being left out, who do not heal quickly from ridicule, who seethe over dents in their reputations. These are the motives of those who need others. They need others for their very sense of self, they live for the responses they elicit from others. When the response is wrong, or never comes, the result is often bloody indeed. Revenge, retaliation, retribution.

These are not the motives that move loners. We do not want those things from others—acceptance and admiration and control and power—that make social people kill. We neither hang nor thrive on what others think, say or do. The fact that we mind our own business saves us from the types of torment that typically lead to violence. We want nothing from others but to be left alone.

We lack the motive. Tell *that* to the newspapers.

WHEN A CRIMINAL is labeled a loner, from what criteria is the label drawn? How do the labelers devise their definition? Largely from what they see on the surface. Lives alone? He is a loner. Not married? A loner. No friends? No kids? Quiet? Loner. Does not confide in coworkers? Loner. All these things indicate a state of aloneness. But is that person alone by choice, as loners are? Most likely not. Aloneness itself tells us nothing. The seven-time deadbeat dad with bad breath and festering chancres and only one hobby, shooting squirrels, is alone—but only because no one can stand him. In his studio apartment, he eats solitary meals and comes and goes in silence, carrying his hunting rifle in and out. Alone, but not a loner.

• • •

WHAT WE HAVE here is a crisis of semantics. The word "loner," based on the shallowest impressions of surface appearances, is being used wholesale to tar an amazing diversity of people—most of them not loners—with the same mucky brush. This crisis not only insults true loners, criminalizing innocent people through wrongheaded logic and myopic observation. It also keeps many actual criminals free, evading suspicion as they bask in the safety of neither being nor appearing to be loners. By sharpening the terminology, providing a language lesson, we could do a lot more justice all the way around.

If by "loner" we mean "someone who prefers to be alone," this is our starting point. Others might quibble with our definition, arguing that "loner" means only "alone a lot." But one of this book's purposes is to refine the word, to put a finer point on it. The term "Arab" was long used to describe natives of every country between Morocco and Pakistan. It has taken the world a long time to understand that many other ethnic groups live in those regions who are not Arabs. The world will use words ignorantly until, and sometimes even after, it has been informed of their inaccuracy or overgeneralization or offensiveness. We must start somewhere.

So this is our definition. Scratch the surface of those killers branded with a big red "L," and more often than not you will find quite the opposite. You will find nonloners in loners' clothing, impostors. You will find not loners at all, but *pseudoloners*.

The most common variety of criminal pseudoloner is the outcast. An outcast has been *in*, or tried to get in, but has been cast out. He has failed to achieve his goals: acceptance, approval, coolness, companionship. This hurts. It really burns.

WHY ARE OUTCASTS cast out? Sometimes because they have done or said something that incensed their peer group. Has he hit up on a buddy's wife? Does he show up on doorsteps in the middle of the night begging for beer, a place to sleep, a loan? Sometimes they're simply assholes. Just because someone is sociable does not mean he is likable. He might be clingy or aggressive or demanding. Who does not remember that desperate kid in school who tried so hard to be accepted by the drama club, the football team, the yearbook staff but, for his fumbling efforts, was always rejected? Sometimes those who shunned him laughed at him. Sometimes they shuddered, saying *He gives me the creeps.* Sociable types are just as capable of being rude, grating, and gross as loners are of being sweet, polite, and gracious.

Ever since Theodore Kaczynski was arrested in 1996 and convicted of being the Unabomber—having maimed and killed his victims with mail bombs for over twenty years—he has been held up as the classic example of a criminal loner. It is virtually impossible to say that one is writing a book about loners without someone's mentioning Kaczynski. In the days and weeks after his arrest, networks around the world screened footage of the remote cabin where he lived alone, virtually friendless. He had cut off contact years before with his family—the family that, ultimately, turned him in. After Kaczynski's arrest, reporters rounded up former classmates and colleagues who had known him at Berkeley and Harvard. They called him standoffish.

Alone he surely was. But why?

As a mathematical genius, the schoolboy Kaczynski would have found few kids with whom he could relate. He tried, though. Former classmates remembered him as a good-humored jokester who played in the school band. A pipe bomb he built as a youth earned him an ironic burst of fame on campus which gave him a warm sense of acceptance. His high-school physics teacher insisted that Kaczynski was "not the loner he's been portrayed to be." But being so far ahead of his peers intellectually, if not emotionally, made bonding difficult. After his arrest, Kaczynski would tell a psychiatrist: "By the time I left high school I was definitely regarded as a freak by a large segment of the student body." As a young adult, he established a relationship with a female coworker. It soured, and Kaczynski's furious reaction was to write nasty limericks about the woman and post them around the office. His boss, who also happened to be the brother who decades later would turn him in to the FBI, fired him. Kaczynski was not a smooth character, not the life of the party, but he was trying. And like nonloners all over the world, he was finding ways of defending himself against the pain of being rejected. He was learning how it feels to nurse hurt, how to seethe, how to blame others for not responding as one wishes. Before breaking off contact with his family, Kaczynski offered in a letter to his mother an eloquent précis of how a nonloner can come to resemble a loner:

"Suppose that for a period of years whenever you touched— let us say—a banana, you got a severe electric shock. After that you would always be nervous around bananas, even if you knew they weren't wired to shock you. Well, in the same way, the many rejections, humiliations and other painful influences that I underwent during adolescence at home, in high school, and at Harvard have conditioned me to be afraid of people."

His fear of social pain, his mental illness and the fact that he happened to be building bombs made him secretive. Right there are three reasons a nonloner might be alone.

James Daveggio was sentenced to death in California in the summer of 2002 for abducting, brutally torturing, and killing a young woman. He has also been linked to several other similar killings. At the time of the crime for which he was convicted, Daveggio might easily have been mistaken for a loner. In fact he was anything but, according to Carlton Smith, whose book, *Hunting Evil*, profiles Daveggio. The killer had been popular, albeit with a rough crowd, as early as junior high school, and had a continuous stream of girlfriends and wives starting at age thirteen. Quoted in Smith's book, Daveggio's ex-wives noted that it was his outgoing personality, in fact, that initially attracted them. Even one of his victims—a woman he was convicted of raping—reported that he had been nice, polite, and friendly when he picked her up at a bar.

Membership in a biker gang brought Daveggio his dream come true: a loyal peer group of the sort who, as Smith puts it, "run in packs."

"With the gang," Smith told me shortly after Daveggio's sentencing, "he was popular." But when Daveggio's irascibility and passion for crystal meth proved too much even for his fellow bikers, "they repudiated him. Even the most antisocial people repudiated him. He became an outcast of the outcasts, and I think that had a very large effect on him." Drowning his sense of rejection in more meth, Daveggio sank farther and farther into an isolation that enraged him. No one wanted him around except the ex-prostitute who was his accomplice in that brutal murder. Virtually friendless, he might have appeared to be a loner. But this aloneness had everything to do with Daveggio's personal failures "and self-destruction," Smith says. The outcast struck back.

For a social creature to whom the presence of others means a great deal, being cast out—of a gang, a marriage, a workplace, a friendship, a family—is serious punishment. Plunged into social solitary confinement, he struggles with strong negative feelings that cut him off both physically and mentally from what he needs most: company. With whom, in his new isolation, can he discuss his pain? For him, aloneness is so gross and so unnatural that it thrusts him beyond the pale. It is a vicious circle. It proves just too much to bear.

OTHER PSEUDOLONERS ARE set apart from others not by will, but pathology. Unkind as it sounds, the mentally ill are not as a rule enjoyable or even easy to be around. So most people avoid them. The outlook of an unsound mind is so singular that it cannot really be shared by others—but the owner of that unsound mind does not always realize this. The mentally ill might want to reach out, might, in fact, imagine bonds where there are none. They might wish for acceptance, might not understand—any more than anyone does—why their affections go unheeded. Homeless or not, harmless or not, outside of institutions the mentally ill are pretty much consigned to lives of isolation. Not by choice in every case. A schizophrenic living under a bridge who murders a hapless passerby, believing it will forestall Armageddon, is not necessarily a loner.

Blue-blooded serial killer Hadden Clark, who has confessed to the murders of at least a dozen women, believes one of his fellow inmates in a Maryland prison is Jesus Christ. Clark, whose family tree leads back to the *Mayflower*, exhibits multiple personalities, most of them female. He says "the ladies" murdered his victims, slashing and dismembering and in some cases dining on them. Adrian Havill, a true-crime author who visited the killer in jail while researching his book, *Born Evil*, describes Clark hoarding food until it reeked and grew tresses of mold, then eating it happily.

During the years when he was preying on and killing his many victims, Clark lived alone in a tent in the woods, far from prying eyes. This remote, solitary domicile, just big enough for one, is what led the media to roundly dub Clark a loner after his arrest. Even the back cover of *Born Evil* calls him a "reclusive loner." Yet, in the book, Havill himself tells a different story. Clark, he writes, had "a social hunger." He was a fixture in local bars where, joking with servers and fellow patrons until closing time, "he needed to be around others. . . . Hadden was a man to whom friends were invaluable." Avidly attending Bible-study classes, "he yearned for acceptance," Havill writes. The pastor who taught these classes is quoted as saying that Clark tried fervently to make friends there but lacked sufficient social skills to win anyone over. Rollerblading around town, "willing to take any odd job that brought him into contact with people," Havill writes, Clark was "just lonely."

Lonely, not a loner. Lonely, which pretty much *defines* him as not a loner. Deranged. Living alone—how else to conduct an extended campaign of killings before being caught? But desperate for friends: not a loner.

MANY PSEUDOLONERS ARE alone because they have something to hide. If *your* freezer were stocked with severed heads or your bookcase with racist propaganda or your cabin with explosives, you might hesitate to have a party.

Other pseudoloners kill because they want attention. John Lennon's murderer, Mark David Chapman, is regularly dubbed a loner. A typical headline that appeared after the 1980 crime was "Loner Shot Lennon." This is a classic case of the public's believing—forging a consensus on—what it wants to believe. Who else, it reasoned, could kill a crowd favorite, loved by billions, but a loner? Who else but a loner would punish the masses that way, destroying not a politician or an ordinary man who will be mourned only by his friends but *John*, a universal phenomenon? That Chapman had been reading *The Catcher in the Rye* that day, that before killing Lennon he asked the singer to sign a copy of this loner anthem, authored by the literary recluse J. D. Salinger, fueled the flame. Yet Chapman had been outgoing. He had been a counselor and the assistant director of a youth camp. Back home in Honolulu, he had worked amid the clubby atmosphere of a YMCA. He courted women—Asian women who resembled Yoko Ono, the wife of his idol. Chapman wanted fame.

It should be noted that while many loners become famous—artists, scientists, inventors, most notably—fame is not the goal but a side effect, often an unwanted one. In Chapman's case, notoriety *was* the goal: the ultimate form of acceptance, if a twisted one. The murder was a nonlonerish matter of *look at me.*

"I was 'Mr. Nobody,'" Chapman has been quoted as saying, "until I killed the biggest 'somebody' on earth."

TIMOTHY MCVEIGH WAS neither crazy nor an outcast. Following his arrest for the 1995 bombing of the Oklahoma City federal building, the young Gulf War veteran was described over and over in the media as a loner. CNN called him "tall, lean, a loner." The *Denver Post* called him an "angry, maniacal loner." Wisconsin's *Beloit Daily News* called him a "hateful, paranoid loner." *Asiaweek* called him a "disaffected loner." An FBI psychologist went on record describing McVeigh as an asocial, asexual loner. Others chimed in, comparing McVeigh's loner status to the Unabomber's, casting him so unanimously in this role that the public could hardly harbor any doubts that it was accurate.

Yet his service in the war earned McVeigh a Combat Infantry Badge and Bronze Star. Being such a good soldier requires cooperation and obedience—neither of which are loner qualities. In the army he made friends easily, including with the two with whom he enacted the bombing plot.

Interviewed in jail while awaiting trial by a *Time* reporter, McVeigh remarked that the media had been misrepresenting him.

"The big misconception," he said, "is that I'm a loner. Well, I believe in having my own space and being on my own sometimes. But that in no way means that I'm a loner, which the press likes to equate with an introvert. That's a complete misconception. Women, social life—." He laughed. "I'm misunderstood through labeling. Speed freak. Gun freak. Loner. All those misconceptions" had given the public, he lamented, "a completely different picture of me. The real me has not been reported to the press."

After his execution in June 2001, the *Cape Cod Times* ran this headline: "McVeigh stays a loner to the end."

He would not have liked that.

McVeigh had longed to join the Green Berets but failed the entrance test, a failure that devastated him. This sense of rejection might have been what fueled his growing anti-government, extremely right-wing sentiments. But in pursuing those sentiments to a violent conclusion, McVeigh saw himself not as a lone crusader on a solitary mission but as one of many: an infantryman in a different kind of army, a brotherhood of patriots.

MANY SUCH BROTHERHOODS are thriving around the world. Their members are not loners, but each group behaves, as a unit, the way the public thinks loners behave. Not as loners *really* behave, but as we are all too often accused of behaving. Secretive. Prickly. Separatist. Obviously hiding something. Volatile.

Hate groups, cults, sinister sects—their members are bound by shared beliefs, goals, agendas, motives, methods. Each group has its system. That system becomes the group's identity. And in such groups, identity is everything. Nowhere else is groupthink so much in evidence, so *de rigueur*, as there.

The secrecy, the prickliness, those other qualities are motivated not by true lonerish instincts but by pseudoloner instincts. As a rule, these groups do not simply feel happier to be by themselves, as loners do, but are actively hostile. In most cases they are actually hiding something. Their goals and methods are unconventional, beyond the pale, illegal. As units, they are outsiders. Typically, when one of their members is implicated in a crime, he is readily dubbed a loner. Yet members of these groups are quite the opposite. Having subordinated their own identity to that of the clan, they cease to operate as individuals. Thriving entirely on the fact of membership, fellowship, groupthink, these people are drones, replicants, Myrmidons.

Men like McVeigh—and McVeigh knew this—are not loners. They need one another. Even if they never meet, it is imperative that they know the others exist, that their voices are not lone cries in a wood but a chorus. *Militia* is a collective noun.

You would think crime fighters could see this. Yet even at the highest echelons, they persist in confusing the group with its members, and even then playing fast and loose with the l-word. On the heels of the Oklahoma City bombing, the Justice Department created a report in 1998 on homegrown terrorists, identifying them as an increasingly significant threat to American security. An article about this report in the

Washington Post was headlined "A Most Dangerous Profile: The Loner."

Along with McVeigh, the main example cited in the article is Eric Rudolph, a fundamentalist Christian charged in the bombing of an Alabama abortion clinic and suspected of placing explosives in an Atlanta park during the 1996 Olympics. Still at large as of this writing, Rudolph is, like McVeigh, described universally in the media as a loner. Yet as the *Post* reveals, from his teens onward, Rudolph belonged to a radical organization, the Christian Identity movement. After embarking on a life of crime, federal investigators agree, he maintained contact with members of Christian Identity as well as with the racist, Idaho-based group Aryan Nations. For Rudolph to have stayed hidden for so long despite a massive manhunt would be virtually impossible without others assisting him. Being a true loner and remaining unnoticed for years is one thing. Being one of America's most wanted criminals and remaining unnoticed takes support, a group effort, and cannot be done alone.

THE UBIQUITY OF the l-word in the press today owes itself largely to its ubiquity in the burgeoning realm of criminal profiling. This crime-solving methodology was pioneered by FBI agents in the 1970s, and draws on a combination of crime-scene evidence and precedent to establish lists of likely characteristics for as-yet-unidentified suspects. As the twentieth century drew to a close, profiling captured the public's imagination. This owes a bit to the Oscar-winning 1991 film, *The Silence of the Lambs*, in which a convicted cannibal helps an FBI agent profile a wanted killer. But no doubt it springs, too, from America's growing fixation on crime. With a terror of kidnappers, pedophiles, serial killers, and terrorists gripping the collective heart, a desperate need arises for saviors—latter-day Hercule Poirots and Sherlock Holmeses who use their brains to deduce, track, and apprehend. Hardly a major unsolved crime is covered in the media today without profilers being interviewed, being implored to aid the search. Featured on numerous TV dramas and offered in university courses around the world, profiling has become an increasingly popular career option.

Critics call profiling mere guesswork. They protest its use of race as a defining factor. Caucasians are as offended by the FBI's announcement that the anthraxer is a white man as African-Americans are outraged at being pulled over just for driving in the "wrong" neighborhood. Yet in the lexicon of profiling, loners take incredible heat. It is us, loners—*who, me? yes, you*—whom profilers peg *pro forma* as serial killers, bombers, arsonists, and assassins.

PROFILERS CREATE *why* + *how* = *who* equations. They take into account such givens as victims' background (friendships, habits, work); details about a crime scene such as its location and condition; objects missing from the scene or added to it by the perpetrator; and forensic findings such as DNA and blood-spatter analysis. Other clues taken into account are any that might suggest an offender's gender, race, language, and style of dress. The premise is that patterns exist and that certain types of people commit certain types of crime.

And serial killers, profilers say, tend to be white male loners between twenty years of age and fifty.

A sweeping statement. And a damning statement.

And a statement based on assumptions that contradict the true nature of loners.

A high percentage of serial killers have suffered some form of childhood abuse. Often they were raised by alcoholic, violent, or incestuous parents. Such experiences might understandably make an individual spend much time alone, but not necessarily because he is a loner. Instead, abuse typically creates shame and anger—emotions keyed inextricably with other people, with their reactions. Abuse survivors might yearn to connect, but fear the pain of revelation and rejection.

Growing up in severely dysfunctional families makes kids secretive. It is never a good idea to invite classmates home when Daddy is on a bender. These kids isolate themselves not for the joy of it, as loners would, but as a defense against ridicule. It is their fear of the reactions of their peers that drives them into solitude. Moreover, growing up in such households might damage a child psychologically. As we have seen, mental illness isolates adults, though it does not necessarily mean they are loners.

A typical profiling Web site cites "traits that seem to be universal" among serial killers. These include "disorganized thinking, bipolar mode disorders, a feeling of resentment towards society brought on by their own failings, sexual frustrations, an inability to be social or socially accepted." Here is a classic description of the pseudoloner who *yearns* for acceptance yet fails to receive it.

The Web site of an instructor who teaches criminal profiling at the university level expands on this picture of what he calls "psychologically harmed boys" whose horrific childhoods have rendered them "unable to develop the social skills that are precursors to sexual skills and that are the coin of positive emotional relationships." The instructor uses the terms "loner" and "serial killer" interchangeably: "By the time a normal youngster is participating in an active social life, the loner is turning in on himself and developing fantasies that are deviant. The fantasies are substitutes for more positive human encounters. . . . All the murderers knew that they had not had normal relationships, and they resented not having them; it was this resentment that fueled their aggressive, murderous behavior."

If we look at some of the last half-century's most famous serial killers—at actual cases—we find that they are anything *but* loners.

Charles Manson had a rough childhood. His mother was a prostitute—but Manson grew into a manipulative, social adult who surrounded himself with suggestible minions. Ted Bundy, who also had a rough childhood, was able to murder as many as thirty-four young women largely *because* of the good-natured charm he displayed when coaxing them into his car or into other lethal situations. John Wayne Gacy, whose father was a violent alcoholic, killed some two dozen young men by using his social skills to persuade them that he would find them jobs in the construction business. Gacy, who performed in a clown costume for hospitalized children, was a community activist and a leader in the Junior Chamber of Commerce. The Jaycees elected him Man of the Year. Andrew Cunanan, whose bloody cross-country killing spree ended with the shooting of fashion designer Gianni Versace, was a notorious partygoer and social climber whose fondest dream was fame. Wayne Williams, convicted of killing dozens of children in Atlanta, had been spoiled and doted on as a child. Williams was a gregarious, energetic music promoter who ran his own radio station and who secured victims' trust by telling them he was a talent scout. The list of sociable serial killers goes on and on.

IT'S NOT JUST serial killing. As profilers would have it, loners are up to a lot of other mayhem as well. In fact, if they are to be believed, we are far too busy hunting and hurting others and burning down their houses to have *any* time left to ourselves.

A profile issued by the Royal Canadian Mounted Police warns that "stalkers exhibit these common behaviours": substance abuse, a penchant for violence and for threatening others, possession of weapons and, of course, "loner, outsider behaviour."

In its official profile of a type of sex offender known as "the Gentleman Rapist"—more talkative, insecure, and nerdish than his muscular counterpart, "the Power Rapist"—the National Center for Women & Policing warns that "this offender . . . is probably seen as . . . gentle, quiet, and passive" and "is considered a loner. His solitary pastimes include reading, watching television, and surfing the Internet."

On a Christian Web site, a list of "Typical Satanism-Related Crimes" includes "Murder (fairly rare, and essentially by loners)." Good to know.

• • •

THE FBI'S JOHN Douglas is hailed as one of profiling's pioneers, and today is in great demand as one of its spokespersons. In his book, *The Anatomy of Motive,* coauthored with novelist Mark Olshaker, Douglas plays fast and loose with the l-word, often using it to describe perpetrators whose behavior and motive indicate anything *but* a true loner.

On the day in 1996 when a gunman massacred sixteen children at a Scottish school, Douglas was asked on TV to profile the as-yet-unidentified killer. In his book, the profiler recalls what he told the interviewer: that the shooter would be "an asocial loner" who was "very, very angry" because "no one will listen" to him. It is not loners but *outcasts* who are angry when no one listens to them, yet Douglas went on to describe this "loner" as a malcontent who believes that "he has nothing of importance left in his life. . . . The entire community is to blame, his entire peer group is at fault." When the gunman was subsequently found, he *was* very angry—about having been dismissed from his post as a Scout leader, and about his neighbors' unkindness to him. Pedophile and creep though he was, Thomas Hamilton was also wholly outer-directed. He wanted company—inappropriate company, perhaps, but company nevertheless.

Douglas also recalls the case of a mental patient whose hobby was "sticking hundreds of pins into naked Barbies." This man, the profiler explains, "was a coward and a loner . . . taking out his anger and frustration about the way he is by punishing a fetish representative of what he aspires to but can never have." Again, this mistakes the reject for the loner. The man's act is a protest against his hated isolation.

Then come arsonists and bombers. Crimes that do not involve face-to-face confrontation tend to be perpetrated, Douglas believes, by "the loner, the asocial who has to put emotional distance between himself and everyone else" and is "among the most cowardly of all." He describes one Washington State firebug as "a loner" yet also, in the same passage, describes this man as "very lonely." Before his arrest, the arsonist had spent much time socializing in bars. A letter he wrote in jail noted that it had been "very painful to lose so many valued friends" as a result of his conviction.

Another non-face-to-face case for which Douglas was consulted involved the discovery that someone had been secretly urinating into bottles of the liquid with which workers cleaned their computers in a busy office. Developing a profile of the mysterious urinator, Douglas speculated on the sort of employee who tends to go in for sabotage: "Is he always sitting by himself at lunch?"

This profiler is not finished with loners yet. "Assassin personalities tend to be white male loners with self-esteem problems—no surprises there," Douglas declares. He cites a San Antonio gunman who began firing at random into a crowd during a parade. The gunman was a truck driver—"an inherently solitary profession," Douglas notes. (As is the composing of songs and the writing of novels.) Moreover, the killer's landlord "characterized him as a quiet loner."

This killer was ill. Suffering from paranoid delusions, he believed the CIA was after him, and he had been struggling with severe post-traumatic stress disorder ever since surviving a bad road accident. "The mere fact that someone keeps to himself doesn't mean he's going to be an assassin personality," Douglas offers. Well, thanks! "But without having anyone around to observe him, you don't know if and when he might become dangerous."

LAW ENFORCEMENT HAS evolved over time. For one thing, police no longer employ phrenology, the study of cranial bumps, as a means of identifying criminals. Will loner-bashing, too, become merely an artifact, a sad thing of the past?

Dean Wideman hopes so. The Houston-based consultant has worked on thousands of cases nationwide involving the collection, preservation, examination, and analysis of forensic evidence. Wideman asserts that in his business the l-word is far too often "too loosely applied, or even misapplied—and the foundation for using it isn't always there." In failing to specify what they mean by "loner," he tells me, profilers and the reporters who quote them don't take into account the finer textures that might better aid the identification process. For instance, "at what point is [the criminal] a 'loner'? Is he *always* alone or is he only alone around the time he does the crime? I try to stay away from that term myself," Wideman says. "In fact, I don't even think I've ever put it in any of my own reports. Investigatively, I've found that it doesn't add any value—although," he admits, "people *do* like to see it. They want to get the idea that [the criminal] is not somebody who's integrated into society. But the reality is often the exact opposite. A lot of killers are real social people whom you couldn't describe as loners even generally. It's rare even in my research for me to come across an actual loner."

Internationally known forensic scientist and criminology instructor Brent Turvey agrees. "Most FBI profiles which are published in the paper include the archaic suggestion that the offender is a loner who lives with his mother, and this is simply not always or even commonly the case. The profiles are quite commonly incorrect. The bottom line," Turvey notes, "is that most offenders have social connections until they are apprehended and then everyone deserts them. Offenders like Jeffrey Dahmer and John Wayne Gacy had lots of friends and very extensive social lives until they were arrested." It was only *then*, Turvey points out, that "nobody wanted to be associated with them. Hence Dahmer, for instance, was considered some kind of social outcast, which is simply untrue."

In her work as CEO of the Sexual Homicide Exchange, a Minnesota nonprofit dedicated to closing unsolved sex-murder cases, Pat Brown constantly finds it necessary to "dispel profiling myths," as she puts it. "I disagree that serial killers and psychopaths are loners," notes Brown, a profiler and investigator herself. Those neighbors so ubiquitously quoted in crime articles declaring that a certain suspect was a loner "are saying that simply because they were not in the creep's circle of acquaintances. For that matter, since neighbors hardly know each other anymore, that description could probably be used to fit a good half of the neighborhood. If he isn't a hell-raiser," Brown points out, "he gets called a loner."

It *is* true, she adds, that perpetrators she encounters in her work "tend to have a tough time keeping any kind of *real* friendship going. They use people, abuse people, and therefore most folks tend to distance themselves from them. Often it is said of suspects that they didn't get along with coworkers or have any close friends. Most of the time that's true. Once in a while you get a rare person completely separating himself from society—but that makes it much more difficult to stalk and abduct people. Many serial killers are married, are parents, are gregarious and friendly. They are also liars, weirdos and psychopathic manipulative failures. To sum it up, the term 'loners' is erroneous."

Reality is just one letter away.

"A *loser* who has a limited circle of people who will put up with him is more accurate," Brown says. "Losers, yes. Loners, no."

FOR THREE WEEKS in the fall of 2002, a mysterious sniper was picking off victims in the Washington, D.C. area, seemingly at random. A terrified nation waited breathlessly for the killer to be caught. During the wait, profilers were called in—and predicted that the sniper would be a white loner. Though they were dealing with an utterly baffling case, there was consensus on that point. Asked to characterize the shadowy figure who was wreaking havoc on his state, Maryland's governor announced, "It's a loner." An article on ABCNEWS.com was headlined, " 'Evil': Forensic Psychiatrists Say Sniper Is Likely a Self-Absorbed Loner."

But when the investigation was over, it had netted not one white man but two African-Americans. The elder, Gulf War veteran John Muhammad, was twice married and a father of three. Those who had known him expressed shock at his arrest. Muhammad, after all, *wasn't* a loner. "We played neighborhood ball together," an old friend told the *International Herald Tribune.* "John was cool." Muhammad's first wife told Britain's *Mirror* that the killer "enjoyed company."

The *New York Times* promptly called this case a prime example of profile glut. "Criminal profilers were the perfect filler" in newscasts during the spree, "always ready to offer an insight when the action lulled." The case was also a prime example of how wrong profilers can be.

"So much for the Chevy Astro van," smirked the *International Herald Tribune.* "And the twenty-six-year-old white loner."

But the matter would not rest. Articles appeared claiming that Muhammad and/or his teenage accomplice were "by all accounts" loners, despite previously published accounts that they were *not.* Loners would not be let off the hook. The press and the public wanted so badly for these killers to be loners.

A few days after the suspects were apprehended, the *New York Times* speculated on the nature of this kind of crime. "These days it is increasingly difficult to figure out who is a terrorist—or what that even means. Terror—as opposed to terrorism—may be inflicted by any loner with a vague political grievance and a gun." The message in the sniper case, the article concluded, transcends the fact of who these particular snipers were. "Leaderless revolutionaries, one-man armies, lone wolves angry at the world: you don't need a plane or a bomb to terrorize America," the *Times* mused. "Just one gun."

13.

bizarre as i wanna be

[ECCENTRICITY]

You might think you're the most ordinary person in the world.
The world begs to differ.

HOWARD HUGHES IS the subject of a lot more books and films than J. Paul Getty is. Both men were immensely rich. But about Getty, personally, all most Americans know is his name. Tell-all books about him do not clog the shelves of the biography sections in public libraries. There are quite likely no published descriptions of Getty straining on a toilet. Of Hughes, however, such details are readily available.

Similarly, we know and care little about the intimate moments of J. P. Morgan or Cornelius Vanderbilt. Their names conjure little in our minds beyond the chill of bank vaults and the thud of moneybags.

But Hughes: The billionaire aviator's name inspires shudders, giggles, clenched shoulders, as if his famous paranoia were contagious. References to Hughes and pictures of him pepper the legendry of vintage Hollywood. He makes cameo appearances in the works of *L.A. Confidential* author James Ellroy. In the twelve years before he died in 1976, Hughes lived as a hermit in the Beverly Hills Hotel. Accompanied only by bodyguards, he sat all day in a semidark bungalow. During those years, he avoided the public eye fiercely. Photographers were not permitted near him. His corporation demanded hefty fees of any newspaper that dared to print his name. While the other hotel guests played in the pool and strolled the grounds, Hughes sat in solitude brooding about germs and Russians.

Billionaires, as such, are interesting only up to a point. To the masses who find Hughes interesting, he is so not just because he was a billionaire, but because he was an *eccentric* billionaire. Not merely an eccentric billionaire, but a *reclusive* one. Crouching amid stacks of film canisters in that bungalow, ordering steaks from room service every few days but fasting in between, he is the classic American icon of eccentricity. He was an eccentric loner, a loner eccentric.

IT HAPPENS. STAYING apart from others—a lot, a little—renders us different. On bad days we are called crazy. On better days, though still not good ones, we are called eccentric. There is virtually nothing you can do about it. There is no escape.

Are you eccentric? *Webster's New World Dictionary* defines the word, which derives from the Greek *ekkentros*, off-center, as "deviating from the norm."

Perhaps you say *no way*. You know yourself as ordinary, even dull—a wage slave with kids and taxes and a Toyota. But we will not escape the raised eyebrow, the watchful neighbors who whisper about us. *She never has anyone over! His bedroom light is on at the strangest hours!* Being a loner might feel natural for you. It might seem nothing, might seem normal compared to some of what is taken for granted in America: tongue piercing, for instance, or eating ground-up spleens and eyeballs cooked in casings and called hot dogs, or keeping an arsenal of automatic pistols in the living room.

And yet even the dullest loners have been called eccentric just for being loners. Those loners might be surprised to hear it, irritated—*Do I look like Howard Hughes to you?* The loner in the plain white shirt and khaki shorts eating at Taco Bell is lumped together with the odd duck who lives up a tree and talks only in iambic pentameter. We need to come to terms with this. If you are a loner, whether you sleep on a bed of nails or a queen-size Sealy Posturepedic beside your perfectly ordinary partner, chances are that someone sometime will call you eccentric. Whether you like it or not. Whether or not you think it is fair.

IN A LANDMARK study launched in 1984, Dr. David Weeks of the Royal Edinburgh Hospital set out to examine the nature of eccentricity. Interviewing well over a thousand acknowledged eccentrics from both sides of the Atlantic, Weeks explored how these individuals perceived themselves and how, throughout their lives, they had been perceived by others. As his research progressed, certain characteristics surfaced which most of his subjects seemed to share. No matter how disparate the manifestations of their eccentricities—whether they dressed exclusively in

Crimean War uniforms or collected hundreds of lawn gnomes—
they had, Weeks found, a set of traits in common.

Most were either the only or eldest children of strict parents.
Most had vivid imaginations, were idealistic, and wanted to help
make the world a better place. Since childhood, they had recognized themselves as different. Noncompetitive, opinionated,
curious, intelligent, creative, these were classic nonconformists.
Largely because they felt no need to compete, they were notably
calm and stress-free and robustly happy. Most had offbeat eating
or living arrangements. Most had hobbies and most loved a good
joke. Many were single and, Weeks found, most were loners.

He was particularly concerned with determining whether
distinctions could be drawn between eccentrics and the mentally ill. They can—and solitude, Weeks found, has much do
with it. Eccentrics use their solitude very constructively, which
Weeks calls the single best indicator of mental health. (It is possibly Weeks to whom Dr. Raj Persaud, quoted earlier in this
book, refers when he marvels that some in his field laud the
ability to enjoy time alone.) By contrast, the mentally ill suffer
and are much worse off when left alone, Weeks writes. More
evidence of mental health among eccentrics is that they see
themselves as different, but feel no compulsion to change.
Mocked, they regard the mocker as the one who has a problem, not themselves. Sticks and stones.

"Simply put," Weeks concludes, "neurotics are miserable
because they think they're not as good as everyone else, while
eccentrics know they're different and glory in it." Rather than
feeling helpless or driven, "eccentrics act wholly according to

their own will," the doctor found, "and for the eccentric it is a positive, pleasurable experience."

Weeks's conclusions apply to eccentrics in general but also to loners specifically. Imaginative, curious, engaged in hobbies— that's us. Making excellent use of solitude—that's us. Creative, sense of humor, sure. Uh-oh.

WHETHER MANY ECCENTRICS are born loners or whether it happens when they learn, as small children, that others do not share their penchant for eating breakfast at 3 A.M. or keeping hornets as pets is a question for the nature-or-nurture department. But not all eccentric loners are treated alike. Some, like Hughes, trigger derision. Others—Emily Dickinson again— are hailed as heroes. Cruelty to some and kindness to others reflects the mob's motivations and favorite prejudices.

The eccentric loners who are admired or at least bemusedly tolerated are those who are perceived as having something to give. Poets, artists, musicians, scientists—when now and then they emerge from their cocoons, they bring beauty, entertainment, or inventions. They sing for their suppers.

Howard Hughes, who suffered from severe obsessive-compulsive disorder, had nothing to show for his solitude. No ouevre, no anthem, not one single transcendent thing. His solitude was a closed circle, shut on itself like the mythical snake that swallows its own tail, the ouroboros. Impatient as Hughes frittered away his years at the hotel, the mob stamped its feet in outrage: *What is he doing in there? What has he got to hide?*

They cannot bear being left out. Of anything—of clubs, of

games, of conversations. *Let me in*, they shout, pounding on doors, often on principle, often by instinct, when they do not even actually want in. It comes down to the old saw that not sharing is not nice. Those who share are, by the rules of the masses, good. Who, after a tornado has leveled every house in town but one, would sit and watch his neighbors starve? Expecting to be shared with is presumption, the myth of entitlement. Those not shared with feel furious and hurt and grapple with the possibility that someone might not like them. Thus loners, in general, who can be perceived as not sharing themselves, are judged harshly. Thus, when it comes to eccentric loners, those who give nothing are judged most harshly of all. They are given no quarter.

Hughes's solitude was "selfish," meant for no one, not an entertainment—paparazzi were not even permitted to "share" pictures of him with tabloid readers, nor reporters stories of him. This is why he became fair game.

In his memoir, *I Caught Flies for Howard Hughes,* the magnate's former bodyguard Ron Kistler describes Hughes's long, solitary stints in screening rooms, where he obsessively stacked boxes of the Kleenex he believed would guard him from disease. Dubbing Hughes "the king of the enema," Kistler recounts how his boss "sat on the toilet for 26 consecutive hours, groaning and rocking back and forth." Other scenes recall Hughes's bad aim in urinals, his dislike for bathing, his body odor, and his nasty domineering personality. Whatever sanctity Hughes found in his expensive inner sanctum drains away as his bodyguard reports on its dirty furniture, its heat, its odor, and Hughes's sitting there stark naked save a hotel napkin draped over his crotch.

· · ·

THE VAST MAJORITY of eccentric loners, being loners, live and die without ever becoming famous. But a few emerge into the limelight, their genius attracting more attention than, as loners, they perhaps relish. Before his death in 1925, the French composer Erik Satie, who collaborated with the likes of Pablo Picasso, Jean Cocteau, and Serge Diaghilev, was a full-blown celebrity surrounded by besotted acolytes. Yet he was forever a loner. As a young man, he founded a church, *L'Eglise Métropolitaine d'Art de Jésus Conducteur*, whose only member was himself. In his memoirs, the composer described his singular diet: "My only nourishment consists of food that is white: eggs, sugar, shredded bones, the fat of dead animals, veal, salt, coconuts, chicken cooked in white water, moldy fruit, rice, turnips, sausages in camphor, pastry, cheese (white varieties), cotton salad, and certain kinds of fish (without their skin)." Even if he was exaggerating in an effort to be an over-the-top Surrealist, it is an eccentric exaggeration.

Britain has always prided itself on breeding more eccentrics than any other country and being more tolerant of them as well. "England is the paradise of individuality, eccentricity, heresy," wrote the philosopher George Santayana. Dame Edith Sitwell, herself born into a family of famous eccentrics, declared eccentricity a peculiarly British trait, a national characteristic.

Tales are told of British aristocrats who never set foot outside their homes for years at a stretch. One of these was Sir Henry Harpur of Calke Abbey, Derbyshire, known during his lifetime in the eighteenth century as "the Isolated Baronet." His reclusiveness was a family trait; one of Harpur's twentieth-century descendants was a lord said to have communicated with his own children, who shared the house with him, solely by letter and never by speech.

Sitwell has written of Matthew Robinson, Lord Rokeby, who after attending Cambridge's Trinity College around 1735, became so fond of mineral baths on a visit to Aix-les-Bains in France that he secluded himself on the family estate in Kent and spent the bulk of his solitary days submerged in water. Sometimes it was the sea, in which he would paddle till he fainted from exhaustion. More often it was a pool in a greenhouselike enclosure near his mansion. His privacy guarded fiercely by a troop of cocker spaniels, Robinson would float on the still surface with his waist-length beard wafting around him.

His membership in the upper class—one cousin was an archbishop—allowed Lord Rokeby to escape most of the responsibilities that would otherwise draw him away from his treasured privacy and what Sitwell calls his "eternal baths." A few years later, another aristocrat, Captain Philip Thicknesse, also went into seclusion at an estate near Bath which he called, significantly, St. Catherine's Hermitage. It was here that Thicknesse wrote what he called "the Hermit's Prayer," in which God is implored "that I may view with rapture the inexhaustible volume of Nature, which Thou hast spread before mine eyes." Ensconced in his self-styled hermitage, the old soldier indulged the sensation of being the master of all he surveyed. He saw "the barks on the Avon, which I considered as messengers whom I have sent forth to fetch me Tea from Asia, Sugar from America, Wine from France, and Fruit from Portugal . . . I have obtained," he wrote, "that which every man aims at but few acquire: solitude and retirement."

During the eighteenth century, a fashion arose in which wealthy British landowners hired hermits to dwell on their grounds. It was felt that these hermits-for-hire lent the landscape an air of romance. "Nothing . . . could give such delight to the eye," Sitwell writes, "as a bearded 'ornamental hermit' clad in 'a goatish rough robe, doddering about amongst the discomforts and pleasures of nature.'" Charles Hamilton set aside a quarter of his large Surrey garden for the purpose. A treehouse-style hermitage was erected in Hamilton's garden, supported high above the ground on cunningly contorted stilts and gnarled roots. The hermit's sole possessions were to be a Bible, spectacles if necessary, a pillow, a floor mat, and an hourglass. He was to drink only water and subsist on whatever food was brought him from Hamilton's kitchen. He was to wear a loose robe at all times, and cutting his hair or nails or exchanging even a single word with any of Hamilton's servants was cause for dismissal. Hamilton's advertisement offered the hermit one hundred pounds a year, but payment would come only at the end of seven years. Another advertiser, this one in Lancashire, promised fifty pounds a year for life to a hermit who would occupy an underground cell equipped with as many books as he desired. Hermits also placed newspaper ads offering their services.

In the summer of 2002, a resident hermit was being sought for Shugborough, a Staffordshire stately home owned by the fifth Earl of Lichfield, the royal photographer. The advertisement specified that the hermit would be expected to dwell in a cave on the estate, shunning all human contact, and would be compelled to stay dirty and hairy—though the job was to last only for a few days, a special "solitude weekend." During that weekend, the public would be taken on tours of the grounds, including a visit with the hermit. Applications poured in from as far away as Pakistan and Poland.

"This is the first time the job of a resident hermit has been advertised in more than 250 years," Corinne Caddy, spokeswoman for the 300-year-old stately home, told a reporter before the hermit was chosen. "We have been stunned by the number of applications."

To many of those applicants, and to some extent the organizers of the job, it was no doubt a lark, a joke. Would it seem so hilarious if instead of a hired hermit the earl put on display a hired deaf-mute? A hired Zulu? Hermits are still safe to laugh at. To puzzle over like beasts at the zoo. To peer at and thus to invade, larking, the solitude for which they stand.

Most of us will never go all the way, will never be hermits. In fact, most of us will never do much that is outrageously bizarre at all. Still, many of us will be called eccentric. Just sitting around, we will. Unlike *crazy*, eccentric cannot be quantified or certified. It is not used in courts of law. They cannot lock you up for it. So, no big thing. We have been called worse.

14.

the sleeve said

[CLOTHES]

They dress for success. They dress for sex.
Clothes bare the soul, and thus betray us.

WHEN I WAS just starting out as a journalist, one of my first stories was about a nudist camp in a hot valley across the bay from San Francisco. When making arrangements to visit, I had been warned that most of the camp was off-limits to anyone clad in anything more than shoes and a hat. If I wanted to see the swimming pool, the shuffleboard court, the volleyball games, and the barbecue pit, I was told, I would have to undress.

This didn't bother me. However, it bothered everyone I told about my imminent visit. *Won't you be embarrassed? Aren't you scared?*

Of what? Of being naked? In front of a lot of strangers? No. That *no* rolled around and around in my mind like a billiard ball. It was so solid, so hard. Yet it made no sense. The prospect of being naked with strangers somehow had nothing to do with sex. I'm not an exhibitionist—well, not particularly. Anyway I knew the camp was not a meat market. Strict anti-ogling rules got offenders tossed right out on their naked heinies. Still, I would be naked in public. Not just in some relatively empty place, either, and not in the dark, but in the full light of day. It wasn't as if I had ever quite done *that* before.

So why was I gladly counting the days? Loner that I was, what bugged me was not the prospect of the camp, but the fact of wanting to go there.

The afternoon came. Beyond the parking lot, over a creek, began a trail barred by a woodburned placard, ranch-style, saying Clothes Cannot Be Worn Beyond This Point. Mine slipped off in a sec. The camp's vice president, who was my tour guide, slipped hers off as well, baring a pudgy body fully browned. We strolled out to the pool, where a country-western song was playing on someone's radio. Dozens of buttocks dipped and bobbed: smooth, slack, flat, fat, furred. Figures lazed around the deck. Buff and bronze. Aged and elephantine. Teenage and tender. One woman sipping a cool drink bore surgical scars across her back like satin stitching.

Some waved. Some glanced my way but, I realized, only because I was unfamiliar, not because I was wearing only a pair of eelskin sandals. Instantly they went back to their dog paddles, their sunscreen tubes, their crossword puzzles. Following my tour guide to the water's edge, I kicked my shoes off. In the blue depths, I could see tufts of pubic hair blooming brown and gold like sea anemones. *Why, oh why, does this feel normal?*

The vice president read my mind.

"Nudity," she said, palms together for a dive, "is the great equalizer."

THAT WAS IT. Not wearing clothes was not something to fear, but a *relief*. A liberation—not from tight buttons or the specter of provocation, as nudists and feminists will say, but, for a loner, from so, *so* much more.

As a signal of civilization, dressing is taken for granted. It is not a question of if, but what. Down these millions of years, it has become so *de rigueur*, so automatic, that many dress with amazing ease. They dress either without thinking or with regal deliberation, relishing the gradual accumulation of effects the way sovereigns must feel as silks and furs are drawn by servants up their arms and fastened at their necks. Each cloth and pattern proclaims some part of the body but, and more importantly, the body as the soul wants it to seem. Dressing is an act. It is, tacitly, a relationship. In any case, besides dressing purely for warmth, it is an intercourse.

This is me! cries the pant leg, the collar, the sock. Clothes prepare wearers to be seen. They are a uniform for an army of one. They signify. They advertise the self, package the self, offer up the self for inspection, for assessment, for classification, for its fate.

For loners, then, the idea of dressing is self-betrayal. Ironically, dressing the body means baring the soul. How can we reconcile the fact that nearly every time we step outside, we are doing the utmost nonlonerish thing? *Hey, lookee here.*

So what is lonerwear?

Some, perhaps without realizing why, wear outfits that hide them like tents. Cargo pants, overcoat, oversize top. *Nobody's here, just this big pile of fabric.* It works. So does dressing calculatedly like others, vanishing thusly into the crowd. Both of these tactics work, solving the problem of how not to tell too much.

But both, for some, cause other problems. Both are stealthy methods of *non*-dressing: so lacking in apparent artifice that they might as well be nudity. They work, but what of loners who love clothes, love their feel and cut, know clothes as art? For them, non-dressing is a wasted opportunity, a heresy. But for them, clothes are a never-ending dilemma, every sleeve a double-edged sword.

Their nonloner counterparts, who know clothes as art, delight in dressing. Theirs is a pure, directed delight. They know they will attract eyes. Strangers will comment, will ask where the shoes were bought, laud the tie. They want this. They are nonloners. They use clothes, as they use everything, to connect.

The loner who looks fabulous is one of the most vulnerable loners of all.

ANDREA SIEGEL, WHOSE book *Open and Clothed* explores how and why people dress as they do, interviewed several loners while conducting her research. "There can be something delicious," she told me afterward, "about the private discussion that goes on between self and wardrobe. One of the many advantages of being a loner is that often there's time to think, ponder, brood, meditate deeply, and figure things out to one's satisfaction. That is not as available," Siegel reasons, to those who must dress in a rush.

Some of her interviewees "were what I'd call 'closet loners,' in the sense that the persona they presented to the world did not reflect the kinds of clothes they kept in their closets. In other words, they had alternate wardrobes for unlived lives—as represented by the evening gown for the gardener, the dress for the male technical assistant, the ladies-who-lunch suit for the mother of toddlers who always wore sweats. These were parts of their unexpressed selves."

GIVEN THE FACT that, by definition, no two loners are alike, you would think there could be no possible thing as a "loner style." You would think. "The eccentric has always been a style enigma," muses the text of a photo essay in *Paper* magazine's fashion section. "No matter how hard designers try, they're never able to emulate the look. Here are some inspired looks from fashion's back door." Along with images said to depict the "Odd Couple" and the "Quirky" dresser is a dramatic photograph captioned "Loner." In it, a stick-slim model resembling Harry Connick, Jr. wears a noirish black suit with matching shoes, tie, and hat—askew—and a striped shirt whose unbuttoned cuffs dangle, enormous, from the ends of the coat sleeves.

A Singapore-based fashion Web site offers a commentary on which colors appeal to which personality types. "If you wear white," the text declares, "you have a positive, well-balanced, and optimistic personality. You are highly individualistic and a loner. You seek a simplified lifestyle free from outside pressures. If you wear gray, you are very much an individual. Many people may get the impression you are self-sufficient as you have excellent self-control and prefer to remain uninvolved. Those who wear gray have a tendency to isolate themselves"—as compared with, in the commentator's view, impatient but engaging orange-wearers and competitive red-wearers.

Nor can crime reporters resist using clothes in their attempts to characterize and create a recognizable uniform for the homicidal psycho-loner. Much was made of the Columbine killers' sunglasses and trench coats—though, as we have seen, their belonging to a "Trenchcoat Mafia" with numerous similarly attired members rendered the two teens not loners, but pseudoloners. After the middle-aged Norfolk farmer Tony Martin murdered a sixteen-year-old Gypsy boy, Martin was denounced by British papers as a loner, yet also, contradictorily, as lonely—appearing at a friend's home at all hours, aching for company. Martin lived alone amid his apple orchards, reported the Manchester *Guardian*, which added that the killer was "said to wear only navy blue."

There is something, I confess, to a uniform. No guesswork, no decisions, no variables. No personal data revealed. No provocations and no clues. Wearing uniforms signifying certain jobs, enrollment in certain schools, military status, and the like is to announce membership in a group. A mob. And thus the opposite of all a loner stands for. Yet, at the same time, it lets a loner disappear, just as we sometimes like to vanish in a crowd. Uniforms can be a relief. They are a type of nakedness.

My husband has a policy with clothes. His goal, as a loner, is to make it clear that his clothes mean nothing at all. That they make no statement about him.

They make statements, but not about him.

He wears beige cotton trousers and T-shirts. He buys the shirts at rummage sales, during the last hour when prices plummet and he can stuff all he wants into a grocery bag for a dollar. If a shirt is his size, if it lacks holes and stains, he takes it. The picture or slogan on it does not matter. Thus his closet is packed with shirts depicting mallards, slot machines, historic landmarks, bottles of malt liquor. *North Shore Surf Shop. UC Berkeley Engineering Club. Club Med. Lowriders de La Cañada.* The logos of cell-phone companies and defunct dot-coms and a magazine about bisexuals.

"If I wear whatever I pull from the closet, totally at random, it means I don't care." Caring would imply making a fashion statement and, for him, being a loner means being elusive, never letting others know what he is thinking. "If the shirt says I'm bisexual or an engineering student or that I went to Ixtapa, then that day whoever sees me will think that's what I am. The next day my shirt will have a completely different message. So what am I? A dorky nerd? A sporting guy? Hawaiian?" In the end, the conflicting messages all cancel each other out, becoming a blur. And in that blur, unseen, unreadable, the loner dwells.

I, on the other hand, have always had too many clothes. Many of them I get cheap, as he does. So I tell myself this is not profligate, not pointless. Thinking *I loooove this!* I picture myself in the platform shoes, the hot-pink jacket. I will never wear them. They will hang forever, waiting in the closet fruitlessly like sad clowns, while every day I seize the same camouflage—jeans, ever-so-unremarkable striped shirt. All those lovely perfect things with every passing year become less plausible for someone of a certain age to wear. Skintight T-shirts printed with pictures of fried eggs, Pokémon, goldfish. Rhinestone hairclips linger untouched in the bathroom, sparkling like foreboding butterflies.

If I were smart, I would resist this impracticable urge to buy and, instead, act like a Parisian: settling on one or two outfits that flatter and that neither say too much nor nothing. On the other hand there are nude islands in the Adriatic—I have heard of some, nudist banks and restaurants and all—where loners can fill their closets with art supplies or sporting goods or CB radios or anything but clothes.

15.

don't go there

[ENVIRONMENT]

We are happy living in one place, suicidal in another.
We ought to figure out why.

PROFESSIONAL HARPOONERS AND cross-dressing flamenco dancers feel more welcome when they live in some places than in others. Loners, too, have much to lose or gain from the landscapes in which we park our belongings. For us the warning signs might not be as obvious as those for cross-dressing flamenco dancers—or for intellectuals, gourmands, mixed couples, dukes. We all too often settle, unsuspectingly, for hell.

First consider the broadest strokes, the backdrop. Should we live in the town or the country?

Urban critics blast the anonymity of city life: the lack of eye contact, the lack of conversation, the coolness with which big-city neighbors ignore one another. Laissez-faire is an urban etiquette. City dwellers are too busy for boredom to stop them in their tracks and make them curious about the new tenant downstairs, the stranger walking a terrier in the park, the patron in the corner booth, dining alone. This is why cities are where fugitives hide in plain sight. And this is why loners who like living in cities like it.

The opposite—living in a remote cottage miles from the nearest paved road or shop—has its benefits, too. No casual visitors, no milieus in which one might run into those whom one does not want to see. Some loners love the countryside. It is a life of extremes, sacrifices, suited only to the very self-reliant.

It is in between these two that loners often feel cornered. Small towns are closed circles in which paths cross back and forth all day. It is an incessant bumper-car ride. *Hello, it's me again!* In small towns, villages, and suburbs, strangers recognize each other in the street, in stores, on line at banks and offices. It would be rude never to nod, never to speak. Idle chatter is the sound track to small towns, a music that drives most loners mad.

Many nonloners have a problem with city life. It makes them lonely. Ditto country life. Lonely. They are happiest in that middle zone, buffered from loneliness by the sight of familiar faces, the ease with which one can find a willing ear, converse, connect. The knowledge of all those connections, low-fi though they are, comforts the nonloner like knowing that a house has electricity even when all its lights are off. Mathematically speaking, loners are just the opposite. We thrive where population density runs to extremes—the city with a thousand residents on each block and the countryside with houses miles apart. The very aspects of city and country that nonloners fear and despise are those that whisper to the loner, *Welcome home.*

Welcome to lonerland.

AS FOR THE finer strokes, what *sort* of countryside, what sort of city, these are personal decisions. With some mitigating factors.

Deanne Stillman spent ten years researching and writing *Twentynine Palms*, her award-winning book about the murder of two young women by a U.S. Marine in the titular Mojave Desert town. Having loved the emptiness and freedom of the desert since childhood, the Midwestern-born Stillman came to a deep understanding of it in those ten years. Desert rats, as self-effacing locals call themselves, tend to share a lonerish outlook. Don't ask, don't tell. Mind your beeswax. Prickly, prohibitive flora and fauna echoed the human ethos. Stillman empathized with that.

"People go out there," she told me, "because they want to be left alone." Some come for the cheap housing. But a lot come "because they're hiding." Desert animals, like their human counterparts, know that heat can kill. For both, hiding is second nature. In an ambience that freeways and phones have done little to change since frontier days, "you're unchecked out there in the desert," Stillman says. "You're not being tracked." Tracked by the law. Tracked by society.

"People say the desert is desolate. Yet for me it's very much alive, full of surprises. As soon as I see those wide-open spaces, I can breathe," says Stillman. The desert's apparent emptiness, rich in hidden life, is a metaphor. Joshua trees make stark spiked silhouettes against the landscape—hinting in their stillness at passion, like loners, Stillman notes.

Deserts as lonerlands offer comparatively few stimuli that demand a response. A desert's colors and occupants and climatic variations are relatively few. Its flat pastels and fuck-you climate make it "a haven for people who can't function in cities," Stillman says. Yes, desert rats "will tell you to go screw yourself. Yes, they want to be left alone. But for the most part, they're happy." Adopting an unwanted spot where what wildlife there is looks like blades, needles, knives, and swords, where stings are lethal and the gila monster will not loosen its bite even after you sever its head, loners feel safe. The desert is one dry, drawbridgeless moat. Seashores and forests, by contrast, share a big disadvantage: Everyone you know will want to visit you there.

FOR LONERS, TRAVELING means never staying anywhere long enough for others to know us. In this way, it is a liberation. Hello, good-bye, without expectations, without obligations. No guilt. *Passing through.* Or not saying hello at all. It is an ideal state sometimes. You get all the advantages of being somewhere, seeing things, living, walking the streets alone or eating in restaurants alone, exploring and absorbing, and no one you know knows where you are. You see just strangers all day.

When I was seventeen, I spent six weeks touring America with a busload of other kids. I'd found the tour company's flyer in a travel agency and begged my parents to pay my way.

Shockingly, they did. It was not the same as traveling alone—that wouldn't happen for another two summers—but all the other teens were from other schools, other parts of L.A., so strangers to me. As time wore on, we got to know each other, but they were all having so much fun smoking and using their parents' credit cards to buy beaded moccasins in Arizona, leather jackets on Fifth Avenue, and elk antlers in Wyoming, that no one minded how I was. They did not require anything of me. Some of them found me funny, silent all day. We shared rooms at night. Other girls liked having me there. It was rather like having no one there. Partway through the trip, votes were taken: best-looking, most likely to succeed. I was voted most easygoing.

For me, every day was encyclopedic. I could not believe so much could be seen. Petrified forest, bayou, gulf, Mount Vernon, Custer's blood-soaked vest at the Smithsonian—tarantulas, June bugs, cockroaches, fireflies—if I could have stayed up all night every night, I would have.

The night of the fireflies—it was Alabama—the tour leader came to get me. A sturdy freckled redhead, probably the age I am now.

Come with me, she said. Leading me by the hand into a corridor. Then when we were alone: *I'm worried about you.*

Why? Blinking.

Because you're depressed.

I laughed. *I'm not.*

No need to cover it up. You'll feel better if you just cry.

I don't want to cry.

Would you like to call your folks?
No!
Well, what else can I do? There's no life in your eyes.

Except that it was the happiest six weeks I'd ever spent. When it was over, it stopped with an awful shudder, like a boulder dropped from a height. Why, I thought, do I ever have to stop moving?

AS CITIES GO, each has its own current and flavor. All offer loners the welcome opportunity to disappear into a crowd, but work, weather, and politics help determine where those crowds are coming from, whether they're mostly cool or mostly Fundamentalist or homophobic. And whether they're clad in shorts and tank tops and smiling on grassy lawns most of the year, or wrapped in overcoats and dashing indoors from the cold.

I have not lived in many cities, but can tell you that Los Angeles, for all the cruel things people say about it, is a loner's paradise.

There are clues in those cruel things. The residents are shallow, you say? Narcissistic? Hedonistic? Fine. To a loner, that means the residents are minding their own business. Too preoccupied with mirrors, too busy pleasing themselves to bother eyeballing the lone figure who does not wish to be examined. As it is, the city has so much else to be looked at. Billboards. Beaches. Stars. So much so that even the act of looking has an etiquette about it. Smooth. Through lowered eyelids.

So much flagrant display leads to endemic blasé. Only hicks stare. And in a town of spectacles, of the spectacular, loners can mutter *Hey! Look over there!* while slipping safely out of sight. There is in L.A. always something to draw attention away from you.

Nor are most things in L.A. precisely real. The fact of ever-present artifice makes for a million ready-made smoke screens and veils.

Sealing its fate as lonerland, L.A. is a freeway town. Virtually everyone over the age of fifteen spends a large portion of every day and night in cars—in most cases, as the brown sky attests, alone. Freeways are mobile empires comprising a million hermitages, each outfitted with its own array of ornaments, its own music. In Joan Didion's novel, *Play It as It Lays,* much is made of freeways by the protagonist Maria—a loner who has trouble even making conversation with anyone besides her sexual partner of the moment.

Life spent in cars affects the act of seeing. Through a moving window, everything seems fleeting. Now you see whatever, now you don't. By force of habit, those who spend their lives in cars tend to glance, rather than really observe. Their eyes slide off you like a freshly cracked egg slides out of its shell.

Weather makes a difference, too. When it immobilizes you, pins you at home, you are a prisoner, a sitting duck. *Then they can find you.* But mild climates offer loners a handy escape route. On lovely days, no one can assume you are at home. Unanswered phones, unanswered doorbells are not so perplexing on a lovely day. You might be anywhere.

BECAUSE LONERS ARE born everywhere, we end up living everywhere. We do not, have not, tended to single ourselves out as special, elite, requiring rarefied environments. Too often we have done the opposite; lived where we lived because our jobs were there, or families, or because we'd heard the schools were good there, or that we would love a place with changing seasons. Then, no matter what, we put our noses to the grindstone. We take living there as a fait accompli, a fact. Too often we are miserable somewhere without realizing why. We blame ourselves for not buckling down, settling in, fitting in. The problem is the place, but too often we do not see this, we will not allow ourselves to see this. It's the same old thing: *This is a friendly town, so what's your problem?*

Asthmatics are better off in arid climates. Gays and lesbians feel more at home in San Francisco than Riyadh. To the nonloner, or the self-reproaching loner, the fact of being a loner is not comparable to those other determinants. It is not a matter of life and death, we tell ourselves. It is not a matter of breathing or of execution by stoning. But home is the crucible of living. Homes have living rooms. So how can living not be a matter of life or death?

16.

absolutely, totally alone

[SOLO ADVENTURERS]

They call us geeks and scaredycats.
Let's see them sail around the world alone.

WE SAY WE are loners. But how alone, most of the time, are we? Aloneness comes in stages, degrees, like those science lessons in which a cross section of the human body is projected on a screen and the teacher removes transparencies, one by one, so that first the renal system disappears and then the respiratory system. Then the cardiovascular, reproductive, and digestive systems. Then the muscles go. Circulatory system. Brain. Until nothing is left but bones.

Alone-in-a-crowd we know best of all. We feel it nearly every time we set foot outside our front doors. The environments taken for granted as most normal, most mandatory—school and office, church and club, restaurant and public-transit system—are guaranteed to make us feel alone in a crowd. Faces fill the entire scene, a repeated motif, like polka dots. A swarm of arms, so close you sometimes touch them. Not on purpose. Brushing past, bumping.

Even this first stage can be further subdivided into crowds you *know* and crowds of strangers. Do you recognize those polka dots? Must you acknowledge those brushes and bumps? Must you speak? In this sense, school is one way and subways are the other.

Alone-in-a-crowd can give curious comfort, like a swath of pillows. It has color. Action. Stuff to see and overhear. And we can disappear. The bigger the crowd, the less chance you will be singled out.

The next stage is being alone out there just out of sight of others, though you know others might appear any minute. Walking alone down the sidewalk of a quiet street. Arriving at the beach before the other surfers.

The next stage is being alone behind walls—armor, either the steel walls of a car or plaster ones at home. This is the safest stage of all, the most controlled. It is the one in which loner-haters think we spend all our time. They picture us hiding behind our curtains, hurting, too hateful or mad or cowardly to face the world.

Which brings us to another stage. The state of being *absolutely, totally* alone. Being the only human life form for dozens of miles, hundreds of miles around. The solitary creature up against the great unknown, the wilderness. Weeks alone, all alone, so far from signs of civilization that you are truly on your own. No one can hear you scream.

An expedition, mission, quest whose primary criterion is that it be done solo. *Sail around the world alone. Survive in the South*

Pole alone. It has been done. Not by your average loner, not by anyone like me. There is solitude, and then there is solitude. The real acid test. It has been met—so who are they calling cowardly now?

SIX HUNDRED YEARS ago, even the most adventurous travelers and the hardiest loners drew the line at traveling alone. The unknown was truly unknown, and in a very real sense Satan was held to be hiding around every corner. Peasants lived and died without ever leaving their villages. Religious pilgrimages were just about the only legitimate reason for traveling, and pilgrims, as Chaucer could tell you, moved in packs. Explorers and navigators had massive entourages. Sailing solo beyond sight of land before the age of ship-to-shore technology was suicide. Even the most lonerish loner might rather spend his life in a busy marketplace than venture out and die.

To the modern loner, the increasing viability of solo travel is a dream come true. Every railway in the world, every hostel, sees a constant stream of solo travelers. It has become no big thing. Teenage girls do it.

The solo *expedition,* traveling beyond reach, is a big thing still and will always be. To the loner, such an adventure promises epiphanies, wonders never to be forgotten, elemental challenges, confrontations with the ultimate and the self. Success or death. The very essence of a loner's life, larger than life.

To nonloners, it promises epiphanies and tests as well, but of the opposite kind, so they take up the challenge, too. To them the prospect of being so absolutely, totally alone is horrific, the closest you can get while still alive to hell. Thus, for both loners and nonloners, the test is of superhuman courage. But for nonloners, the self-reliance on which survival depends is a terrible hardship—thus momentous. For loners, the self-reliance is bliss—thus momentous. For nonloners, the victory is that of having survived torture. For loners, the victory is that of having lived truly alone, thus truly lived.

BEFORE SETTING OFF to row alone across the Atlantic in 1969, John Fairfax had had a wild life. His roller-coaster romances had been punctuated by stints as a smuggler, a pirate, and an Amazon explorer. Yet a loner he certainly was, and was not afraid to admit it.

Training in London for the voyage—in which he would man a small rowboat single-handedly from Gran Canaria to Miami—Fairfax looked forward to being at sea for months on end with only himself for company. Rowing on a Hyde Park lake, he found that "on sunny days, surrounded by cheerful couples and boatloads of kids merrily bumping into each other, I had trouble concentrating. . . . I preferred the cold, windy, gray days, when I found myself almost alone. My mind could then retreat into itself, tentatively tasting the loneliness . . . and liking it." His experiences up until that point, his brushes with all manner of characters on water and land across three continents, had made Fairfax "more than convinced that rowing across the Atlantic in itself would be peanuts compared with my struggle against humanity."

He assessed that struggle with a wry and unapologetic

humor. A less secure man might have wasted his energy on self-doubt or futile attempts to "fit in," but not Fairfax, who indulged what some might call disparate facets of himself: athlete, happy loner, shameless show-off.

At sea, Fairfax slipped immediately into the carefree lifestyle that he had anticipated so eagerly. Charting his course, rowing nonstop for hours at a stretch, he was his own boss. Laziness or sloppiness and their repercussions would be entirely his fault. Everything depended on him. A small human being and a small boat seem smaller and smaller the farther out they go on an open sea. Fairfax observed the changing weather, the vastness of water and sky, the fishes that followed his boat: quintessential fullness and quintessential emptiness all in the same stretch of horizon. Loners know this feeling, the *all* that lies in seeming nothing, the vibrancy of stillness. Waking with the sun every day, Fairfax came to realize what mattered to him and what did not. Seeing no use for the synthetic measurement of time, he threw his only clock overboard. He did not despatch his transistor radio, but scorned it, switching it on for shorter and shorter periods each day and sometimes not at all. A sailor who was less of a loner might have welcomed even battery-operated companionship, but "I loathed having my solitude shattered by the sound of human voices chattering," Fairfax would later recall. "All I craved, and even this only now and then, was a good concert." Even the diary in which he recorded his progress came to feel like a hindrance. "I want to think," Fairfax complained to the diary itself. "Writing simply spoils everything; it's like having company."

He missed his girlfriend. "It is not a thing I yearn for very often," he noted, "but today I really wish I were home . . . a beautiful girl sprawled all over me, purring. Gee, how many times I have done so—and yet, at the end, I always got bored with it and wished I were where I am now." After months without human contact, Fairfax was invited aboard a passing German ship. The German crew was kind and gave him delicious treats, but "the whole episode struck me as odd and unreal," Fairfax reflected afterwards. "I very much needed the goods they could supply me with; but once these had been supplied I craved for the solitude that had been my own for so long." Back on his boat, he felt only relief. "Loneliness" was for a loner like himself not "a specter to be feared, but more a cherished companion without whom I was at a loss." So much so that, spotting another ship a few nights afterward, "I switched off my torch, lest they see it . . . and watched it disappear."

SAILING ITSELF IS a lonerish pursuit, sweeping the sailor away from land and all it represents. Sailing solo is one step beyond. The San Francisco Bay Singlehanded Sailing Society—a recreational club that stages solo boat races between San Francisco and Hawaii—is one of many such clubs around the world.

"The running joke," says solo sailor Rob McFarlane, "is that it's the club for people who don't have friends. It's a racing club, *not* a social club."

For McFarlane and the other members, sailing alone "is the best way to travel. It's like breathing. It's absolutely normal. You don't even think about it. Everything is on your own terms, and you get to sidestep all those 'people' issues that get in the way" when a crew is involved.

McFarlane used to do the crew thing, but it wearied him. "People would show up late and be all grumpy, and that spoiled it." He still relishes the day he bought an autopilot, which makes a crew unnecessary. Today he lives alone on his boat in a marina and commutes to his job at a nearby lab.

On a long solo voyage—the Hawaii jaunt takes about fifteen days—solo sailors face the problem of leaving their vessels unguarded while they sleep at night. Club regulations urge members to "keep a sharp lookout at all times," though this is pretty much a contradiction in terms if one is to sleep at all. There are ways to illuminate a boat so that larger vessels can see it from some distance away, but absolute vigilance around the clock just isn't possible.

"Either you get run over or you don't," McFarlane shrugs. "You're risking basically everything. It's up to you whether you choose to think of it as stupidity or as fun."

He knows which it is for him. During Hawaii runs, he tosses a "dinner line," a fishing line outfitted with large lure, over the side. Bobbing in the wake, the lure attracts tuna and mahimahi—dinner.

"People always ask, 'Aren't you scared of sailing alone?'" McFarlane says. "Well, if you're good company for yourself, you're going to like it. If you're not, you're going to hate it. I've never been good with people." Sailing solo "means you're not dependent on anyone to enjoy anything. And it's a total blast. It's unbelievable."

· · ·

GERARD D'ABOVILLE was one of those who was going to hate it. When he decided to row solo across the Pacific in 1991, solitude stood out in his mind as a handicap, a hardship akin to storms and sharks. The Frenchman was no loner. Waiting in Japan to begin the sojourn that would land him, four months later, in Washington State, d'Aboville steeled himself "to grapple with my own solitude . . . before it seized me in its own invincible grip." His sense of dread was further reinforced by port officials, the press, and the public in Japan, a nation "where individual exploits are uncommon, where group decisions are the rule"—and where as a result the very idea of his project "ran into a stone wall of incomprehension."

"I have chosen the ocean as my field of confrontation, my field of battle," d'Aboville wrote, tellingly applying a military metaphor. "I am a resistance fighter in a war I invented for myself. . . . The enemy is me."

RICHARD E. BYRD was no loner, either. Yet when a group expedition turned into a solo engagement, the celebrated Arctic adventurer came to see merits and marvels in solitude that were—for him—utterly unexpected. An adventurous admiral whose exploits were magazine fodder for an enthusiastic public, Byrd elected to establish a weather station deep in the Antarctic, near the South Pole, in 1934. A team of hardy men was originally to occupy the Boston-built hut along with Byrd, but the last minute found his would-be companions turning back and Byrd settling in alone. And thus he stayed for four and a half months, as temperatures outside the hut dipped to 83 degrees below zero. Even a lifelong loner would find such surreal conditions harsh. Byrd could only describe the early days of his adventure in the most sepulchral terms. Sunk in "a funereal gloom," he speculated that "this is the way the world will look to the last man when it dies."

But time changed that. Byrd became meditative. "Harmony, that was it! That was what came out of the silence . . . a gentle rhythm, the strain of a perfect chord. . . . I could feel no doubt of man's oneness with the universe." Just as the sailor John Fairfax would observe aboard his tiny boat on the Atlantic a generation later, Byrd in his chilly hut discovered that "I wish very much that I didn't have to have the radio." Day by day, he was learning many things that nonloners seldom learn. They neither wish to learn these things nor ever are, as Byrd was, forced to learn.

"My thoughts seem to come together more smoothly than ever before. . . . I am better able to tell what in the world is wheat for me and what is chaff," the admiral observed. "Solitude is an excellent laboratory in which to observe the extent to which manners and habits are conditioned by others. . . . A life alone makes the need for external demonstration almost disappear . . . when I laugh, I laugh inside; for I seem to have forgotten how to do it out loud. This leads me to think that audible laughter is principally a mechanism for sharing pleasure." It sounds remarkable, coming from the pen of a celebrity whose charm was a fulcrum for his fame. "How I look is no longer of the least importance; all that matters is how I

feel." Byrd later called it "a great experience" despite a ventilation problem in the hut that nearly killed him. "I felt more
alive than at any other time in my life," he declared in his memoirs, "my senses sharpened in new directions, and the random
or commonplace affairs of the sky and the earth and the spirit, which ordinarily I would have ignored if I had noticed them
at all, became exciting and portentous."

FOR HIS BOOK, *The Story of a Shipwrecked Sailor,* the novelist
Gabriel García Márquez interviewed Luís Alejandro Velasco,
who had been a crewman aboard a cargo vessel that sank
abruptly off the coast of South America. Velasco, who made
his way to a life raft, was the sole survivor. His solitude was not
only unplanned, but also was spawned by tragedy. Nor was
Velasco a loner. He told Márquez how much he had enjoyed
his crewmates' companionship, what a team they had been.
Floating on the raft just after the sea closed over the sunken
ship, "I thought it would take them at least two or three hours
to rescue me," Velasco recalled. "Two or three hours seemed
an extraordinarily long time to be alone at sea."

But the hours stretched into a whole night. As darkness
spread, Velasco believed "I wouldn't be able to overcome the
terror." Then at daybreak, "the sea's surface grew smooth and
golden." To the sailor's surprise, "for the first time in my twenty years of life, I was perfectly happy."

GROWING UP AMID the green hills and wild, rocky shores of
the New Zealand countryside, Naomi James savored being a

loner. Nor did her first trip abroad, a solo stint in Europe soon after finishing high school, change anything: "I liked the feeling that being alone in a crowd gave me. I liked to feel myself apart from the people and their worries," she later recalled. "I found that I preferred not knowing anyone." Biking around Austria, "I spoke to no one."

When, in 1977, James set out to sail single-handedly around the world, old salts warned her that the route she had chosen entailed months at a stretch with no hope of human contact. "To most people," she observed, "the most daunting feature of this voyage would have been the length of time spent alone. To me that wasn't important at all. I don't even have the patience to talk over the trivialities of life with people" under ordinary circumstances, on land, which "has driven me to prefer silence because I don't have the strength of mind or the lack of manners to tell people I'm bored to death."

At sea, she was contented with just a cat for company. Pragmatic after the cat was swept overboard to its death, and after she herself sustained injuries during an accident, James shatters the image of the loner shackled by melancholy, nursing every sorrow. Mishaps tested her, and she bobbed to the surface emotionally and physically every time. Fond as she was of her faraway fiancé, another solo sailor, "I'm a natural loner because as long as I know that Rob is alive and well I don't really worry about him. He has his life to live and I've got mine, and if I can survive then I'm sure he can." Throughout the voyage James displayed courage, a defiant optimism that she carried like a flag even after her boat capsized several times—

and, single-handedly, she righted it. While relatively unafraid of the open sea, "I have always been slightly afraid of other people," she confessed in her account of the voyage, "imagining that they are looking down at my faults and finding obvious inadequacies. I feel that I am out here," James explained, with a loner's logic, "to escape criticism . . . to prove that I am a rational, self-dependent and capable human being." It is onshore, among others, she wrote, that the real pains and perils lie. Processing these gave James a purpose, a goal that demanded more bravery and led to a grander accomplishment than ordinary people can imagine. Aboard, alone, "I succeed or fail by my own endeavours without any influence from the outside world."

After a two-and-a-half-month stretch with no human contact, James was thronged by reporters as she sailed into Cape Town for supplies. One journalist "asked me if I was glad to see people again," James confessed, "and I'm afraid I pulled a face."

Many nautical miles and near misses later, the voyage was done. "I was," James concluded, "never ever bored."

WHAT IF YOU were alone at sea? How would you do? *What* would you do? What if you were marooned? Once in a newspaper I saw a tiny article about a woman who had been rowing in the South China Sea, got lost, and wound up on a tiny islet, where she survived for three weeks by eating toothpaste before being rescued. She had lived in the dorm room next to mine at UC Santa Barbara. I kept wondering what she had thought about all those days under the turquoise satin sky, feet in the sand. Most of us will never be that alone. So alone that even all our fantasies about being alone, our desert-island dreams and Captain Nemo dreams and *Twilight Zone* dreams of depopulated towns in which we wander, loose-limbed, picking what we need off store shelves—would be revealed as cartoons, counterfeits. There is a real thing.

Solo adventurers are our version of Olympians. Of Nobelists or Green Berets. Elites. Showing the world what loners can do. Loners at their bravest and sanest and strongest. Buff loners. Loners who laugh at death.

And who prove that not only they but we are not afraid of the one thing that is for nonloners one of the scariest. It frightens admirals. It is solitude and we are not just unafraid of it, but love it. We are totally at home in it, as pilots are at home in the sky and sailors at sea. Solo adventurers reveal that in this arena we win, we *kick nonloners' asses* and when the ship wrecks, we will survive.

They are our proof. They are legends in real life whose sagas should be required reading for every new loner generation. Archives that can comfort, inform, inspire. Are we all recluses? Failures? Wimps? We can be heroes.

17.

smiling bandits

*For fear of raising little killers, parents persuade
little loners to play volleyball.*

O N WINTER VACATIONS in desert towns, I paddled back
and forth across motel pools, peaceably alone. I floated on
inflated rafts. I dove for dimes I threw myself. I did handstands,
holding my breath. I acted out scenarios in which I was cast
overboard from pirate ships or was a dugong. I would glide, submerged, alone, glassy sunbeams slicing the shallow end.

In pools, the idea of needing playmates was especially
ridiculous. Around me other kids, siblings and strangers to each
other, formed phalanxes for a day, head-butting and cannon-
balling, caroling *Maaarco. Pooolo.* So it was that after I had
played alone for ten minutes or so, my mother would come up
and seize my swimsuit strap.

Swim up to that kid this instant and say hi.
To who?

To someone. That girl. Anyone.
What for?
Because they'll all think you're weird if you don't.
Who cares? I'll never see them again after to—
Get the hell over there.
So I would go. Watching my mother watching me.
Hello, my name is—
I played. I was not all there, but I played. At sunset, the families toweled themselves dry and went back to their rooms to change for dinner at the smorgy.

On vacation and at home, I played alone if I could get away with it. Playing alone means never being forced to put Barbie and Midge and Ken through halfwit dialogues somebody else thought up. Playing alone means never having to play someone else's favorite game.

MY FRIEND JANE remembers her childhood, like mine, spent very much alone. She had three siblings, and the neighborhood was full of kids. Sometimes she joined a game but mostly she went wandering alone. Strolling to Sav-On or the vacant lots, climbing a giant elm and reading every last Hercule Poirot mystery.

Looking back on that, Jane marvels. She has three kids of her own now and marvels at how much has changed since she charted her singular course across her own youth. Children's social lives today are almost wholly in the hands of grownups. The informal, magical spontaneity with which Jane shaped her afternoons back then has been replaced with the rather clinical convention of playdates, in which kids' rendezvous are arranged days or weeks in advance by their parents.

"This playdate mentality," Jane seethes. "It really bothers me. It isn't natural."

Jane's eleven-year old, eight-year-old, and four-year-old do not wander the neighborhood as she did, or play in the front yard or the street. Nor do they play alone. Instead, they make lists and submit them to her, stating which of their classmates they would like to see after school. From a photocopied chart sent home by their teachers, including all the students' addresses, phone numbers and parents' names, Jane calls the mothers of the children in question so that dates and times can be arranged. It must be planned in advance: at whose home the kids will play, and who will drive whom where. This is the price we now pay for a world that seems no longer safe, where kids are plucked from their trikes and pulled into hell. Parents face all sorts of new fears: Will their children be attacked by criminals or become criminals themselves? Will their children be lonely, be loners, or be too socially inept to grow up and get jobs?

All elements of chance are taken out of it, Jane says, and once the kids are brought together for a playdate, they are watched by the adult whose home it is. Afterwards, when the visiting child's mother or father arrives to collect him, the adults discuss what the kids did. *First they played with their Gameboys. Then they had a snack. Then they watched cartoons.*

It's awkward, Jane says, and contrived. But also the vigilance bothers her, "the hovering parent constantly ensuring that everything is going fine." Combined, it puts all social interaction onto a microscope slide, controlled and watched. It enforces the concept of right and wrong ways to socialize.

And *not* socializing is not an option.

YOU WOULD THINK parents would be pleased with a child capable of entertaining him- or herself. Think of the advantages. Such a child learns to be resourceful, independent, learns to concentrate. Playing alone, a child will not get into fights. Solo pastimes hone creativity. Reading. Writing. Crafts. Acting out dramas in which the lone player must devise the plot, portray every character, come up with costumes and a denouement. You would think parents would appreciate this. You'd think they'd be grateful. But they're not.

Parents today are all too well-versed in tales of friendless children who grow into murderers.

One day in March 2001, San Diego-area high-school student Charles Andrew Williams sprayed his classmates and school administrators with gunfire, killing two and injuring a dozen. Papers in the aftermath ran a quote from a classmate calling Williams a "loner type." It was an echo of the coverage following 1999's Columbine shootings, after which papers promptly called killers Dylan Klebold and Eric Harris the l-word. The day after the shootings, the *Seattle Times* called both boys "loners, misfits."

But the mislabeling of pseudoloners as loners which affects adult criminals applies to youthful ones as well. Some kids, like Jane and me, *like* to play alone. Others, on the other hand, are outcasts.

Charles Williams wanted acceptance. He strove to impress peers with his bass-playing and skateboarding, but his efforts backfired. They teased him for bragging and for not being very skilled. The BBC reported that kids at school had called him names: dork, freak, nerd. Days before the shooting, Williams told classmates what he was going to do. One of them reportedly sneered, accusing him of being too much of a coward to go through with it.

Klebold and Harris were not quite loners, either. The "Trenchcoat Mafia" of which they were the leaders numbered as many as fifteen kids who affected attention-getting garb and habits: black berets and sunglasses, copies of *Soldier of Fortune*, Nazi salutes. A far cry from the little loner floating calmly in the swimming pool.

In a less fearful era, little loners did not worry their parents. Then again, those were times when kids were considered best seen and not heard. It was expected that they should amuse themselves. William Morris, who throughout his solitary youth was close only to his sister, was impassioned instead with forests, gardens, flowers and birds—which would be his favorite subjects when the adult Morris became a poet, an artist and one of his era's most prolific designers.

It is different today. *Don't be shy* comes the chorus from parents, teachers, counselors, coaches. Dr. Mel Levine, childhood expert and author of *A Mind at a Time*, has said he receives numerous queries from parents worried about a child who always plays alone. The parents, Levine says, make a point of asking the child to go out and play with others, to no avail. So they come to him asking, "How hard should we push?"'

Levine wisely tells them that the answer depends on the child. Some kids, he says, play alone by choice, and some do not. And even the choices of the small should be respected.

So the bully or the sad-sack outcast is not the same as the child who chooses to play solo games. The first two have a problem. The loner has no friends or few friends not because of failure or bad behavior but because he chooses so carefully. Loners *can* play well with others—the *right* others, maybe just one other. Certainly not tons of others, picked for them at random.

Children are not born with social skills. They must be taught to say please and thank you. Loners should learn these things as well as others should, if not learn them even better, so that later in life their politeness and empathy can get them through sticky situations.

BUT WHAT ARE parents to do when everywhere they look are warnings that they might be raising psychopaths? One Massachusetts clinical-case manager, interviewed for her local paper, offered a list of "warning signs for violent children and adolescents." On the list, typically, was "isolation, being what is known as a loner." Yeah, but that could also be on a list of ways to identify a genius.

Gifted children walk and talk at an early age, have vivid imaginations, high powers of concentration, love to read, and spend a significant portion of their time alone. Parents who fear raising snipers might be raising composers.

. . .

AND THEY MIGHT be doing everything they can to keep such children from becoming what they were born to be.

In his book, *The Blank Slate*, MIT psychology professor Steven Pinker confronts the nature-versus-nature question. Firmly on the "nature" side, he decries the conviction—dominant in the West for the last several decades—that babies are born "blank slates" whose eventual talents and tendencies are solely products of their environment. The idea that children are born equal in every way, and equally malleable, has in Pinker's view wrought incalculable damage.

"The 1990s," he writes, "was the Decade of the Brain and the decade in which parents were told they were in charge of their babies' brains. The first three years of life was described as a critical window of opportunity. . . . Parents of late-talking children were blamed for not blanketing them in enough verbiage." He quotes Hillary Clinton's declaration that the first three years "can determine whether children will grow up to be peaceful or violent citizens, focused or undisciplined workers, attentive or detached." There is, Pinker warns, "no science behind these astonishing claims."

By contrast, he cites research evincing that "all human behavioral traits are heritable"—that is, genetically determined, inborn. Such traits, as discussed elsewhere in this book, include amiability or disagreeability, aptitudes for language, and the like. As profound an orientation as lonerism surely counts among them as well.

Thinking of children as blank slates, Pinker writes, "can make us forget they are people."

Thus, when parents force—or persuade, which is the word nice parents with nice kids use for forcing—little loners to join sporting teams or the Scouts, they think they are writing on blank slates. The result, as adult loners know who have lived through Little League, can be disastrous. Catcalls. Alienation. Feelings of failure. The presumption that kids together are *happy* kids is like the presumption that all plants need the same amount of water.

Too young to defend themselves—too young to realize what it is about them that requires defense—little loners go along with the game. Wanting to please parents who say *This is for your own good*, they pick up the bat. And part of themselves, deep down, switches off.

In Bluebirds, I did not learn what they wanted me to learn. I did not have the fun they wanted me to have. This went on for years—from Bluebirds into Camp Fire girls.

Largely in an effort to raise stronger, more self-confident girls, the past decade saw an unprecedented rise in the profile of female athletes and athletics. Not just girls' teams but boys' and coed teams abound: in 2002 it was estimated that more than 20 million American children were enrolled in some kind of out-of-school sports program. While this is fine for many energetic, social kids, it is a nightmare for the quarterback who wants to be home, reading *Madeleine* books or building a robot.

Team time, for loners, is wasted time. The minutes tick away.

Lost. Stolen. Minutes that might have been fun, minutes spent feeling normal. Stolen.

WHEN PARENTS ARE in charge of children's social lives, and when parents know that networking leads to success, they enforce networking from the cradle onward, now more than ever, whether it suits the individual child or not. Parents are "so determined for their children to be popular," my friend Jane complains, and so certain that they can finesse that popularity by making the right phone calls, that some mothers she knows keep track of how many play dates their children attend from year to year: "They worry if the number drops." Ditto for birthday parties. Some of these parents "are so insistent," Jane says, "that they'll eagerly arrange playdates with kids they don't really like and that their *kids* don't even really like. It's the contact that matters." Constant contact, fueled by fear. "The current wisdom," Jane says sepulchrally, "is: *Never let your kids be alone.*"

She often hears other parents fretting when their children wish to play alone. The parents wonder whether this is a sign of depression, a danger sign, a cry for help. Jane knows better.

"My daughter likes to be in the basement alone and skip around the room conversing with people who aren't there. I hear her laughing and I can't help but think, *I wish she was a normal kid instead.* Her need for people is really low-dosage and she'll just come out in the middle of a play date and say she wants to leave. At eight years old, she already perceives herself as weird. 'I know I'm different,' she says."

Jane's eleven-year-old son is careful about what he says to

whom. He has only one good friend, and spends hours alone at the computer keyboard, writing stories. One day during a play date, the child he was visiting invited him to spend the night. Jane's son called her to say he was going to stay. But something in his voice "made me suspicious."

So she asked him whether he had been invited while the other boy's whole family was watching. He said yes. She asked whether he had accepted the invitation so as not to hurt the other boy's feelings. He said yes. She asked whether the boy and his family were standing there still, watching her son make this phone call.

His voice came across jerky and high, a tone some might call cheery but which Jane recognized as shrill.

Yes!

And would you rather come home instead?

Yyyyessss!

"I got his classmate's mother on the phone," Jane says, "and I made up a lie. I told her he needed to be here because his grandmother was visiting. Anyway, it worked. I went over and picked him up. When we drove off, he sobbed as he was thanking me."

Because he is a conscientious child, Jane worries that all his life he will agree to do things that compromise his nature.

She also hates play dates for a reason that has nothing to do with her kids' welfare. This time it's personal: play dates force Jane to interact with a lot of other parents when she'd rather be alone. Typical was one night not long before we talked when a mother, arriving at Jane's house to pick up a child, sank onto the sofa for a long chat. She and Jane had never met before that night. Jane had nothing to say. She sat there thinking of the plans she'd made for the evening—dinner, then work, then a cable show—which were now on hold.

"Kids' friendships aren't just theirs anymore," Jane says. "They become ours." Watching the stranger on the sofa, Jane was watching the clock.

"I thought: I can't believe the price I'm paying for my little girl to spend a few hours playing with somebody. Would I do her such a great disservice if I said, 'Why don't you stay by yourself in the backyard and play with the dog?'"

As most loners have learned to do, Jane smiled politely and waited for the chat to end.

"I seem friendly." She scowls. "But this voice inside me is shouting, 'No! Don't make me do the play dates!' It's a terrible responsibility."

EVEN THE MOST lonerish child has relationships, of a kind, with toys. And synthetic as they are, mass-produced and heartless as they are, toys can still teach loners and nonloners a lot.

The standard toy for little girls—the clichéd toy—is a doll. One girl, one doll. This image has changed much over the last several decades, sparked by feminism and other forces. But it is a *boys'* doll whose evolution holds crucial messages for loners.

Girls' dolls impose a mother-and-child dynamic—or, in the form of fashion dolls like Barbie, impose fantasies about how the child hopes someday to look. Such motivations would be useless in designing dolls for little boys. Thus, G.I. Joe had to be more than something to cuddle, something to stare at. He had to inspire *action*—or, at least, a fantasy of action.

Appearing in American stores for the first time in 1964, G.I. Joe stood twelve inches high and wore combat fatigues. He was an unprecedented success. In that first year alone, the Hasbro toy company sold six million of him. The first-ever male action figure had struck a chord. And he was an indefatigable loner.

Soldiers are team players on the battlefields of the real world. So toy soldiers had always been small and were sold squadrons to a box. Joe was different. Lacking companion dolls, Joe embodied the American fighting man as bold explorer, swift decision-maker, problem solver, lone wolf. Sold alone, he had to fight alone and, for the sake of his own popularity, had to make it look worthwhile and fun.

Creating scenarios with only a single doll validates the power and wonder of the individual. Even if this is only a molded-plastic individual with painted-on hair and a mass-produced costume, it is a vessel through which the child projects his own visions of himself as an independent thinker, doer, adventurer, and winner. With only a single doll, the child celebrates self-reliance, learns to strategize, and learns the most potent lesson of all: The doll—or the real person the doll represents—requires nothing in order to do things and have experiences. Its adventures are sparked and carried out through ingenuity, imagination, creativity. In playing with a single doll, the child discovers how to entertain himself. A lone doll gives the message that one is enough.

But America's romance with G.I. Joe turned sour in the 1970s, on the heels of the Vietnam War. It was then that an entirely new type of toy eclipsed the bold soldier and, coincidentally or not, made his self-reliance appear outdated and obsolete.

Anticipating the release of George Lucas's first *Star Wars* film in 1976, the Kenner company produced action figures based on its characters. Han Solo, Darth Vader, Luke Skywalker, Princess Leia, the robots—it was a numbers game. Rather than release a single doll, the company released a whole ensemble of interrelated dolls. At under four inches high, each doll commanded a smaller retail price than G.I. Joe. This, it was hoped, presented customers with yet another reason to buy the dolls in large quantities, collecting the whole ensemble.

It was a risk. But *Star Wars'* astounding popularity ensured huge sales for Kenner, which on the basis of these dolls soon soared to the top of the American toy industry. Some ten years after the film's release, the company had produced well over a hundred different models and vehicles, and had sold hundreds of millions. Other companies followed its example, and today tie-in toys appear with the release of every Hollywood blockbuster intended for young audiences. Often tiny versions are given away free at fast-food restaurants as teasers for the full line of products on sale at stores.

This has changed the way children play.

Action figures give a wholly different message than a solo-adventurer toy like G.I. Joe. At the most basic level, they inspire a restless desire for quantity, *more*. One is never enough. One is ridiculous, pathetic, incomplete. And playing with an ensemble of toys might theoretically teach social skills such as cooperation, but it also limits each doll's putative abilities. It pigeonholes them, diminishes each of them, diminishing the individual. This is exacerbated by the fact that action figures replicate specific characters in famous films. They not only have names, but also quirks and pasts and dialogues. Their personalities come predetermined, known already by the child even before she plays with them. So much for creativity. So much for strategy. It is as if tie-in toys were designed to train children how *not* to be loners, not to think as loners, not to like loners or understand loners—or shop like loners.

Trying to keep up with the times, Hasbro eventually launched a new line of assorted characters to accompany G.I. Joe. A female intelligence ace, a snow-combat specialist—he's not a loner anymore.

Yet another type of toy has eclipsed action figures. Computer and video games are most often played alone. Thus, social critics lambaste them for turning today's kids into pallid, overweight isolationists. At first glance, these electronic playthings might be seen as "loner toys," but are they really? Yes, solo protagonists playing these games dispatch villains, solve problems, and blow things to bits. But the player hardly needs to think, only to click. Hours go by in a kind of daze. The child has not created a unique character, story, dialogue, or situation. In this sense, clicking away, he is even worse off than he would be with a boxful of *Star Wars* figures. Playing this way, he is cut off even from himself.

CHILDREN, WARNS STEVEN Pinker, "are not indistinguishable lumps of raw material waiting to be shaped." On the contrary, he asserts, we are all born with personalities. If tampering with

afterword

HE WAS A loner all his life. As a boy he fled the swarming tenement for "nature walks," as he called them, at Sheepshead Bay and Coney Island. He had one friend—a cousin, actually—but they parted ways at fifteen. None followed. He was a loner in the war, happy alone working night shifts in tropic outposts with the Signal Corps, the South Pacific sky like sequined velvet hung over a satin sea.

He was a loner learning electronics, suffering in office towers after the war and company cafeterias, happy left at his desk with the door closed. Happy at home in the backyard, tending the bougainvillea with its papery pink bracts, the spider mums, the succulents that thrived in salty soil and asked for nothing. He was happy in his garage, spending Saturdays polishing stones, sawing wood, making jewelry, making furniture, the radio on. *Leave me alone.* He gave the bookcases and pendants away, then rushed back to the garage, shutting the door.

He was happy on the road, driving down some desert highway or over a mountain pass. If he tried hard enough, he could forget that he was not the only person in the car.

His only child, I, too, preferred closed doors, preferred the road, bristled at interruptions, shut out all distractions, abhorred kits when things could be made to one's own design. His only child, I, too, preferred eating alone, wearing clothes it did not matter if no one saw, the beach when no one else was there.

Not that I knew it then. Not that we ever said anything of the kind. He was in his garage working the saw, listening to Mantovani. I was in my room gluing doll eyes and pipe cleaners to seashells.

When he had a stroke, I was grown up. I flew back to Los Angeles.

"He can understand everything we say," the doctor intoned at his bedside. My father was twitching, rigged to tubes, babbling gibberish. "He just can't speak properly. Because of what has happened to the brain, he can't formulate responses and just talks nonsense, but he understands."

My mother nodded slowly, horrified. Her eyes darted like fish. "Will he—?"

No one could say. And as the day went slack, the January sky gone royal blue and nurses rolling carts with dinner trays, but not for him, who ate through tubes, I saw that alone could mean many things. My mother was alone now in an awful way, was already alone, rendered alone the instant his vessel misfired. And her aloneness would go on, would resound like the bells in that poem by Poe. There is a kind of alone when you miss someone, I realized, someone in particular. Most alones are grand; *he* would have said so himself if he could say something besides *theswitchisontheladderisababa.* But there is a kind of alone that can be hell. Don't you think I know that?

And what about him? He knew. He knew exactly what had happened.

The nurse had taken his bifocals and shut them in a drawer. His right arm was clenched in a rictus like when children mimic horses. The other lay limp against his hip, an aspic stillness.

"You'll be fine," my mother said.

He gabbled a phrase that sounded like "chuckburger."

His sister Roz was there. She kept calling him *baby brotha.*

The nurse said, "Gosh, he looks healthy."

"He spends lots of time outdoors. He *spent,*" my mother said.

We sat in chairs around the bed, sharing Chex from a box. My aunt straightened his blankets, turning to me.

"Have a baby."

"What?"

"I said, will you please have a baby."

To fill in the missing space, she meant. Because if my father died there would be too few people in the world, one less, make more, fill it up.

I massaged his feet. The nurses had said it was worthwhile to keep his muscles toned, in case. His soles were soft as chamois. He jerked, fussed, looking the same yet different, as if being portrayed by a clever actor. My aunt unwrapped an Almond Joy bar. "There's a candy machine down the hall. If anyone wants candy, there's a—"

I scooted my chair up to the head of the bed from the foot.

"Dad," I whispered. "Can you hear me?"

beezisindabakeryrr.

"Dad?" I touched his forehead. He jerked and said the clearest thing he had said since the stroke, the clearest thing it turned out he would ever say.

Leave me alone.

endnotes

INTRODUCTION

"his outward appearance": Carl Gustav Jung, *Psychological Types* (Princeton, NJ: Princeton University Press, 1976), 134.

[I. • VILLAGE PEOPLE]

"an unacceptable return": Richard Critchfield, *Villages* (New York: Anchor Books, 1991), 9.

"immensity of African space": Ryszard Kapuściński, *The Shadow of the Sun* (New York: Vintage Books, 2002), 19.

"no chance of surviving": ibid., 31.

"disposed to the other": ibid., 29.

"misfortune, perdition": ibid., 49.

"This is impossible": ibid., 109.

"curt replies, if anything": Tim Nollen, *Culture Shock! Czech Republic* (Singapore: Times Editions, 1997), 32.

"know your neighbors": ibid., 35.

"keep a low profile": ibid., 36.

"Unlike many cultures": Patricia Levy, *Culture Shock! Ireland* (Singapore: Times Editions, 1998), 14.

"an essential history": ibid., 53.

"there is relentless pressure": Boye De Mente, *Behind the Japanese Bow* (Chicago: Passport Books, 1993), 40.

"spending more time alone": editorial, *Mainichi Shimbun*, July 11, 2000.

[2. · LISTEN TO US]

"the means of communication": Thorstein Veblen, *The Theory of the Leisure Class* (New York: Macmillan, 1902), 69.

"much more complex": Wendy Cavenett, "Jürgen Vollmer: An Artist's Progress." *iGallery*, April 1998.

"I'm full of dust and guitars": Jenny Fabian, " Fond memories of a crazy diamond who shined." *The Age*, January 21, 2002.

"not living in a field": Interview with Paul Breen, Syd's brother-in-law by BBC Radio One DJ Nicky Campbell, October 27, 1988.

"room full of chowderheads": Gina Arnold, "There's no replacing Paul Westerberg." *San Francisco Examiner*, April 23, 2002.

"building something slowly": David Wild, "Axl Speaks." *Rolling Stone*, January 10, 2000.

"a kind of male Garbo": Dave Kindred, "When baseball mattered the most, no one mattered as much as Joe DiMaggio." *The Sporting News.com*, 2000.

"arrogant, ungrateful athletes": David Whitley, "Pure Hitter: Ted Williams." ESPN.com, August 27, 2002.

"Not everybody liked him either": Bob Nightengale, "How do you like me now?" *USA Today*, July 3, 2001.

"enjoy the show": Bob Carter, "Bonds lets his numbers do the
talking." ESPN.com, October 3, 2001.

[3. • DO YOU FEEL LUCKY?]

"Who wants to be reminded": Tim Grierson, "*One Hour Photo:
Only the Lonely.*" *Knot,* September 29, 2002.
"hoary movie archetype": Stephen Holden, "*The Postman:
Neither Snow, Nor Rain, Nor Descent to Anarchy....*" *New
York Times,* December 24, 1997.

[4. • MARLBORO COUNTRY]

"$1.09 worth of cola": Bob Garfield, "How Coke Advertising
Has Lost Its Way." *Advertising Age,* February 18, 2002.

[6. • JUST CATCH ME]

"sexual predators are loners": Bill Briggs, "Best dating-service
advice: Be careful." *Denver Post,* May 2, 2000.
"the crack cocaine of sex": Mike Santangelo, "Internet is a good
place to get an STD." United Press International, July 25,
2000.
"a wondrous love": Sharon K. Elkins, *Holy Women of Twelfth-
Century England* (Chapel Hill, NC: University of North
Carolina Press, 1988), 26.
"a life-enhancing state": Alexander Ávila, *The Gift of Shyness*
(New York: Fireside Books, 2002), 27.
"those who date a shy person": ibid., 44.

"the gift of listening": ibid., 46.

"the worst thing you can do": ibid., 207.

"being a quirkyalone": Sasha Cagen, "The Quirkyalones." *To-Do List,* June 2000.

[7. • POWER SURGE]

"their tendency to ostracize": Patricia Kitchen, "Introverts Struggle to Fit Into An Extroverted Workplace." *Newsday,* June 23, 2002.

"on personal references": Nancy Senger, "Exceptional Service Takes the Cake." *Business Solutions,* December 1999.

"if they're sociable or not": Jeff Zbar, "Secrets of a virtual company CEO." *NetworkWorldFusion,* April 30, 2001.

"Keep score": R. Bruce McFarlane, "How to Gung-Ho Your Orthodontic Office." *Clinical Impressions,* volume 8, 1999.

"do not want to conform": Richard Florida, *The Rise of the Creative Class* (New York: Basic Books, 2002), 77.

"most of the technological": ibid., 172.

[8. • THE DIVING BELL]

"Mr. Munch hates all contact": *New York Times,* February 14, 1937.

"a *grand solitaire*": Frank Elgar, *Mondrian* (New York: Praeger Books, 1968), 182.

"as our ancestors did not live": Rainer Maria Rilke, *Letters to a Young Poet* (1934. Reprint: New York: W.W. Norton & Co., 1994), 127.

$$\left[\text{ E N D N O T E S } \right]$$

"very little is published": William Roberts, *Five Posthumous Essays and Other Writings* (London: Valencia, 1990), 71.

[9. • SINGULAR GLAMOUR]

"the secret of my whole existence": Jules Verne, *20,000 Leagues Under the Sea* (1873. Reprint: New York: William Morrow Books, 2000), 23.

"never to speak of them": ibid., 22.

"greater solitude or silence": ibid., 24.

"pursue a female wolf": Hermann Hesse, *Steppenwolf* (1929. Reprint: New York: Owl Books, 1990), 42.

"how could I fail": ibid., 30.

"without wanting to": ibid., 77.

"this fear of people": Franz Kafka, *Letters to Felice* (New York: Schocken Books, 1973), 279.

"We are social beings": Robin Dunbar, *Grooming, Gossip, and the Evolution of Language* (Cambridge: Harvard University Press, 1998), xvi.

"I'm a loner, an individualist": Sinda Gregory, Toshifumi Miyawaki, and Larry McCaffery, "It Don't Mean a Thing, If It Ain't Got That Swing: An Interview with Haruki Murakami." Center for Book Culture.org.

"refused to communicate": Paul Alexander, *Salinger* (Los Angeles: Renaissance Books, 1999), 236.

"met us at the driveway": ibid., 295.

"leave me alone": ibid., 268.

"feeding tetchy disdain": ibid., 298.

[10. • JESUS, MARY, AND JENNIFER LOPEZ]

"there is not a door": Jacques Lacarrière, *The God-Possessed*
(London: Goerge Allen & Unwin, 1963), 100.

"a shower of arrows": ibid., 118.

"once and for all": Elkins, *Holy Women of Twelfth-Century England*,
152.

"She shall hold it": Linda Georgianna, *The Solitary Self*
(Cambridge: Harvard University Press, 1981), 52.

"I had to escape": Toni Maraini, *Sealed in Stone* (San Francisco:
City Lights Books, 2002), 42.

"this world of evil": ibid., 123.

"stole my space": ibid., 50.

"be truly recollected": Georgianna, 69.

"Such thoughts as these": Elkins, 158.

"and this is good": Thomas Merton, *Dancing in the Water of Life*
(San Francisco: Harper San Francisco, 1997), 176.

"A few birds": ibid., 22.

"run to their shame": Thomas Merton, *Learning to Love* (San
Francisco: Harper San Francisco, 1997), 342.

"return to truth": *Dancing*, 175.

"I become anxious": Thomas Merton, *The Other Side of the
Mountain* (San Francisco: Harper San Francisco, 1998), 252.

"Once in a while": *Dancing*, 33.

"that is that": *Learning*, 68.

"The hermit crab": Kamo No Chomei, *Hojoki: Visions of a Torn
World* (Berkeley, CA: Stone Bridge Press, 1996), 67.

"openness to experience": Steven Pinker, *The Blank Slate* (New
York: Viking Press, 2002), 375.

[ENDNOTES]

"I was drawn": Rabbi Yosef Yitzchak Schneersohn, "The Baal Shem Tov's Sixteenth Birthday." Chabad.org

"Life as a hermit": Ernie Garcia, "Modern hermits turn lives around in Yonkers." *Journal News*, August 11, 2002

[11. • NEW DISORDER]

"hacking Perl scripts": Steve Silberman, "The Geek Syndrome." *Wired*, December 2001.

[12. • THE L-WORD]

"all the more baffling": "Typical or Terrorist? Teacher, Police Descriptions of Plane Crash Teen Differ." ABCNEWS.com, January 8, 2002.

"Suppose that for a period": John E. Douglas and Mark Olshaker, *The Anatomy of Motive* (New York: Scribner, 1999), 287.

"any odd job": Adrian Havill, *Born Evil* (New York: St. Martin's Press, 2001), 140.

"is at fault": ibid., 17.

"a coward and a loner": ibid., 44.

"by himself at lunch": ibid., 145.

"no surprises there": ibid., 219.

"a quiet loner": ibid., 229.

"It's a loner": Tom Baldwin, "Sniper not likely a terrorist," *The Trentonian*, October 23, 2002.

"A black sniper": Jeffrey Gettleman, "Arrests confound profiling 'experts.'" *New York Times*, October 25, 2002.

"So much for the Chevy": Jeffrey Gettleman, "Most clues and hunches missed sniper suspect." *International Herald Tribune*, October 26, 2002.

"with a vague political grievance": Jeffrey Gettleman, "When Just One Gun Is Enough." *New York Times*, October 27, 2002.

[13. · BIZARRE AS I WANNA BE]

"glory in it": David Joseph Weeks, *Eccentrics* (New York: Kodansha Globe, 1996), 14.

"the king of the enema": Ron Kistler, *I Caught Flies for Howard Hughes* (New York: Simon & Schuster, 1976), 200.

"groaning and rocking": ibid., 93.

"before mine eyes": Edith Sitwell, *English Eccentrics* (New York: Vanguard Press, 1957), 166.

"solitude and retirement": ibid., 165.

"pleasures of nature": ibid., 48.

[16. · ABSOLUTELY, TOTALLY ALONE]

"My mind could then retreat": John Fairfax, *Britannia: Rowing Alone Across the Atlantic* (New York: Simon & Schuster, 1971), 31.

"my struggle against humanity": ibid., 22.

"All I craved": ibid., 149.

"it's like having company": ibid., 152.

"watched it disappear": ibid., 165.

[ENDNOTES]

"before it seized me": Gerard d'Aboville, *Alone* (New York: Arcade, 1993), 50.

"The enemy is me": ibid., 80.

"when it dies": Richard Byrd, *Alone* (Covelo, CA: Island Press, 1984), 74.

"I wish very much": ibid., 87.

"what is chaff": ibid., 160.

"exciting and portentous": ibid., 120.

"I was perfectly happy": Gabriel Gárcia Márquez, *The Story of a Shipwrecked Sailor* (New York: Knopf, 1986), 25.

"I found that I preferred": Naomi James, *Alone Around the World* (New York: Coward, McCann & Geoghegan, 1979), 19.

"to prefer silence": ibid., 71.

"He has his life to live": ibid., 98.

"I pulled a face": ibid., 101.

[17. • SMILING BANDITS]

"attentive or detached": Steven Pinker, *The Blank Slate* (New York: Viking Press, 2002), 86.

"fighting and praying": ibid., 375.

"make us forget": ibid., 99.

bibliography

Abrams, M., ed. *The Norton Anthology of English Literature*. New York: W. W. Norton & Co., 2001.

Alexander, Paul. *Salinger*. Los Angeles: Renaissance Books, 1999.

Ávila, Alexander. *The Gift of Shyness*. New York: Fireside Books, 2002.

Baxter, John. *Stanley Kubrick*. New York: Carroll & Graf, 1997.

Byrd, Richard. *Alone*. Covelo, Calif.: Island Press, 1984.

Colegate, Isabel. *A Pelican in the Wilderness*. Washington, D.C.: Perseus Books, 2002.

Colgrave, Bertram. *Felix's Life of St. Guthlac*. Cambridge, UK: Cambridge University Press, 1989.

Cooper, David A. *Silence, Simplicity, and Solitude*. New York: Bell Tower, 1992.

Critchfield, Richard. *Villages*. New York: Anchor Books, 1991.

d'Aboville, Gerard. *Alone*. New York: Arcade, 1993.

De Mente, Boye. *Behind the Japanese Bow*. Chicago: Passport Books, 1993.

Dickinson, Emily. *The Complete Poems of Emily Dickinson*. New York: Little, Brown & Co.: 1976.

Douglas, John E., and Mark Olshaker. *The Anatomy of Motive*. New York: Scribner, 1999.

Dunbar, Robin. *Grooming, Gossip, and the Evolution of Language.*
Cambridge: Harvard University Press, 1998.

Elgar, Frank. *Mondrian.* New York: Praeger Press, 1968.

Elkins, Sharon K. *Holy Women of Twelfth-Century England.* Chapel
Hill, NC: University of North Carolina Press, 1988.

Fairfax, John. *Britannia: Rowing Alone Across the Atlantic.* New York:
Simon & Schuster, 1971.

Florida, Richard. *The Rise of the Creative Class.* New York: Basic
Books, 2002.

Georgianna, Linda. *The Solitary Self.* Cambridge: Harvard
University Press, 1981.

Havill, Adrian. *Born Evil.* New York: St. Martin's Press, 2001.

Herdan, Innes. (translator). *Three Hundred Tang Poems.* Taipei: Far
East Book Company, 1973.

Hesse, Hermann. *Steppenwolf.* 1929. Reprint: New York: Owl
Books, 1990.

James, Naomi. *Alone Around the World.* New York: Coward,
McCann & Geoghegan, 1979.

Johnson, Kurt, and Steven L. Coates. *Nabokov's Blues: The
Scientific Odyssey of a Literary Genius.* Cambridge, Mass.: Zoland
Books, 1999.

Jung, Carl Gustav. *Psychological Types.* Princeton: Princeton
University Press, 1976.

Kafka, Franz. *Letters to Felice.* New York: Schocken Books, 1973.

Kamo No Chomei. *Hojoki: Visions of a Torn World* . Berkeley,
Calif.: Stone Bridge Press, 1996.

Kapuściński, Ryszard. *The Shadow of the Sun.* New York: Vintage
Books, 2002.

Kistler, Ron. *I Caught Flies for Howard Hughes*. New York: Simon & Schuster, 1976.

Koch, Philip. *Solitude: A Philosophical Encounter*. Peru, Ill.: Open Court, 1994.

Márquez, Gabriel Gárcia. *The Story of a Shipwrecked Sailor*. New York: Knopf, 1986.

Lacarrière, Jacques. *The God-Possessed*. London: George Allen & Unwin, 1963.

Levy, Patricia, *Culture Shock! Ireland*. Singapore: Times Editions, 1998.

Maraini, Toni. *Sealed in Stone*. San Francisco: City Lights Books, 2002.

McClatchy, J. D. *Poems of the Sea*. New York: Everymans Library, 2001.

Merton, Thomas. *Dancing in the Water of Life*. San Francisco: Harper San Francisco, 1997.

Merton, Thomas. *Learning to Love*. San Francisco: Harper San Francisco, 1997.

Merton, Thomas. *The Other Side of the Mountain*. San Francisco: Harper San Francisco, 1998.

Nollen, Tim. *Culture Shock! Czech Republic*. Singapore: Times Editions, 1997.

Pinker, Steven. *The Blank Slate*. New York: Viking Press, 2002.

Red Pine (translator). *The Collected Songs of Cold Mountain*. Port Townsend, Wash.: Copper Canyon Press, 2000.

Rilke, Rainer Maria. *Letters to a Young Poet*. 1934. Reprint: New York: Norton, 1994.

Siegel, Andrea. *Open and Clothed*. New York: Agapanthus Books, 1999.

Sitwell, Edith. *English Eccentrics*. New York: Vanguard Press, 1957.

Stacey, Michelle. *The Fasting Girl*. New York: Tarcher Books, 2002.

Storr, Anthony. *Solitude: A Return to the Self*. New York: The Free Press, 1988.

Taylor, Barbara Erakko. *Silent Dwellers*. New York: Coninuum, 1999.

Veblen, Thorstein. *The Theory of the Leisure Class*. New York: Macmillan, 1902.

Verne, Jules. *20,000 Leagues Under the Sea*. 1873. Reprint: New York: Morrow, 2000.

Waite, Terry. *Footfalls in Memory*. New York: Doubleday, 1995.

Weeks, David Joseph, and Jamie James. *Eccentrics*. New York: Kodansha Globe, 1996.